VISION IN THE DESERT

VISION IN THE DESERT

Carl Hayden and Hydropolitics in the American Southwest

Jack L. August, Jr.

with an introduction by Bruce Babbitt

Texas Christian University Press
Fort Worth

Library of Congress Cataloging-in-Publication Data

August, Jack L.
Vision in the desert : Carl Hayden and Hydropolitics in the American Southwest / by Jack L. August, Jr.
p. cm.
Includes bibliographical references and index.
ISBN 0-87565-310-3
1. Hayden, Carl Trumbull, 1977-1972. 2. Legislators—United States—Biography. 3. United States. Congress. Senate—Biography. 4. Water conservation—Political aspects—Southwest, New—History—20th century. 5. Water resources development—Political aspects—Southwest, New—History—20th century. 6 Arizona—Politics and government—1951-
I. Title.
E748.H387A94 1998
328.73'092—dc21
[B]

98-16386
CIP

Unless otherwise indicated the illustrations in this volume can be found in the Arizona Collection, Arizona State University Libraries. Hereafter cited as ASU followed by the call number.

Design: Hal Normand

Contents

For My Family;
Nuclear and Extended

Acknowledgements

My maternal grandmother, Inez Sanchez, and my father, Jack L. August, Sr., a most unlikely duo, spurred my earliest interest in the history and culture of the American Southwest and northwestern Mexico. My grandmother, with her amusing and sometimes strange stories of *brujos* and supernatural occurrences—from St. Johns, Arizona, to Hermosillo, Sonora—anticipated the tales of the late 1960s cultural icon Carlos Casteneda and left my high school and college friends shaking their heads and wondering if Grandma Sanchez needed more air conditioning in her home at 920 West Madison in downtown Phoenix. Significantly, my grandmother, whose idiosyncratic behavior still causes laughter among family members years after her passing, first brought Carl Hayden and Southwestern political culture to my attention. My father, whose abilities as an artist and student of history, lay hidden beneath his career as a much-beloved grade school physical education teacher, provided guidance, encouragement, and reading materials. To this day, his 1950s era textbook from some long-forgotten political science course at Temple University (Stefan Lorant's *The Presidency*) sits on my nightstand. I still take time to gaze at Theodore Roosevelt's 1904 inauguration portrait—much as I did as a seven-year-old wondering what kind of man this Roosevelt must have been.

A noteworthy triad of historians—Howard R. Lamar, Gerald D. Nash, and Richard Etulain—through their distinguished careers as writers, teachers, and mentors, provided inspired direction and guidance at various stages of this study. A. Tracy Row, editor at Texas Christian University Press, whose gentle humor and intimate knowledge of the material discussed in this volume, deserves much credit for the final product. His many years as editor of the *Journal of Arizona History* gave him special insight into the broad contours of Senator Carl Hayden's career and the Arizona senator's preeminent role in the nearly century long struggle over the waters of the Colorado River system. In short, Tracy was uniquely qualified to edit this book. I continue to value highly his professional skills, friendship, and opinion.

Funding from various institutions and foundations made completion of the research and writing possible. The Dorothy Woodward Foundation at the University of New Mexico, the Moody Foundation at the University of Texas, the Charles T. Hayden Library at Arizona State University, the National Endowment for the Humanities, the U.S. Canada Fulbright Commission, and the Humanities Center at the University of Oregon, to name a few, provided financial assistance and encouragement along the way. Those dedicated professional librarians and archivists, from Phoenix to Austin to Washington, D.C., maintain my undying gratitude. More often than not these professionals directed me to the appropriate manuscript collection or repository.

A few close friends and family members interested in the life and career of Carl Hayden require special acknowledgement. James Chilton, who worked with Senator Hayden during the 1960s and his retirement years (1969-1972), provided help, support, and first-hand knowledge of the senator's activities. He and his wife, Sue, always welcomed me warmly to their homes in Arizona and California. Roy Elson, two-time U.S. Senate candidate and the senator's long-time chief of staff, provided guidance, friendship, and a comprehensive knowledge of Washington D.C.'s power structure and night life. Christine Marin of the Chicano Studies Collection at Arizona State University and James Allen of the Arizona Historical Foundation survived my years of research at the Arizona Collection in the Hayden Library with little discernible irritation or injury. Finally, Kathy Flower and her children, Sommer, Shannon, and Natalie, and my son, Sam—through this project and several others—merit special recognition and thanks for accommodating a writer's unpredictable and self-absorbed hours. Without the help and understanding of these individuals, institutions and countless others this project would not have come to completion. To them I owe a debt of gratitude.

Jack L. August, Jr.
Prescott, Arizona
July 18, 1998

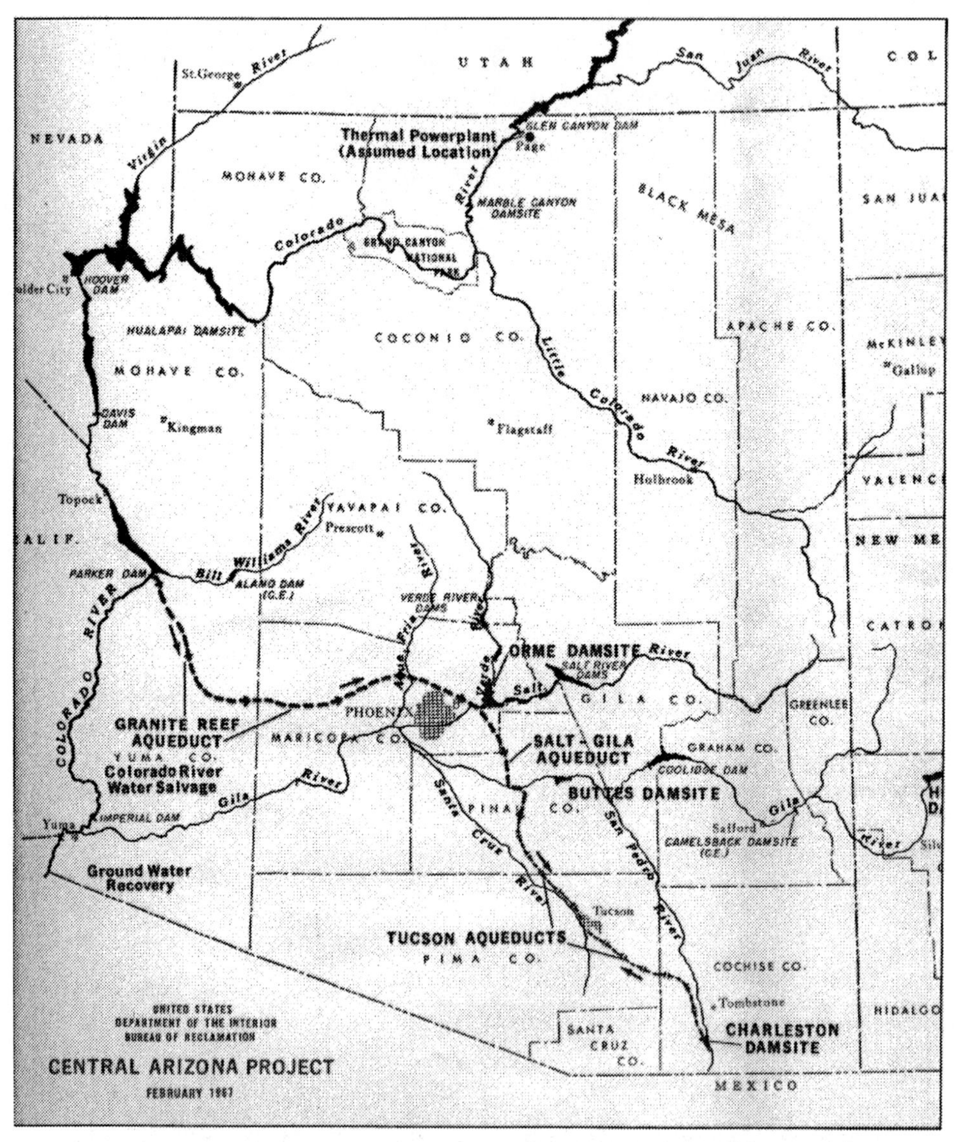

The Central Arizona Project as it was envisioned in 1967. A number of the projected dams and aquaducts have never been built (ASU: CE EPH QPCAP-31)

Introduction

We are now approaching the last phase of a productive century of federally sponsored reclamation in the American West. With the development of a few remaining authorized dams and delivery systems the era of the construction of the great reclamation project will come to an end. A major contributor to the process of water resource development in the American West was longtime Senator Carl Hayden of Arizona. A native of Arizona's Salt River Valley, Hayden experienced first-hand the often cruel vicissitudes of flood and drought in the arid Southwest. He saw Arizona grow from a raw territory of a few thousand hearty pioneers to a desert oasis of millions. Central to his efforts in the service of his Arizona constituents was the development and use of the Colorado River, the controversial interstate stream that serves the needs of the seven basin states (Arizona, California, Nevada, New Mexico, Utah, Colorado, and Wyoming). And while he devoted his public career to the residents of his state, the man who became affectionately known as the "Silent Senator" had an impact and significance that reached far beyond the borders of the Grand Canyon state.

The most striking feature of Hayden's political career was its longevity. He spent sixty-seven of his ninety-four years of life in public office. Between 1900 and 1912 he learned the art of politics by serving in a variety of local and county positions in territorial Arizona.

When statehood was achieved in the latter year voters elected their native son to the House of Representatives, kept him there for seven terms, and in 1926 promoted him to the Senate where he remained until his retirement in 1969. During his fifty-seven years in the federal government he served with ten presidents, beginning with William Howard Taft and ending with Lyndon Baines Johnson.

Any public official in Arizona quickly learns that Hayden's lengthy tenure in the federal government benefited Arizona in a multitude of ways, and to attempt to catalog his accomplishments would require volumes. In 1912 when he first stepped into the well of the House of Representatives, Arizona was one of the most sparsely settled states in the union. When he retired from the Senate in 1969, Hayden returned to one of the fastest growing states in the country. Today, dams and reservoirs, thousands of acres of productive reclaimed farmland, power transmission lines, highways that helped create Arizona's important tourist trade, a healthy commercial and industrial economy, Indian and veterans hospitals, and aircraft and military bases stand as testaments to the public career of Carl Hayden.

Hayden's labors, however, aided not only Arizona but also the other states of the American West. In the 1960s, for example, Oregon Senator Wayne Morse announced to his fellow lawmakers that he considered the Arizona solon an honorary legislator because of his support for the Bonneville and other dams that harnessed the Columbia River's resources to the work of man. Westerners living in the modern era and those of future generations would always be indebted to Hayden for his help in bringing life-giving water to arid lands and the countless benefits that flow from multiple-use developments of the river resources of the western United States.

Even California, often a bete noire in Arizona's nearly century-long quest for a share of Colorado River resources, received much needed and appreciated help from the Arizona senator. Hayden played a crucial role in the support and procuring of federal financing for northern California's Central Valley Project. He also helped southern California in his support for the activities of the Metropolitan Water District. As one southern California water leader aptly put it,

"The West owes him much and recognizes that most of the great federal projects have some imprint of Carl Hayden."

In spite of these noteworthy accomplishments, few people outside Arizona or Washington, D.C., knew of Arizona's senior senator. This lack of recognition resulted from a unique political style notable for its avoidance of ostentation. Moreover, staffers who worked with Hayden knew that the public image was largely natural, partly cultivated, yet immensely effective in achieving desired results. As one longtime observer of Arizona politics assessed the Hayden political style: "Hayden's deportment in conducting his daily duties seemed better suited for a judge or a minister rather than a politician."

Fellow senators who spent time with and around Hayden commented on his kindness, humility, and modesty. Indeed, in what became an almost biannual ritual for senate newcomers, Hayden evinced amazement among the newly elected members for never sitting in the front row of the Democratic side of the Senate as he was entitled. Instead, he maintained the seat he took in March 1927, on the aisle, one row removed from the back.

Another well-known Hayden quality that cut against the grain of conventional political wisdom was the Arizonan's propensity for silence. Especially in the Senate, a political body notable for its lack of oratory, Hayden stood out as the soul of brevity. His remarks in the *Congressional Record* consumed less space, perhaps, than any other senator in recent history. Yet as any careful observer of western politics knows, the absence of Hayden verbiage gave no hint of his power, knowledge, or effectiveness. Upon his fiftieth anniversary in Congress, the *New York Times* declared, "few individuals in the history of Congress have done so much with so little talk." Furthermore, when Hayden chose to appear before a committee with a project or a request, most members were certain it was worthy and justifiable. If Hayden wanted something, it needed little persuasion or rhetorical advancement. In a great political incongruity, Hayden fashioned silence into a form of legislative power.

More than any other of these key qualities, Hayden, arguably, was one of the most powerful senators in the history of the United States.

Besides chairing the Appropriations Committee he served as president pro tempore of the Senate and was third in line for the presidency. Although he held such vast political power, one of Hayden's most useful political attributes, according to President Lyndon Baines Johnson, was the high degree of affection in which his colleagues held him. With this combination of endearing qualities and immense power, Hayden chose most often to use his influence behind the doors of committee rooms or in persuasive conversations in the cloakrooms of Congress. At the same time he did his homework with consummate care until he knew, as one of his Republican colleagues recalled, "the front, back, and middle of everything." Perhaps my good friend and another political legend, Senator Barry Goldwater, stated it best: "Let me put it this simple way, whenever my service in the Senate is terminated, I hope that my service to my country and my state equals a small fraction of what Carl Hayden has provided in both areas."

Also, as Senator Goldwater or any other Arizona resident could tell you, Hayden outgrew party personality early in his political career. Nevertheless, he always proclaimed with pride that he was a Democrat. His voting record not only supported this assertion, but also reflected remarkable continuity through a half-century of intraparty transition. He entered the House of Representatives as a Wilsonian Progressive, a staunch proponent of the programs embodied in the New Freedom. He supported Roosevelt's New Deal and Truman's Fair Deal. Toward the end of his career he championed Kennedy's New Frontier and Johnson's Great Society. Still Hayden never let political partisanship interfere with friendship or helping a constituent. "I have friends in both political parties," he often said, "and I do not forget that fact when there is an opportunity to be of service to them, regardless if they are Republicans or Democrats."

While Hayden developed a renowned expertise in the field of federal reclamation, he could also boast of several other areas of legislative proficiency that aided the growth and development of the western states. Hayden, for example, was one of the great leaders in federal highway legislation, coauthoring a New Deal measure—the Hayden-Cartwright Act of 1934—that established the formula for the distribution of federal aid to highways to the states on the basis of area rather than population. This legislation helped tremendously in providing transportation links between the West's far-flung cities. He introduced and supported measures that advanced mining operations throughout the country. His efforts provided for fair prices, protection against unfair imports, and subsidization for strategic metals. He was the sponsor in 1919 of the 19th amendment to the Constitution, extending the right of suffrage to women and he sponsored and managed the House bill to establish Grand Canyon National Park. He worked for social security legislation and in 1950 fostered an amendment to that law that allowed American Indians to be included within its framework, thereby preventing the withholding of benefits from a large number of Arizona and other western citizens. Other broad areas of federal legislation attracted his attention: forest conservation, national parks, labor, public lands, agriculture, and veterans affairs, to name a few. Significantly, most of these issues were crucial to the growth and development, as well as the conservation and preservation of the American West.

Water, however, and its use and distribution, more than any other issue, lay at the heart of Hayden's public career. He became most famous as a statesman who helped bring water and life to a vast region of the country. Unquestionably, the fortunes of his Arizona pioneer family were tied to water, or more specifically, its diversion onto land. As a local politician he lobbied for one of the first, and most successful, federal reclamation projects—Arizona's Salt River Project. During his first term in the House, he further displayed his understanding of the importance of water to his home state by obtaining authorization of an engineering study that led to the construction of Coolidge Dam on the Gila River and the San Carlos Irrigation Project. He also helped shape federal reclamation policy in its early years by writing and securing passage of the provision that allows local water-user associations throughout the country to take over the care, maintenance, and operation of federal reclamation projects. In nearly six decades in Congress reclamation issues occupied more of his attention than any other legislative subject, and Colorado River development took up a significant portion of that time.

As noted, Hayden's interest in water resource development bore enormous implications for his home state. During his tenure in Congress Arizona's population multiplied eight times, due in large part to economic benefits derived from federal reclamation. In 1962, on the fiftieth anniversary of statehood Hayden, in a rare moment of public self-evaluation, commented on his contributions to Arizona. Characteristically, he refused to take direct credit for his role in the state's remarkable growth and development. "The basic factor in making Arizona's spectacular agricultural and industrial development was the Reclamation Act of 1902, sponsored by that great and energetic president, Theodore Roosevelt." That law, he told his constituents, made possible the use of federal funds to develop water for irrigation and hydroelectric power, both of which were essential to the state's prosperity. "Needless to say," he continued, "I have helped that basic program move forward." The then eighty-four-year-old senator concluded, not dwelling on the past, but urging Arizonans to look toward the future: "I hope to see the day when central Arizona and other important areas of the state have the water required to continue the pattern of growth and progress attained in the first half-century."

The senator alluded to Arizona's decades-old obsession, the Central Arizona Project (CAP) which channels Arizona's hard-won share of Colorado River water to the central portions of the state, including the rapidly growing metropolitan areas of Phoenix and Tucson. The project not only altered dramatically the course of reclamation history in the American West, but also it will have an impact on the delicate desert environment in countless ways. The environmental, social, and economic impacts of this landmark federal initiative are now only becoming apparent to residents of Arizona and the other Colorado River basin states.

In 1962, approaching his mid-eighties and growing increasingly infirm, Hayden considered an unprecedented seventh term in the Senate because of CAP. Indeed, since the 1920s he had worked for the project and after decades of legislative horsetrading, compromise, and maneuvering, he submitted the first bill to authorize CAP in 1947. The Senate passed bills in 1950 and 1951, but the House, under pressure from the more numerous California delegation, refused to take action. After the lengthy and legendary Supreme Court case *Arizona v. California* which in 1963 awarded Arizona a significant portion of Colorado River water, the way was cleared for legislative action on the project. Despite his advanced age and plans for retirement, state leaders convinced Hayden to run for one more term. A widely circulated *Phoenix Gazette* editorial best summarized voter sentiment at the time: "The CAP is the keystone to Arizona's future. By such a combination of circumstances that seldom happens in history, the future depends tremendously on one man, Carl Hayden, America's most powerful U.S. Senator."

Hayden won his final and most gratifying legislative battle in 1968 when CAP was authorized through passage of the Colorado River Basin Project Act. He could look back at the broad contours of his political handiwork and realize that he had helped shape and improve the quality of life in the American West in the twentieth century. Also, he realized that he influenced the quality of life of westerners in the twenty-first. Yet the builder of so much of the dynamic new West was a product of the legendary old West. Carl Hayden, born at Hayden's Ferry in 1877, reached adulthood before the twentieth century; before women's suffrage or collective bargaining, before Anzio or Alamogordo. He grew to maturity on the American frontier where his parents and his austere desert environment shaped his character. Importantly, the senator from Arizona who contributed so much in creating the American West of the future possessed roots that reached deep into the heart of the American experience of the nineteenth century.

Bruce Babbitt
U.S. Secretary of the Interior

1

The Vision

In 1962 an Arizona public school teacher asked her sixth grade class to name the three great branches of the federal government. One twelve-year-old girl, with a degree of accuracy that few of her classmates could appreciate, answered, "the President, the Superb Court, and Mr. Carl Hayden." When informed that the venerable Arizona senator was not a separate branch of the federal government and that her answer was incorrect, the student shot back, "But he has always been there, hasn't he?" When local newsmen reported the story, former governor and longtime Hayden friend Howard Pyle, chuckled and offered that he found an underlying truth in the schoolgirl's answer. "Carl is like the Arizona sun," he surmised, "he is always there." The governor and the schoolgirl, in their separate ways, said much about the relationship between Carl Hayden and Arizona; their histories were inseparable. And as one chronicler of the American West has suggested, "Carl Hayden was Arizona. His life came as close as anyone's to spanning the various interests of the state." Hayden, however, had an impact and significance that reached well beyond the borders of the Grand Canyon State.[1]

Carl Trumbull Hayden, born at Hayden's Ferry, Arizona Territory in 1877, served in the U.S. Congress for fifty-seven years, the second-longest legislative tenure in American history. After a decade-long career in local territorial politics, he represented the new state of

Arizona—first in the House of Representatives from 1912 until 1927, then in the Senate from 1927 to 1969.

Significantly, it was a career tied closely to the environment and the federal government. Reared in the arid reaches of Arizona's Salt River Valley, when much of the American Southwest benefited from and chafed against the U.S. territorial system, Hayden early in his life became aware of the pervasive if arbitrary influence of Washington, D.C. As a young elected local official during the early decades of the twentieth century he saw firsthand the influence of the federal government increase even further as it established national parks, forests, highway programs, military installations, and, of course, water projects. In time, as Hayden grew and matured as a professional politician he emerged as a classic example of the twentieth century western lawmaker, encouraging and fostering this apparently inexorable and enduring federal involvement in regional growth and development. As congressman and senator from the West's desert heartland—Arizona—he pursued what one recent historian has called, "a unique relationship with Washington," in which several hundred billions of dollars were pumped into the region during his over half-century on Capitol Hill.[2]

Indeed, as the Arizona schoolgirl anecdote suggests, Hayden's political longevity poses noteworthy challenges for the historian or biographer who embarks upon the task of producing a one-volume work on this lawmaker. The question of choice confronts the researcher; what aspect of Hayden's public career best reflects his historical significance? What area of congressional, legislative, or political activity can provide a window of perspective, an opening wedge, a thread of continuity, or a critical insight into the essence of his tenure in government? His legislative involvement, for example, in the areas of Indian affairs, mines and mining, public lands, transportation and highway development, national parks, forestry, agriculture, immigration policy, political patronage, and veterans affairs, to name a few, provide material enough for volumes of scholarly analysis.

Without question Hayden maintained several areas of legislative specialization and expertise. Upon closer scrutiny and critical evaluation of the voluminous Carl Hayden Papers Collection at Arizona

State University in Tempe, Arizona, however, one must conclude that a regional interpretation of his activities, beginning with the consequences of the land and its aridity, charts the way in which the longtime Arizona senator's historical role can be evaluated most effectively. Put another way, Hayden's political life reveals primary concern with the implementation and perceived benefits of the federal reclamation program in his arid region. Thus, Hayden's prominent and enduring role in the politics of water resource development in the American Southwest, above all else, best illustrates the broader significance of his public career.

From the turn of the century onward Hayden focused the majority of his energies on the single most important factor confronting his arid land constituents—the search for large quantities of fresh water. In congress he represented the "heart of the West," which was, to historian Walter Prescott Webb, "a desert unqualified and absolute ... a gigantic fire" that mitigated against human settlement and economic development, yet vividly defined the region as a unique place on the American landscape. From Hayden's perspective, at least, Arizona and the arid Southwest, in contrast to other parts of the country, were deficient and the most notable deficiency was water.[3]

In effect, Hayden sought to ameliorate the desert's influence by using the power of the federal government to develop scarce regional water resources for the growing urban oases of the twentieth-century West. While Webb and his intellectual descendants might interpret Hayden as one of those westerners who helped adapt political, legal, and scientific institutions to the environment—the quiet builder of a remarkable and vigorous reclamation civilization—a later generation of scholars like Donald Worster, William Kahrl, Marc Reisner, and others, might characterize the Arizonan as yet another of the cynical tyrants of modern hydraulic society. For Hayden was one whose actions helped bring about the modern western social order based upon large scale manipulation of water resources in an arid environment.[4]

That interpretive debate notwithstanding, Hayden's overall career mirrors other important elements in western American political culture. This turn-of-the-century politician from the desert West developed his electoral instincts and political ideology in a distinctly different environment than that of the East. During the first half of the nineteenth century, for example, mass political parties grew in the East, shepherding causes like universal suffrage and partisan politics. Yet as Hayden grew to political maturity in the territorial West of the Gilded Age and Progressive Era, parties and partisanship had come under attack and were comparatively weak. Hayden and other western political activists were no more vigorous in their denunciation of party politics than their eastern counterparts. Yet eastern party organizations, with longer traditions and entrenched bureaucracies, effectively resisted the assault on party organization.

Hayden, on the other hand, affiliated himself with an Arizona Democratic party that had little chance to develop any semblance of organizational strength. With his election to Congress in 1912 he burst upon the national political scene when state and local party organizations were far more developed in the Midwest and Northeast. And as recent studies have indicated, these traditional regional party organizations endured well into the 1960s—but they did not in the West. Unquestionably Hayden, who many contemporaries said "outgrew party organization early in his political career," benefited from and personified this western political predilection.[5]

Given Hayden's central role in the environmental politics of the region and the institutional political status he achieved within Arizona, the Colorado River controversy, most striking for its longevity and complexity, occupied more of his time in office than any other single political issue. His direct involvement in the legendary struggle can be traced to its earliest emergence as a problem of national and international significance. In May 1919, for example, he presented a bill during the first session of the Sixty-sixth Congress to authorize a Colorado River reclamation project along the lower reaches of the river. Thereafter he was involved in all legal and legislative phases of Colorado River development—from the Colorado River Compact negotiations of 1922 to the passage of the Colorado River Basin Project Act of 1968 which authorized construction of the

Central Arizona Project (CAP). The 300-mile-long CAP, for many Arizonans the fulfillment of a decades-old dream, has recently put a portion of Arizona's hard-won share of Colorado River water to "beneficial use" in the central portions of the state. For the Grand Canyon State especially, and other Colorado River Basin states as well, the enactment of CAP legislation holds important economic, environmental, and demographic implications that reach far into the next century. For Hayden, passage of the CAP bill was a personal victory, a fitting triumphant exit to his political career. "My efforts in behalf of the Central Arizona Project," he told his constituents shortly before his retirement, "began while I was still a Congressman and I consider it ... the most significant accomplishment of my career."[6]

Yet this massive tribute to the engineering profession, which today channels water from the mainstream of the Colorado to Phoenix, Tucson, and the agricultural sectors between these two urban oases, had its inspiration in the late-nineteenth-century civilization of the desert Southwest. Hayden's father, Charles Trumbull Hayden, upon his arrival in what was then territorial New Mexico in the mid-1850s, confronted the daunting environmental and economic limitations of the arid Southwest. As the elder Hayden crisscrossed the region supplying miners, merchants, and government employees stationed in remote desert outposts with a variety of eastern-manufactured goods and supplies, he, like few other pioneer visionaries, foresaw possibilities in this apparently forbidding and hostile territory. And in the mid-1860s, on one of his numerous freighting forays, the desert sojourner, almost by accident, camped upon the future location of his pioneer reclamation community.

As he approached the south side of the flooding Salt River in 1866, Tucson trader and probate judge Charles Trumbull Hayden realized that he would not be able to cross. Forty-one-years-old and well-traveled, he had never journeyed north of the Gila River. Before leaving Tucson for Fort Whipple, he had stopped there and conferred with Pima Indians who informed him that the best crossing was at a place where a large and small butte stood opposite rock hills on the north side of the river. With little else to do but wait out the high water, Hayden climbed the larger of the two buttes. From his vantage point, 300 feet above the desert floor, he looked out upon a wide stretch of inhospitable desert landscape. Stranded for two days, he contemplated the forty-mile-wide valley that lay before him.

During his solitary vigil, Hayden had a vision. He saw more in the Salt River Valley than an arid, forbidding land; he envisioned an agricultural empire reclaimed from the desert. Canals would irrigate verdant farms, and, at the base of the butte, he would construct a water-powered flour mill. As the flood receded he climbed down from his perch and vowed to return. A New Englander by birth, the stranded trader had spent most of his life moving westward on the American frontier. The notion of pioneering a new community in the desert Southwest seemed an inviting challenge.

Charles Trumbull Hayden was born on April 4, 1825, in the village of Haydens, Windsor Township, Hartford, Connecticut, where his Puritan ancestors had lived for six generations. The only children of Joseph and Mary Hanks Hayden, Charles and his sister, Anne, helped their mother operate the family farm after their father had drowned in the Connecticut River when Charles was six years-old. At age sixteen while attending nearby Windsor Academy, Hayden began clerking in a store at Warehouse Point. With three years of formal education and some work experience behind him, in 1843 Charles ventured away from his Connecticut home.[7]

Over the next four years, Charles Hayden migrated south and west, earning his living as a school teacher. A series of short pedagogical stints in Virginia, New Jersey, Indiana, Kentucky, and Missouri hastened young Hayden further westward, where, influenced by the spirit of Manifest Destiny along with a touch of "Oregon Fever," his career plans broadened. By 1847, Charles found the Santa Fe Trail trade more to his liking, and by the mid-1850s he had broken away from the mainstream of westward expansion and was pushing toward the cutting edge of the southwestern frontier. In 1856 Hayden, by then a seasoned Missouri-New Mexico traveler, left Independence, Missouri, with an especially large stock of goods. His destination was the recently acquired Gadsden Purchase south of the Gila River in southwestern New Mexico Territory.[8] Although Tubac, a few miles north of the newly drawn border with Mexico was his original goal, within two years Hayden consolidated his growing interests in Tucson, where he wore the hats of freighter, trader, merchant, and civic leader, expending much energy in the pursuit of each vocation. In fact, in 1864, Hayden accepted an appointment as First District probate judge of the newly formed territory of Arizona. "Judge Hayden," as he was often called, maintained a high profile presence in Tucson until 1873 when he decided to devote the entire wellspring of his considerable energies to his vision of an irrigated agricultural empire in the Salt River Valley.[9]

At this juncture Hayden acted on his vision of creating a farming community in the Salt River Valley. In fact, as early as December 1870 he gave notice in the *Arizona Miner* that he claimed "for milling, farming, and other purposes, sections 28 and 29, Government Survey, on the south side of the Salt River taking in two buttes on either side of the main road from Phoenix to the Gila River." In addition, his newly formed

Charles T. Hayden in front of his Tempe mercantile outlet about 1899 (ASU: CP CTH 1539).

Hayden Milling and Farming Ditch Company claimed 10,000 miner's inches of water from the river. Along with some partners, he planned to homestead the two sections and dig an irrigation ditch to bring the land under cultivation and provide water power to operate a grist mill.

By the mid-1870s, Charles Hayden's pioneer irrigation community, clinging to the south bank of the Salt River, boasted a variety of bustling enterprises; fields of grain, the grist mill, orchards, and Hayden's Ferry which shuttled travelers back and forth for a modest fee and from which the little town took its name. Significantly, in the context of establishing an economic foothold in the desert Southwest, Hayden, at fifty-one-years of age and still a bachelor, met and married his wife, Sallie Davis Hayden. He had met the Arkansas-born school teacher on a freighting trip to northern California in 1874 and after a secret engagement, the couple married in Nevada City, California, on October 4, 1876.[10]

On October 2, 1877, the Haydens became a family with the birth of their first child, a son whom they named Carl. As the first Anglo child born at Hayden's Ferry, young Carl was in the public eye from the very beginning. Local newspapers hailed him as the "prize baby of Maricopa County." Down in Tucson, the *Arizona Citizen* announced: "Born at Hayden's Ferry, Maricopa County, to the wife of Judge Charles Trumbull Hayden, a son. We are advised this newcomer weighed nine pounds, ten ounces at birth." Eventually, the Haydens were blessed with three more children, all girls. Sarah Davis Hayden, often called Sallie, was born June 25, 1880; Anna Spencer Hayden on March 3, 1883; and Mary Calvert Hayden, nicknamed "Mapes" by her older brother, on November 21, 1886. Two-and-one-half-year-old Anna, however, died unexpectedly in 1885, after eating too many green peaches from the family orchard, and, her mother thought, from not receiving sufficient medical attention. The Hayden children were close-knit, but Carl, undoubtedly, became the favorite child of both sisters and parents. Clearly, the hopes and expectations of the family fell on the shoulders of the first-born male.[11]

Carl Hayden's earliest memories centered on his parents' unremitting efforts at making a living in an often hostile environment. At the same time and in spite of the profound environmental limitations, the

Haydens never ceased searching for new ways to broaden and enhance the economic base of their irrigation-dependent community. In the late 1880s, for example, Carl worked long hours at his father's side as they conducted large-scale experiments with citrus trees, grains, and several other crops. The resulting lush orchards and robust fields made the Haydens the envy of Maricopa County.

To a significant extent, young Carl Hayden's hometown became a testing ground for a variety of new ideas. Yet the unpredictable flow of water in the Salt River tempered the hopes of the most optimistic and innovative pioneer farmers. Young Carl knew that Hayden's Ferry, renamed Tempe in 1878 when he was still an infant, was a small and insignificant oasis in the desert, which, at any moment could dry up and blow away on the desert winds, or conversely, could be washed away by an unexpected spring flood. Moreover, as Carl and his family experienced, not all of his father's ideas were successful. Although Charles Hayden had become a man of considerable property and achievement—by 1882 he was the fourth largest taxpayer in Maricopa County—as he grew older he invested unwisely or trusted unscrupulous men. Carl, during his early adolescence, besides observing his father invest foolishly and develop a mania for starting new projects, also witnessed his father devote a major portion of his final years struggling helplessly against environmental forces that threatened Tempe's survival.[12]

In mid-February 1891 Carl experienced for the first time the awesome destructive power of the unharnessed Salt River. Described by contemporaries as "the biggest flood of the Salt River that had ever been known," it erased two decades of human effort and toil in the Salt River Valley. Heavy and continued rains from late January through February on the Salt and Verde River watersheds created the great flood of 1891 and although the crest did not reach the valley until February 20, the railroad bridge washed out on February 18, leaving Phoenix without this important transportation and communication connection for three months.

According to one observer, "white people and Indians scrambled to high ground around Mesa," and flood refugees looked back into the valley with its scores of washed out bridges and weir dams that previously laced together the Salt River Valley community. Frantic letters from relatives and friends outside the valley took weeks to reach their destination. And in mid-March, when Carl and his fellow townsmen looked out upon the ruination, they saw unprecedented destruction. Fortunately for the Hayden family they had moved their living quarters to a ranch on high ground two miles from the river. The family's buildings and businesses located downtown near the river's edge, however, suffered extensive damage and twelve-year-old Carl labored with his father salvaging and repairing items long after the flood receded. In ensuing months, Carl noticed his parents and other valley farmers and businessmen clamoring louder than ever for some type of government assistance that would lead to flood control and water storage.[13]

In what became a cruel irony, a decade-long drought followed the flood of 1891. One Salt River Valley resident recalled that "the big drought started in the 1890s and extended into 1903, practically ten years." Another chronicler interpreted the drought as "the blackest period in the history of the Salt River Valley." A nationwide depression that lasted locally well into the new century compounded the human suffering. By 1897, one of the worst years of the drought, water scarcely trickled in the Salt River. Crops failed, water shortages for livestock and domestic uses became acute, and the local economy ground to a halt. The following year the desert began reclaiming the Haydens' empire: livestock died, and settlers abandoned once-prosperous farms. Those who stayed prayed or hoped for a change in the weather. As the century ended desperate residents from various districts throughout the valley called meetings to take action against the extremes of flood and drought.[14]

Significant private and public sector activity on water storage and flood control preceded valley farmers' calls for organized action in the late 1890s. In 1889, for example, local businessmen and county officials prepared assiduously for a visit from a U.S. Senate sub-committee on irrigation. Earlier that year the Maricopa County Board of Supervisors assigned funds for a study to locate a suitable dam site upstream from the valley. The survey crew, headed by W.M.

Breakenridge, reported that the best location was at the juncture of the Salt River and Tonto Creek, nearly sixty miles northeast of the valley. The "Tonto Site" possessed a hard-rock narrow canyon that opened up to a wing-shaped double valley, where, according to the surveyors, there "was storage capacity for all the floods of an average season." Valley leaders presented the "Breakenridge Plan" notes to the sub-committee, but the legislators took no action.[15]

Discouraged but undaunted, in 1895 local leaders attempted again to construct water storage and flood control facilities on the Salt River. County officials attempted to finance the work through private capital. The New York-based Hudson River and Canal Company filed on the site and maneuvered around bureaucratic obstacles, but after a few years of planning, the company concluded the project was too costly. These unsuccessful efforts at regulating the Salt River in addition to the drought and the exigencies of the eepression, formed a significant part of the physical and social environment of Tempe during Carl Hayden's formative years.

These environmental challenges unfolded against the backdrop of the national irrigation movement of the 1890s. This confederation, headed by reclamation pioneers William Ellsworth Smythe and George Maxwell, combined with the local water shortages of the period, had a major impact on Carl Hayden and his family. The Haydens became involved in several trying water rights cases. Water scarcity led to overdrafting of existing supplies and Carl watched as the family spent considerable sums of money on litigation. One time, when his father left town on business, Carl stood beside his mother as she defended Hayden water rights with a shotgun.

As a direct result of these troubling events, Carl began reading any material available related to irrigation and reclamation. He awaited anxiously the return of his father, who participated in several of the early National Irrigation Congresses, spearheaded by reclamation proponents Smythe and Maxwell. From these meetings, attended by irrigation leaders from throughout the West, Charles, much to the delight of his son, returned with copies of Smythe's magazine, *Irrigation Age*, or Maxwell's published tracts. The writings of these late-nineteenth-century activists, dedicated to "the conquest of arid America," provided Carl with his earliest understanding of the issues and problems relating to his community and to the other western territories and states.[16]

At age sixteen Carl seized an opportunity to act upon a local water issue. During his teenage years he often worked for Curt Miller, editor of the weekly *Tempe News*. In 1894, during the middle of the great drought of the 1890s, Miller took an extended vacation, entrusting his teenaged worker with the printing and delivery of the paper. At this time a major local issue raged as to whether to erect a water tank on top of the butte to provide municipal water works. Miller had expended much energy editorializing against the idea, claiming it would be too expensive to construct and that Tempeans would not support the bonding required to pay for municipally operated water works.

While Miller vacationed, however, Carl rode around town on his bicycle taking a poll on the water project. "Most people were for it," he recalled later, "so I boosted it in the paper and it was built soon after that." Editor Miller returned to Tempe somewhat chagrined at Carl's insubordinate behavior, but later gave the water project his blessing because, as he decided after analyzing the situation, "it was what the people wanted." During the first decade of the twentieth century, the water tank on Tempe Butte stood as a concrete monument to what was, perhaps, young Carl Hayden's first attempt to obtain public benefits for his hometown.[17]

Besides this early demonstration of concern and leadership in local public issues, young Carl's family provided him with the opportunity to travel, not only within Arizona Territory but also throughout the United States and Mexico. Family trips to the East Coast, Washington, D.C., and the Columbia Exposition and World's Fair at Chicago in 1893 were interspersed with solo adventures on horseback into the Grand Canyon and to Mexico. At age fourteen, for example, he traveled to Mexico City alone. Indignant family friends questioned the propriety of such a thing, but Charles Hayden responded to the gossip: "If he can't take care of himself at this age, it's high time he was learning." Unquestionably, the opportunity to travel, whether to Chicago by train or to the Grand Canyon on his favorite horse, provided young Hayden with a perspective on his world that few, if any, of his Tempe contemporaries possessed.[18]

In addition to travel, formal education played a crucial role in shaping Carl Hayden's character, helped him form increasingly sophisticated views about water resource development and other environmental issues, and produced in the young Arizonan a powerful attraction to the political arena. From ages fifteen to eighteen Carl attended Arizona Territorial Normal School, an institution his father played a major role in creating. He attained high marks throughout his three years there, earning especially high grades in U.S. History, Reading, Geography, Botany, and Pedagogy. He also submitted articles to the school literary magazine, *The Record*, and along with the standard subjects Carl studied a new discipline, Political Science, "with unusual depth" according to one of his professors. His classmates, moreover, allowed that their quiet but ambitious classmate displayed "a degree of magnetism seldom found in one of his years." In June 1896 he graduated from the Normal School and, like the majority of his twelve fellow graduates, he intended to pursue a career in teaching. At the commencement exercises, however, he revealed another burning interest when he delivered an address on one of the most controversial issues of the day, the Initiative and Referendum. Reflecting the progressive political mood in the territory, Hayden argued to the audience that Arizonans should adopt these forms of direct democracy, inveighing that "the time had arrived in the affairs of men when government and the people should be made one."[19]

Graduation from the Normal School, which was more like a modern-day high school, prepared Carl for the next stage of his formal education. In the fall of 1896 he entered five-year-old Stanford University, one of the West's pioneer academic institutions, the product of the labor and money of Leland Stanford, one of California's leading citizens. He arrived at Stanford in early September 1896 and immediately faced challenges that tested his ability to adapt to his new environment. He arrived short on credits but was able to enroll as a special student on "probationary status" for one semester. Given a chance to prove himself, Hayden, after completing the first semester with good grades, gained regular student status. Adapting to new academic and social standards proved difficult, but surmountable, and Hayden soon began to enjoy much of what Stanford had to offer. Importantly, he thrived in an academic environment that offered a wide selection of courses.[20]

The variety of elective courses, however, caused a degree of tension between Carl and his father, who envisioned his son taking over the family businesses after graduation. The elder Hayden wrote long, philosophical letters to his son strongly suggesting, if not ordering, Carl to enroll in particular courses. The overzealous but well-meaning father even wrote to Carl's professors, urging them to steer the young Arizonan in the right direction. When Carl confided in a letter to one of his sisters that he intended to study French, Charles fired back a reply to his son: "We recognize your letters as common property. A clear knowledge of the Natural Sciences is more important than knowledge of the French language or any other but your own." As late as November 1899, during the first semester of Carl's senior year, Charles reminded his twenty-two-year-old son that he would do splendidly in business and looked forward to his coming home and "taking charge."

Young Hayden's responses to these admonitions were preserved in a series of letters written at Stanford and reveal clearly that he had formulated definite ideas about his career goals. In one long letter written during his freshman year, Carl wrote, "I have received several letters from you of late and in them you have asked me to leave Stanford next year and help you what little I could in running the business." Carl explained that he foresaw problems in conducting the business: "Did I live under conditions prevalent fifty or sixty years ago I might take the business and make a comfortable success of it. But our competitors today are not J.Y.T. Smith of Phoenix or the store up the street. The corporation owned mills of Kansas and Minnesota fix the price of our flour. To sell meat we must bow to an Armour or Cudahy. We pay for coal at what a Rockefeller asks and if we oppose him he blasts us with his wrath. C.P. Huntington charges all the traf-

Carl T. Hayden upon his graduation from Tempe Normal School in 1896 (ASU: CP CTH 1525).

fic will bear and leaves no profit for me." He called for a truce with his father and told him, "I must say that I would rather have a university than a business education."[21]

Young Hayden had an alternative plan. In reference to his father's hopes that he take over the business, Carl stated flatly, "Both by nature and by habit I love other things. I do not see it that I was born into the business as you say. I am not of the merchant cast." Instead of business, the then twenty-year-old continued, "I was born a lawyer, a politician, a statesman. I have always dreamed of power and the good I could do." In rejecting his father's pleas, Carl asserted his individuality and independence; he possessed direction and purpose.[22]

At Stanford Carl Hayden grew to view politics as his future vocation. Ongoing events in the Salt River Valley reinforced his decision. His family, in the late 1890s lost a major water-rights suit, prompting Carl to wonder if the "Judge had been bought." He looked forward to a time when "honest men can have some say in running public affairs." He charted out an academic program that would best prepare him for a political career. Immersion in philosophy, history, economics, and language, followed by law school, appeared the best plan to follow. He confided to his mother, "I want to make water law a specialty not only because it is a new and open field where the prizes are large to the winner, but also because through it I can have a greater power for good and evil than at any other branch of the law. I know that the law of water is not taught in schools nor found in books, but that is all the more reason why it will be so valuable when known." A growing confidence prompted Carl to declare, "I have no fear of not getting along in this world. Just let me train rightly for the fight and the result is not in doubt. I am going into politics—I shall make honest water laws and see that they are honestly executed."

As an afterthought to this bold pronouncement, he asked his mother to "Burn this letter" lest someone think he suffered from "enlargement of the cranium." And, when he wrote his father that he planned to run for sophomore class president, he asked his father to tell no one for, he theorized, "Silence equals Politics."[23]

In September 1897 Hayden tested his developing political skills in his first campus-wide campaign. After he overwhelmed the opposition for sophomore class president an Arizona family friend wrote him, "I am somewhat surprised by the size of the political bee in your bonnet." The victory came with such ease, in fact, that in his next political endeavor, the race for student body president, Carl ran an overconfident campaign. His friends told him that he had nothing to worry about and convinced him to do little, if any, campaigning against his opponents, among whom was Thomas Hoover, younger brother of recent Stanford graduate, Herbert Hoover. Hayden lost by two votes, the only electoral defeat he experienced in his life. The Stanford student body election of 1899, however, taught Carl a valuable lesson that he never forgot—"always run scared."[24]

An unforeseen event, however, ended Hayden's formal academic career (which, in addition to campus politics, included football, track, debate, and fiction writing) one semester before graduation.[25] In December 1899 Charles Hayden grew very ill, and Carl, rather than staying in Palo Alto and participating in the first Rose Bowl game, rushed home to his family. The elder Hayden became so ill that Carl dropped out of Stanford, took charge of the family business, and incorporated it as C.T. Hayden Company with himself as president and his sisters as vice-president and secretary. With Charles Hayden's death on February 5, 1900, his wish that his son take over the family business was fulfilled. He left Carl the flour mill, the general merchandise store, and several farm properties. Carl also inherited large debts resulting from a combination of his father's generosity and bad luck. In spite of these difficult times, Carl kept the family going. He sold store merchandise to John S. Armstrong and he received a good rental for the mill from Alfred J. Peters, a local businessman and longtime family friend, for $450 per month. Carl tried in 1901 to return to Stanford to finish his degree, but family responsibilities and local political obligations proved too burdensome and again he returned to Tempe before finishing his studies. Resigned to his fate, twenty-three-year-old Hayden decided to make the best of an adverse situation and directed his considerable energies toward support of his family and the fulfillment of his father's dream. Noting the burst of activity, the *Tempe News* commented that "Carl Hayden is getting away with the Phoenix flour trade in big chunks. In fact, the celebrated Hayden flour is taking the lead over the central and southern portions of the territory."[26]

Carl, however, had fixed his eyes on political horizons and moved quickly to divest himself of his business responsibilities. By August of 1901, he had "completely sold out the mercantile interests of the store" and hired accountant L.P. Moore and banker W.H. Wilmer to manage the mill and other rental properties. The rental income enabled him to send his mother, Sallie Davis Hayden, and his sisters Sallie and Mapes to Palo Alto, California, where the girls attended school. With practical considerations thus disposed, he turned his attention and energy to public issues and politics.[27]

In November 1900, twenty-three-year-old Carl Hayden had tested the political waters and found them much to his liking. Tempe voters —by a "flattering vote"—elected young Hayden to a two-year term on the town council. Thus, Hayden embarked on a career of public service that spanned nearly three-quarters of a century. Immediately, the councilman-elect faced the important issue of water. In a letter to Arizona's delegate to Congress, J.T. Wilson, Hayden emphasized that the chief interest of Tempe citizens "lies in a system of water works." In an astute political move, he promised support for Wilson "in Tempe and on the south side of the Salt River," if the territorial congressman would support the Progressive Era concept of public rather than private ownership of the proposed project.[28]

To Carl's satisfaction, Tempe voters approved, 102-17, the sale of bonds to establish public, municipally-owned and operated city water works. Wealthy Phoenix businessman Dwight Heard bought the bonds, and by 1902 a $28,000 stone-and-cement reservoir stood atop Tempe Butte distributing water to local residents. The successful completion of the publicly financed project marked the beginning of Hayden's fruitful involvement in Arizona politics.[29]

As Hayden neared the end of his council term, President Theodore Roosevelt, on June 17, 1902, signed the Progressive "Newlands Reclamation Act." With proceeds derived from the sale of public lands, the government planned to build-water storage projects on western streams and rivers, hoping to encourage settlement of the arid lands west of the hundredth meridian. Hayden and other local leaders quickly recognized the potential economic benefits of the new federal policy and launched an all-out effort to attract a reclamation program to the Salt River Valley. Federally sponsored reclamation, proponents believed, could alleviate vexing problems of urbanization by dispersing population away from the East and encouraging settlement in an agrarian western environment. Under the auspices of the newly organized Salt River Valley Water Storage Committee (later the Salt River Valley Water Users Association-SRVWUA), transplanted New Englander Benjamin H. Fowler traveled east to press the Valley's case in Washington, D.C.[30]

As the time approached for project site selection, Carl Hayden emerged as a spokesman for Tempe and "south side" water rights interests. Under the doctrine of prior appropriation, Tempeans had the longest-standing water rights in the Valley and were determined that those rights should be protected. They became alarmed, however, when National Irrigation Association Director George Maxwell—in Phoenix in early 1903 to help draft the SRVWUA articles of incorporation—proposed eliminating all existing traditions and starting anew.[31] Hayden believed that Maxwell harbored "good intentions," but certainly his "socialist ideas" had rubbed Tempe people the wrong way. In February of 1903, Hayden complained to his mother that he had been "busy every day for a week at various meetings on water storage" and admitted that "the situation is so complex that I doubt if I could explain it all in forty typewritten pages."[32]

At a meeting on February 7, south side water users voted not to subscribe for stock in the SRVWUA. Even so, one Tempe resident fatalistically predicted: "All of the rest of the valley will probably go in for the scheme for they have no way of getting more water and have very little to lose and much to gain by the building of the reservoir." Hayden agreed, stating that "the reservoir will certainly be built," whether Tempe water users joined the association or not. "The boom time," he announced, "is coming before very long."[33]

Somewhat reluctantly, Hayden departed for Washington in early March to lobby for the Tempe Canal Company and south side water interests. He admitted to his mother that he "did not like the idea of making the trip"; nor did he think it would accomplish anything. Hayden, nevertheless, welcomed federal reclamation even if it meant losing Tempe's vested water rights. But, as a leader of his community, he felt duty-bound to represent their concerns.[34] Hayden arrived in the nation's capital in time to witness Secretary of the Interior Ethan Hitchcock "issue the order authorizing the Geological Survey to take up the plans and do all other things preliminary to the construction of five reservoirs among which ours is included." On March 14, 1903, Fowler, Hayden, and other Arizonans in Washington were notified that the Salt River Project was the first of twenty-six reclamation projects authorized by the Interior Department during the first decade of the national irrigation program. Jubilation spread throughout the valley when the news reached Phoenix.[35]

Young Hayden plainly reveled in walking through the halls of power during his three-week stay in the nation's capital, and he proclaimed Washington "the most beautiful city that ever was." "I don't blame a congressman for working by hook and by crook to be returned here," he confided to his mother, "and it is worth all the labor and worry of a political campaign just to be able to live in Washington for two years." Unquestionably, the brief, intoxicating interlude in Washington further stimulated his political ambition.[36]

Hayden returned to Arizona invigorated by his Washington experience, and threw himself into Democratic politics in Maricopa County. The local central committee surpassed Carl's expectations by selecting him to preside over the county convention, which opened in Phoenix on April 26, 1904. When the meeting adjourned three days later, W.B. Cleary—"one of the old chiefs of the wigwam"—expressed his opinion that the Maricopa Democrats should send their thirty-five delegates to the territorial convention in Tucson pledged to vote as a unit for Hayden as territorial delegate to congress. "Hayden for Congress" rumors circulated throughout the Valley, but Carl assured his mother that "there is nothing to the talk."[37]

In Tucson the following month, Hayden achieved his first significant political victory as he was selected to chair the Arizona delegation to the Democratic National Convention in St. Louis. The *Phoenix Daily Enterprise* described the budding politician as "a sterling young Democrat" and proclaimed his selection to head the delegation "an appropriate, deserved, and graceful compliment both to the party and the gentleman in question."[38]

Hayden boarded a train for St. Louis on June 17, eager to rub elbows with national party leaders. He performed his sole duty at the convention, booming out when called upon: "Arizona casts four votes for William Randolph Hearst!" The contest for Democratic standard bearer waged hot and furious. "The political pot is boiling," he wrote his mother, "and only God knows who will be nominated, and He is

Like the Great Flood of 1891, the spring flood of 1905 convinced government officials that the Salt River Valley required one of the country's first federal reclamation projects (ASU: CP CTH 503).

very reticent." Ultimately, Judge Alton B. Parker won the nomination, only to be defeated easily by Theodore Roosevelt in the general election a few months later. Hayden returned to Tempe in August, 1904, with an enhanced reputation and increased respect.[39]

Back in Tempe, Hayden honed his promising talents in the rough-and-tumble arena of local politics. A tireless campaigner, he would win elections as Maricopa treasurer, sheriff, and finally Arizona's first congressman. On November 25, 1904, his hometown *Tempe News* reported: "Carl Hayden won the County Treasurer seat, defeating his Republican and Prohibitionist opponents by a plurality of 341 votes."[40]

Though Hayden had wished to run for the sheriff's office (he had been dissuaded by longtime party members), he viewed the treasurer's office as a political stepping-stone. Hayden's two years as Maricopa County's chief fiscal administrator were years well spent, for he learned much about the budgetary process and public finance. As his term of office expired, Carl informed the party central committee that he intended to run for sheriff. By 1906, party leaders agreed that Hayden deserved his chance.[41] Because the shrievalty was one of the more lucrative county offices—the sheriff received travel money, a percentage of fees collected, and other perquisites—the election was hotly waged and attracted much attention. Citing his record as county treasurer, Hayden promised the same diligence in service and rectitude in conduct. He assured the voters: "I will not be too diligent or strenuous in the pursuit of fees that my bills and charges will be excessive in amount." Rather, he advocated a "middle course" where he received "just and lawful compensation for actual and necessary services."[42]

Voters responded on election day, November 6, 1906, by giving Hayden the largest majority of any candidate in a county race—2,350 votes to John G. Hardin's 1,155. S.S. Green, the Prohibitionist candidate, garnered only 73 votes. On January 1, 1907, Carl Hayden took over the office he would hold for the next five years.[43] Reflecting on his three terms as Maricopa County's chief law enforcement officer, Hayden later recalled, "Being Sheriff required common sense rather than gunplay." Although the six-foot, two hundred pound Hayden cut a colorful and imposing figure, with his cowboy hat, his .45 strapped to his hip, and polished six-point silver badge (with the word "Sheriff" spelled with one "f"), he never shot at anyone nor did anyone shoot at him. Carl traversed the territory, tracking wanted men, serving warrants, or transferring prisoners to Yuma Territorial Prison. His job held important political implications for Hayden, bringing him into contact with influential Arizonans in every corner of the Territory. Most came away with a favorable impression of the Maricopa County sheriff. In the words of a California colleague, "He was a square man."[44]

Hayden experienced two significant changes in his personal life during his term as sheriff. On September 16, 1907, Carl's mother, Sallie Davis Hayden, died unexpectedly after a short illness. Friends and acquaintances throughout the Southwest consoled Carl and his sisters, and mourned the loss of "a great and remarkable woman." Although grief-stricken, five months later Carl tempered the loss of his mother with his marriage to Nan Downing in San Bernardino, California.[45]

The circumstances surrounding the February 14, 1908, marriage illustrated Hayden's penchant for silence, and his attempt to avoid

Nan Downing Hayden (center) upon her graduation from Stanford University in 1902 (ASU: CP CTH 1583).

ostentation and display. Many Tempeans knew Nan Downing, for she had frequently visited the valley as a guest of Sallie Hayden, Carl's sister, with whom she attended Stanford. Upon graduation in 1902, Nan accepted a position teaching English Literature at Los Angeles Normal School. Following a long courtship, Carl and Nan decided in late 1907 to get married; but, at Carl's insistence, they informed only their immediate relatives of their plans.

On Thursday morning, February 12, 1908, Carl notified friends and newspapermen at the sheriff's office that he "was going over home to attend to some business." Word soon got out that the sheriff had left for Los Angeles, and local reporters speculated that he had gone to the coast to pick up a dangerous criminal. Two days later, headlines in valley newspapers announced, "Sheriff Hayden Marries," and "Sheriff Carl Hayden is Now a Benedict." Local friends, surprised at not being taken into the sheriff's confidence, held a belated reception for the couple after their honeymoon trip to the Grand Canyon. The *Arizona Republican* described the festivities: "Thirty-five of his friends visited Carl Hayden and his bride and turned loose their sweet strains of innumerable oil can horns, cow bells, and other melodious contrivances. The serenade was notable not so much for its harmony as its volume." When the noise died down, Carl introduced his bride and passed out cigars.[46]

Nan Downing Hayden quickly experienced what she undoubtedly already knew—her husband was involved in a wide range of activities that placed great demands on his time. In addition to managing the family business, performing the duties of sheriff, and keeping abreast of politics, Carl—a reluctant warrior—was an officer in the Arizona National Guard. Sallie Davis Hayden had not been impressed when, in 1903, by unanimous consent, Carl was elected Captain of Company C. "I don't feel very proud of your new title," she informed her son, "and I shall not address you as anything but Carl Hayden." "I will be lots prouder," she continued, "seeing you with your old blue overalls on riding on a load of hay." Nevertheless, she concluded her protest on a conciliatory note, letting Carl know she trusted his judgment: "I want you to do as you think best and as you will be happiest." Hayden accepted his election as captain, and won reelection as captain until July 1909, when he succeeded E.M. Lawson as major of the First Regiment of Infantry.[47]

* * *

In 1911, Carl read in a local newspaper President William Howard Taft's announcement that if Arizona dropped from its proposed constitution the provision for the recall of judges, he would sign the proclamation granting statehood. The constitutional convention had already set a December date for the election of a governor, two senators, and a congressman, all of whom would take office when Arizona became a state. Hayden turned to his wife and calmly informed her that he intended to run for the House of Representatives. "You certainly have your nerve," Nan replied.

Late in the summer of 1911, Hayden announced: "I am a candidate for the House of Representatives and will begin my campaign as soon as Governor Sloan issues a call for the primaries."[48]

Carl Hayden (second from right) with Arizona Territorial National Guardsmen at Camp Perry, Ohio in 1910 (ASU: CP CTH 1507).

Sheriff Carl Hayden of Maricopa County, Arizona Territory, 1906-1911 (ASU: CP CTH 1533).

II

A Man of Sterling Character

On September 20, 1911, Governor Richard E. Sloan announced that primaries would be held on October 24, followed by general elections on December 12. Forged in a Progressive mold, Arizona's new constitution allowed Arizonans to vote directly for their senators, congressmen, and governors. Moreover, as President Taft well knew, Arizona was a heavily Democratic state with a southern stripe which, in addition, harbored a forceful, politicized labor movement. Winning the Democratic primary, therefore, became tantamount to gaining political office.

Sheriff Hayden faced two formidable opponents, however, in his bid to become Arizona's first congressman. Lamar Cobb, a popular Greenlee County Democrat and member of the state constitutional convention, had strong support in the eastern mining communities. Mulford Winsor, the other Democratic candidate, represented Yuma County's diverse interests, had strong ties with Democratic power broker and future seven-time governor G.W.P. Hunt, and had served as secretary of the state constitutional convention. Few political insiders, including Hayden himself, gave him much chance of defeating either Cobb or Winsor.[1]

Even more discouraging for Hayden, only one Democratic newspaper, the *Phoenix Arizona Democrat*, supported his candidacy. The *Democrat* was prophetic in its assessment of the Maricopa sheriff's political attributes:

> Carl Hayden will make the best Congressman that Arizona will ever send to Washington. A man of sterling character, sound convictions, and a dominating personality, Hayden will make himself known in the halls of Congress. He will accomplish a vast amount of good for Arizona. Hayden is a born fighter and he will not allow the interest of the new state to be overlooked. Hayden is young in years and in full perfection of sturdy manhood. He is a native son of Arizona. Pulsating through Hayden's blood is the innate love for his mother state that ranks second only to the holy tie that binds between offspring and parent. Hayden has tramped over Arizona from the Grand Canyon to the tropic land of the Santa Cruz. To Hayden there is not a spot in all the state that does not teem with thousands of pregnant possibilities. He knows the mineral wealth; the timber wealth. He knows the ranges over which browse the lazy herds of sheep and cattle. Hayden knows the needs of every county and knows them well.[2]

At the outset of the campaign, Carl initiated an agreement in which the three candidates promised not to say "anything bad about each other." The subsequent primary was relatively clean, as the other candidates focused on state, regional, and national issues, and avoided personalities.[3]

Armed with copies of the one favorable editorial and two circulars addressed to "The Water Users of Yuma Valley" and "The Salt River Valley Water Users Association," Hayden gained an early advantage over his two Democratic rivals by defining reclamation as the most crucial issue facing the voters of the new state. In 1905, after years of hydrographic research, Reclamation Service workers had broken ground on a federal irrigation project in the Yuma Valley. "The Salt River Project will be finished in a little over a year," Hayden reminded voters in 1911, "and at Yuma about two and one-half years should see the project completed." Repayment of federal money spent on the two projects worried users because, under the terms of the Reclamation Act, the secretary of the interior would determine the number of annual installments (not exceeding ten) and the "time when such payments shall commence." Hayden stole the political thunder from his two primary opponents by quickly seizing upon an issue of direct economic significance to the voter, defining it, and offering a thoughtful, realistic course of action to the repayment issue.[4]

First, the congressional candidate sought to educate Arizonans on the obstacles in the way of refinancing the debt owed the federal treasury. "The first objection will come from Washington," he predicted, "and the Director of the Reclamation Service will report that we are able to pay our debt and will insist that it be paid promptly in order that completion of other work may not be delayed for lack of money." Fearful that lack of funds might jeopardize present or future projects, representatives from other reclamation states would agree with the Reclamation Service, and insist that Arizona should be made to live up to the letter of the law. For opposite reasons, eastern congressmen and senators, who had always opposed the Reclamation Act as unwanted federal paternalism, would likewise object to adjusting the repayment schedule for Arizona.

Hayden realized that most landowners who would benefit from the Yuma and Salt River projects could not immediately bear the full burden of the payments upon completion of construction. "A congressman who fortified himself with the facts," he argued persuasively, could convince easterners that developing the arid West would benefit the entire country by providing homes and a market for manufactured goods. "If it can be demonstrated that the cost of construction has necessarily far exceeded the original estimates," he concluded, "we should in all justice at least be given a longer time to pay the debt."[5]

Time was the critical element in solving the debt problem facing troubled Yuma and Salt River water users. The federal government had inaugurated the reclamation program as an experiment and, in Hayden's opinion, had arbitrarily and unrealistically fixed the repayment period at ten years. "Delay of any kind will be to our benefit" he argued, "for it will allow Arizonans time to prove to the East that the reclamation of the desert lands of the West will benefit the whole nation."[6]

Candidate Hayden offered a three-point "practical program" to avert the impending crisis. Initial payment should be delayed as long as possible, and subsequent payments graduated so that the largest came last. Finally, and perhaps most important, the Secretary of Interior must extend the period of payments from ten to at least twenty years. If appeals to reason fell on deaf ears in the East, then "the senators and congressmen from Arizona should fight to the last ditch to prevent the passage of any river and harbor bill unless Arizona's just demand was granted." Hayden concluded his well-researched presentation with moving political rhetoric: "I want to see the people who are living in Arizona now, those that have been the pioneers, those that have endured the lean years, to achieve prosperity."[7]

In addition to federal reclamation, the three Democratic contenders addressed a variety of other issues, ranging from women's suffrage, which Hayden strongly supported, to prohibition. The Arizona Constitution, overwhelmingly approved by voters in February of 1911, generated much debate, with Hayden supporting the progressive but controversial document. On a campaign stop in Tucson, he reminded his audience that "The constitution of Arizona is not self-executing. Its mandates must be carried out by men in spirit with the document. The Democratic Party will nominate men who will give you the progressive government that you have long desired to see established in this state." Hayden singled out an issue that especially irked conservative and legally trained President Taft. Referring to the provision for the recall of judges, Hayden stated flatly, "If it is right to recall a state judge it is also right to recall a federal judge, and I will vote for the recall of the federal judiciary."[8]

Fueled by reform sentiment, Hayden and his opponents each tried to convince the voters that he was politically the most progressive. In 1911, and for the decade thereafter, Carl Hayden "wore the label of Progressive Democrat with pride." The issues and causes he supported reflected the spirit of the Democratic Platform of 1912, which went by the slogan "Progress in Every Plank."[9]

Progressivism attracted many groups in Arizona, the most visible —if not the most numerous—of which was labor. "An important segment of the Progressive coalition," during the early days of statehood, Arizona labor possessed a block of votes that no candidate could afford to ignore. Lamar Cobb from copper-producing Greenlee County counted on strong, vocal support in his home county, as well as Cochise and Graham counties, the other eastern Arizona copper mining areas. Hayden and Winsor faced the difficult task of broadening their agricultural and ranching constituencies to include a portion of the mining labor vote.

Hayden responded by urging comprehensive, statewide labor reform, including an employer's liability act, a compulsory compensation law, the abrogation of the fellow-servant doctrine, and the extension to the limits of federal jurisdiction of all provisions in the Arizona Constitution for the benefit of labor. With his Progressive Democratic credentials prominently displayed, the hopeful candidate spent a hectic month on the campaign trail, visiting old National Guard friends as well as all the county court houses and sheriffs' offices he knew so well.[10]

Hayden's careful work paid off and he easily outdistanced his opponents in the October 24 Democratic primary. The final tally listed the Maricopa sheriff with 4,327 votes, to Winsor's 2,685 votes, and Cobb's 2,662. Hayden won ten counties, Cobb two, and Winsor one. Each candidate carried his home county by a handsome margin; Hayden carried Maricopa County overwhelmingly, receiving 1,574 votes, compared to Winsor's 422, and Cobb's 91. As he celebrated his victory, however, the Democratic nominee warned his wife and close friends not to become overconfident.[11]

Hayden had good reason to be cautious. Although a minority party in Arizona at the time, the Republicans had nominated a colorful, popular, and able candidate to face Hayden in the general election, Cochise County Attorney John S. "Jack" Williams. Like many newcomers to southern Arizona in the 1880s, Williams had hoped to find riches in the Tombstone silver mines. Abandoning a legal career back East for "the enjoyment of the free life of the hills," he eventually settled at the railroad town of Benson, sixty miles north of the legendary silver camp. A typical prospector in flannel shirt and khaki trousers, Williams unexpectedly found himself back in the courtroom representing a destitute friend in a personal injury suit against one of the large mining companies. The *Globe Silver Belt* later recalled that Williams' eloquence astonished the jury and won an epic victory. Shortly thereafter he opened a law practice in Tombstone and, in 1908, was elected Cochise County attorney. Three years later, Williams captured the Republican nomination for Congress.[12]

In the six weeks between the primaries and the general elections Hayden spread his Progressive message to the Arizona electorate. With Sidney P. Osborn, the Democratic nominee for secretary of state, and attorney general candidate George Purdy Bullard, he rented an Apperson Jackrabbit, and conducted one of the country's first political campaigns by automobile.

The campaign was memorable for the hardships encountered. Beginning in the southern counties—Pima, Santa Cruz, and Cochise—the intrepid candidates slogged over poor roads in heavy rain and mud, covering the sixty miles from Nogales to Tombstone in fully twenty-four hours. Between Safford and Globe, in Graham and Gila counties, the automobile became stuck in quicksand along the banks of the Gila River. Fortunately three Apache cowboys happened along, tied their lassos to the front bumper, and freed the politicians in time to make their next speaking engagement. Hayden recalled that he learned to shift gears on the Apache Trail near Roosevelt Dam. The three candidates began a campaign tradition of sorts by swinging from Flagstaff, via Winslow, to the Hopi villages, where, in later years, most politicians timed their visits to coincide with the celebrated Snake Dance. Hayden took the time to visit all the Hopi villages; an observer recorded that he stopped at every home in the albino settlements, "asking detailed questions about their health, their education, their happiness."[13]

Also on the northern swing of the campaign, the legacy of Charles Trumbull Hayden resurfaced. Stopping by a spring near Winslow, Hayden spotted a prospector tending to two of his burros. The candidate immediately jumped out of the car, shook hands with the man, and handed him his card. The prospector looked at the card and said, "I never saw you before—you might be a crook or a damned scoundrel for all I know. But you had an honest father so I'll vote for you—once."

Although the automobile was still somewhat ill-suited for Arizona's primitive roadways, Hayden appreciated its mobility, which enabled him to reach many otherwise isolated voters. It also provided him with firsthand experience of the need to improve roadway transportation in the state. Despite the mechanical difficulties encountered during the 1911 canvass, three years later Hayden had purchased a $600 Overland automobile that carried him throughout the state during subsequent campaigns.[14]

Hayden returned to the Salt River Valley in early December, sensing victory. Most of the Spanish language press, including Tucson's *La Democracia* and the *Douglas Industrial Semenario Democrata,* supported his candidacy. At home, *La Voz del Pueblo* devoted an entire issue to Hayden, proclaiming him the only candidate "with the ability to represent and to work for the progress of our new state of Arizona."[15]

At a rally at the Tempe Airdrome, Hayden assured a capacity crowd of 600 people of a clean sweep by the Democratic ticket. The *Tempe News* commented that the congressional candidate had just returned from "a triumphant campaign of the counties of Arizona," and reported that "the crowd of men and women shouted and clapped hands for three minutes" when Hayden rose to speak. In the concluding address of the campaign, Hayden reiterated his support for federal reclamation and again defended "the recall for all public officials, especially the judiciary." But above all, he promised, if elected, to cast in the forthcoming Democratic Congress "one more vote for progressivism and for the principles so dear to the hearts of the people of Arizona."[16]

As most political forecasters had predicted, Hayden and the Democrats swept the Territory in the December 12 general election. The Democratic congressional candidate defeated his opponent in all but three counties—Apache, Coconino, and Pima. The final vote—11,556 to 8,485—appeared a comfortable victory and, indeed, Hayden outdistanced all other Democratic victors in the territory. Unquestionably, Williams' popularity, combined with the 1,252 votes garnered by Socialist candidate John Halberg, contributed to the comparatively narrow victory.[17]

The 1911 campaign revealed an unusual dimension of the understated Hayden political style. At no time, in either the primary or general election, did Hayden mention an opponent's name in public. The tradition would carry over into subsequent political contests. Hayden once remarked that if he ever mentioned an opposing candidate's name in public he "must have been sleepwalking."[18]

Jack Williams remained good-humored to the end of the campaign. When the returns were all in, he wired a telegram from Tombstone saying: "Congratulations Carl. Send my garden seed to dear old Cochise."[19]

On February 14, 1912—the day President Taft signed the bill admitting Arizona as the forty-eighth state—Sheriff Hayden turned over the keys to the jail to Deputy Jeff Adams, and congressman-elect Hayden and his wife boarded a train for Washington, D.C. At Maricopa, the couple met future Secretary of State William Jennings Bryan, who had been visiting his son at the University of Arizona in Tucson. Hayden fondly remembered the chance meeting with the "great populist": "He was kind enough to talk with me and gave me good advice based on his experience as a member of Congress. He told me never to make Fourth of July speeches, because everyone knows how to make them and no one listens."[20]

The Haydens and Bryan arrived in Washington on Sunday, February 18, and the following day Carl was sworn in as Arizona's first congressman. Reporters flocked around the tall, thirty-five-year-old representative from the country's newest state. They found a shy, modest man who responded to questions in monosyllables. After interviewing the awkward legislator, one reporter predicted, "Hayden was all right as a frontier sheriff but he'll never amount to a damn in Congress." When told of the remark, Hayden was "inclined to agree."[21]

III

The Indian Card

Congressman Hayden began the job he held from 1912 to 1927 while President William Howard Taft, whom Hayden remembered as "a kindly man," tried to put Arizona's lone representative at ease, and welcomed him to Capitol Hill. During his fourteen years in the House of Representatives, Hayden witnessed a marked change in the temper of American society. When he entered Congress, agrarianism, the small town, decentralization, and competition reigned in America's constellation of values. The romantic, voluntaristic world of the Arizona Roughriders and the Spanish American War, however, soon gave way to the efficiency-minded state of the Progressive era and the systemization of World War I. By the time Hayden advanced to the Senate in 1927, the distinguishing characteristics of a new America could be foreseen — urbanized, centralized, industrialized, and secularized.

Serving his far western constituency in a rapidly changing America, Hayden, nevertheless, went about his work with an almost singular purpose; extending the benefits of the 1902 Newlands Reclamation Act to his region. Equally important, in the process of furthering federal reclamation in Arizona and the other western states, he helped shape and influence evolving federal reclamation policy during its early and often tumultuous years.[1] "Arizona and reclamation," U.S. Commissioner of Reclamation Floyd Dominy later recalled, "literally grew up together, and Carl Hayden nurtured them both."

Campaign portrait of Congressman Carl Hayden about 1916 (ASU: CP CTH 1929).

As Hayden began his congressional service, federal reclamation, "the great experiment conceived in a spirit of wise and lofty statesmanship," had produced several well-publicized successes. Indeed, Reclamation Service Director Frederick Newell's office churned out annual reports filled with glowing statistical data, claiming "the reclamation of arid lands had brought unparalleled growth to the sixteen states concerned." Beneath the surface, however, serious problems existed within the organization, undermining the apparent progress made during the first decade of the program. Removed from the Geological Survey and made a separate agency within the Department of Interior in 1907, the Reclamation Service had become a veritable snake pit, rocked by "palace revolutions," scandals, and political crises. Moreover, other federal agencies, especially the Army Corps of Engineers, viewed the Reclamation Service as a threat to its "turf," and Hayden, like many other western congressmen, spent considerable time maneuvering around professional jealousies and easily bruised egos. Yet the Arizonan worked with and supported the activities of the Reclamation Service, consulting with engineering personnel and drawing upon the agency's well of expertise. As early as 1914, during his second term in the House, congressmen and senators from both sides of the aisle—Oscar Underwood (D-Alabama) and William Borah (R-Idaho), for example—regarded Hayden as an expert in the politics and economics of federal reclamation. Agency engineers commented on Hayden's grasp of the technical aspects of their work. As he developed a growing reputation in Washington, defining his political identity and expertise in reclamation circles, Arizonans scrutinized carefully their lone representative's activities. And though many important issues faced the Arizona electorate during the second decade of the twentieth century, Hayden knew the bulk of his political fortunes lay in the area of water resource development.[2]

During his tenure in the House of Representatives Hayden wrestled with the practical problem of campaigning for reelection every two years. Since he first arrived in Congress at mid-session, he faced a reelection campaign ten months later. Toward the end of his freshman session, Hayden asked several senior members of the House how they managed to stay in office for so many years. John Moore (D-Tennessee) gave Hayden some predictable advice: "Take care of your folks at home and they will take care of keeping you here." Dorsey Shackelford (D-Missouri) added: "Now you're a young man and you're going home and you're supposed to be a congressman, but you have not yet learned how to be one. Shake hands on the street but if anyone stops to ask you about some piece of legislation, say that you must go on to keep an appointment. If you stop to talk to him, he will soon find out that you do not know any more than he does." Although doubtful that Hayden utilized Shackelford's somewhat cynical advice, he returned home, and recalling his unwelcome surprise in Stanford student politics, "ran scared." Unopposed in the 1912 Democratic primary, he conducted a "runaway race" in his first reelection contest, receiving 2,602 votes more than his Republican and Socialist rivals combined.[3]

From the time Hayden entered the House during the Sixty-second Congress, he devoted most of his time, or as he put it, "the better part of my political career," on issues related to western water resource development. In 1914, for example, he made his first important contribution to evolving federal reclamation policy, playing an active role in the passage of the Reclamation Extension Act, the first significant modification of the nation's national irrigation program. On February 26, 1914, Arizona Senator Marcus A. Smith introduced the bill, describing it as "a broad scheme that will ultimately reclaim the West." The Senate acted promptly, approving the bill on March 18, 1914. When it reached the House, however, strong opposition from midwestern, southern, and eastern congressmen developed, forcing Hayden and other proponents to compromise on several issues.[4]

Eastern, southern, and midwestern congressmen opposed loaning federal funds to western states without interest and convinced the majority of the House that their view should prevail. Yet Hayden and other westerners won a significant victory when they defeated a similar effort requiring interest to be charged on all outstanding water obligations. "Fortunately," Hayden informed his constituents, "we succeeded in defeating this proposition so that the payments to be made will not amount to as much if the money was furnished by private capital." "Even the highest payout under this act," he continued, "is at a lower rate than the interest charge which the average American farmer must pay when he mortgages his land."[5]

Although westerners won concessions over interest charges, Hayden parted ways with the majority and, consequently, with Democratic floor leader Oscar Underwood from Alabama when the Arizonan opposed the Underwood Amendment, which required that Congress vote for appropriations from the Reclamation Fund instead of allowing the Secretary of Interior to allocate the fund. Hayden claimed that the Underwood proposition reverted to the old system of political pork barrel and, therefore, saw no advantage in changing the system. Farmers depended upon prompt completion of irrigation works, he argued, and this could be better accomplished with the

Arizona congressman Hayden campaigning for reelection circa 1920 (ASU: CP MCL 90458).

existing centralized system. Hayden found "no inherent virtue in passing a bill through the Appropriations Committee, for the committee does not necessarily imply economy." "Somebody must show me," the Arizonan contended, "where there is more virtue and more economy in the mere fact of getting a bill through the Appropriations Committee than to leave the expenditure of a limited sum to the discretion of a responsible Secretary, a member of the cabinet who has pride in his work."[6]

Although the Underwood Amendment passed, Hayden expressed his gratitude to the Democratic floor leader because he helped defeat the interest charge provision and aided in the overall passage of the act. The Reclamation Extension Act, as the House of Representatives finally passed it on July 30, 1914, extended payments for construction costs on reclamation projects from ten to twenty years. The bill also allowed flexibility in the actual amount made during the early years of repayment. On August 7, 1914, shortly after President Wilson signed the bill into law, Congressman Hayden delivered a short speech thanking those who supported the bill. "I am of the first generation of Americans grown to manhood in the arid West. I was born in an irrigated valley. I have watered my father's fields at night. I have led the liquid life on to the parched earth, and I know the goodly smell when water touches the dusty clods." Then, referring to the great drought of the 1890s, Hayden told his listeners, "When the dry years came I saw fair fields and fruitful orchards go back to the desert. I saw the horses pawing the alfalfa, for there was no green thing for them to eat. Even the trees on the ditch banks died." He concluded his testament with an endorsement of the Newlands Reclamation Act of 1902: "And then I have seen it all return. This same land has blossomed again under the beneficence of the Reclamation Act.... I speak for every water user in the West when I thank the members of this House who have assisted in the passage of this bill."[7]

Praise from throughout the two-year-old state greeted Hayden for his "clear presentation of the Twenty Year Extension Act." Many water users recalled the special election campaign of 1911 and how the recently passed legislation closely mirrored Hayden's own ideas for reform of the Reclamation Act of 1902. L.B. Hitchcock, a worker for the Arizona Eastern Railroad, "studiously read" Hayden's speeches and congratulated the congressman for the "fearless manner" in which he sought to "keep the reclamation fund from the pork barrel." Hayden himself, in an exceedingly rare example of self-aggrandizement, informed Salt River Valley Water User Association President John Orme: "I feel proud of the fact that I have had some significant part in the preparation of four out of five of these measures, and I am sure that their enactment into law will be of great benefit to the public land states."[8]

Hayden sensed that with the passage of the Reclamation Extension Act, westerners were reassured of long-term federal commitment to water resource development. Most western congressmen, including Hayden, were generally pleased with the new political and economic features of the program and turned their attention to the more mundane yet politically crucial aspects of federal reclamation—securing projects in their districts and handling the multitude of complaints aimed at reclamation personnel. Hayden, however, continued to work on refining reclamation policy. In 1917, for example, he championed the concept of local, yet public ownership of federal reclamation works when he convinced a hesitant Secretary of Interior Franklin K. Lane to transfer the daily "care, operation, and management" of the Salt River Project from the U.S. government to the Salt River Valley Water Users Association.

He explained the motivation for sponsoring this administrative change: "The water users began to complain that the management of the great dam was tied up altogether with too much government red tape." "Everything had to be referred to Washington," and "every suggestion and complaint had to take its course through a routine system, annoying the farmers who were using the water." A staunch proponent of public ownership of utilities, Hayden announced that the Salt River Project's ownership "was public still, but on the ground, not at a distance." "Whenever it works at all," he advised, "local management is better than management from a distance." The Salt River Project was the first reclamation project the federal government began and then turned over to local operation. And, with the continued growth and success of the project, the pattern of government construction and local operation became an organizational framework for future reclamation projects throughout the West.[9]

Hayden next turned his attention to the problem of financing the maintenance and operation charges on reclamation projects. He believed that receipts from the sale of surplus hydroelectric power should be applied to financing operation and maintenance. Interior Secretary Lane, however, opposed the idea, and in a tersely worded missive on December 6, 1916, informed Hayden: "Your claim that power receipts should be credited to operation and maintenance would be violating rules in force." Hayden disagreed with Lane and six weeks later introduced H.R. 20294, "The Power Payment Amendment." In typical Hayden fashion, he inserted the measure into the Sundry Civil Bill. It authorized "receipts from the sale of surplus power to be applied to the payment of operation and maintenance on reclamation projects." Although the amendment passed the House, the Senate, under pressure from the Department of Interior, struck the amendment.

Undaunted by the setback, Hayden began organizing a block of congressmen from Colorado, Utah, Wyoming, New Mexico, and California behind his plan and by the summer of 1917 Lane dropped his opposition. On June 17, 1917, the Arizona congressman wired SRVWUA President John Orme, informing him, that the "House has agreed to conference report on Sundry Civil Bill so that hereafter power receipts will be a credit to the project and can be used immediately to reduce annual payments." Hayden's resolution, authorizing the application of revenues derived from the sale of power to repay the cost and maintenance of reclamation projects, continues to be a prominent feature of the program.[10]

Early in his first term in the House, Hayden obtained a federal appropriation for the Army Corps of Engineers to assess the feasibility of building an irrigation and flood control dam on Pima Indian land along the Gila River in central Arizona. This apparently insignificant legislation was the first step that eventually led to the construction of Coolidge Dam and the San Carlos Irrigation Project. For Hayden, passage of the San Carlos Act was the most important victory of his career in the House. As time would prove, his legislative triumph held significant implications for the larger regional struggle in the 1920s over the Colorado River system. Significantly, historians have ignored the important role Pima Indians played in gaining congressional and public support for the San Carlos Project.[11]

In its first three decades, federal reclamation emerged as one of the most divisive political issues among the Colorado River Basin states. Although the Reclamation Service claimed that conservation had brought "unparalleled growth to the sixteen states concerned," federal largess was unevenly distributed. As a result, western congressmen waged fierce competition for reclamation projects and the federal appropriations that went with them. Indeed, political careers rose and fell with the use and distribution of western waters. In many ways, Hayden's political survival depended upon his ability to bring the benefits of federal reclamation to his arid state.[12]

Throughout most of the nineteenth century the Gila River, a tributary to the Colorado, sustained Indian and Anglo settlers. Water shortages became acute, however, after subjugation of the Apaches in the late 1880s enabled ambitious Anglo-American settlers to take up homesteads along the river above Pima lands. Consequently, by the mid-1890s United States Geological Survey (USGS) hydrographers began looking for storage facilities. In December of 1899, the agency issued a report "strongly favoring" the construction of a reservoir in Box Canyon on the Gila. With the passage of the Newlands Reclamation Act of 1902, landowners in Florence and Casa Grande, along with "friends of the Indian," took heart that they would receive one of the first projects under the new law.[13]

Their optimism faded when Phoenix launched a well-capitalized and highly organized lobbying effort to win the project for the Salt River Valley. The rhetoric of early federal reclamation policy emphasized delivering water to public lands. Because much of the land abutting the river was in the public domain, many Gila River residents assumed that they would have an edge over Phoenicians. Then too, they expected the federal government to take into account abuse of the Pimas' prior rights to Gila River water. However, in the early days federal policymakers favored potential profits over reclamation of public lands. On this basis the Department of the Interior selected the Salt River for one of the West's reclamation projects. It was only the first of many disappointments for the Pimas and for Florence and Casa Grande landowners in their quest for water.[14]

Between 1900 and 1910, Hayden watched the frustration of his Gila River neighbors fifty miles south of Phoenix. No sooner had they braced themselves for a period of government inaction in the wake of funding the Salt River Project (and another project at Yuma), than the floods of 1906 ravaged Indian and white farms along the Gila. Despite their repeated pleas, Gila River valley residents received little relief from the Roosevelt or Taft administrations. Hayden assumed his duties in Congress vowing to do all he could to assist his beleaguered constituents.[15]

Hayden's committee assignments reflected his commitment to reclamation. "I had to build a territory into a state," he later recalled, "so I asked for committee assignments that had legislation that would affect Arizona." Because he hailed from the Salt River Project region, Hayden easily prevailed upon Speaker of the House Champ Clark to place him on the Committee on the Irrigation of Arid Lands. He also asked for and received an appointment to the Indian Affairs Committee. Arizona's mineral wealth, especially copper, placed Hayden on the Committee on Mines and Mining. The federal government owned more than half the land in Arizona, so he welcomed the opportunity to serve on the Committee of Public Lands. Finally, Arizona sent 14,000 men to World War I and soon had more than 30,000 veterans within its borders, entitling Hayden to a seat on the Veterans Affairs Committee. Significantly, at one time or another each of these five committees dealt directly or indirectly with reclamation issues.[16]

Almost at once, the new congressman influenced the legislative direction of the San Carlos Project. In one of his first meetings with the Indian Affairs Committee, he learned about proposed legislation that would direct the attorney general to file suit on behalf of the

Pimas against all appropriators of Gila River water above the reservation. Hayden stunned his fellow committeemen by arguing against the provision. Throughout his boyhood he had heard of nothing but lawsuits over water. His father and neighbors had wasted thousands of dollars on litigation. No court could make rain fall, and no court could stop the torrential floods that washed away the brush dams. The only relief for the Pimas, Hayden explained, was through the Reclamation Fund. Congress should authorize the construction of a great dam on the Gila—like Roosevelt Dam on the Salt River—to store the floodwaters that annually washed down to the sea. In the end, he convinced lawmakers to abandon the idea of a court suit. In its place, Congress instructed army engineers to report on the feasibility of building a dam at the San Carlos site.[17]

For thirteen years conflicting reports had mired the San Carlos Project in controversy. Based on the favorable 1899 USGS study, the Reclamation Service in 1903 had recommended construction of a flood-storage reservoir on the Gila. Two years later, it reversed itself. By 1910, Indian Service engineers joined James Schuyler, a private engineer hired by the Casa Grande Water Users Association, in advocating a reclamation project. The following year, the Southern Pacific Railroad further complicated matters when it took up an old application for a right-of-way through Box Canyon, the proposed damsite. Consequently, Hayden reminded the secretary of war of the importance of the Corps of Engineers' study. If it recommended against construction of the reservoir, it would save taxpayers millions of dollars. On the other hand, if the corps decided that the project was feasible, it would open the way for cultivation of large tracts of desert land, provide homes for thousands of citizens, and ensure a constant supply of water for Gila River Pimas.[18]

Early in 1914, the Corps of Engineers issued a favorable report, calling for the construction of a large dam at Box Canyon, diversion dams downstream, and canals and laterals to complete the delivery system. Much to Hayden's consternation, the corps recommended the adjudication of water rights as a prerequisite to starting the project. Fearing delay and increased costs, the Arizona congressman confided

Coolidge Dam under construction, 1928 (ASU: CP CTH 177).

to Casa Grande landowner Elmer Coker that the proposed lawsuit would let loose the "watchdogs of the Treasury in Congress who make a specialty of preaching economy, particularly when the improvement is outside their own districts." Nevertheless, the favorable report was a starting place, and Gila River farmers rejoiced at the prospect of the $6,311,000 reclamation project. J.F. Brown, President of the Casa Grande Water Users Association, praised Hayden's efforts on their behalf and promised local residents to deliver a "solid vote" in the next election.[19]

Hayden acted quickly to organize influential water leaders in Arizona behind the San Carlos plan. He especially urged them to settle their water rights disputes swiftly in a "friendly" federal court proceeding. "The way to get water is not to quarrel over the meager supply," he admonished, "but to store the water that goes to waste in the sea during flood season." Assigned to Cochise County Judge A.C. Lockwood in June 1914, the proceedings were limited to Pinal County water users and took eighteen months. In early 1916, Lockwood assigned priorities in order of appropriation between 1869 and 1919. The Pimas, the earliest users, received first priority.[20]

While judicial proceedings were still underway in Arizona, Hayden started the legislative machinery rolling on June 3, 1914, when he introduced in Congress the first San Carlos Project bill (H.R. 17106). Unfortunately the Reclamation Service remained cool toward the project. Its engineers pointed to the marginal quality of the damsite, and administrators argued that Arizona had already received a disproportionate share of reclamation funds. Hayden and his Senate colleagues, Henry F. Ashurst and Marcus Smith, therefore, pondered other bureaucratic avenues of support. Careful not to offend the Reclamation Service or its capable but harried director, A.P. Davis, Hayden ruled out seeking support from the rival Army Corps of Engineers. Instead, he adopted an old strategy to new circumstances.

Sensing the reform sentiment that gathered force in the teens and twenties, Hayden convinced the other members of the delegation to play their old "Indian card." Although the plight of the Pimas had failed to sway politicians in the first attempt to win support for the

San Carlos Project, with a unified congressional delegation and backing from white landowners in Florence and Casa Grande, Hayden's new campaign seemed to have a better chance of success.[21]

Hayden very early orchestrated a skillful campaign to shape public perceptions that the San Carlos Project would benefit the Pimas. In March 1914, before the bill had been officially introduced in the House, he informed political leaders, newspaper editors, landowners, and businessmen throughout the Gila River Valley that "our best, and in fact our only avenue of approach is by reason of the fact that the Pima Indians will be benefited." By the following year, Indian Service employees referred to the San Carlos legislation as the "Hayden Indian Bill."[22]

Hayden was well acquainted with the Pimas, whose irrigation and flood control needs played such a key role in gaining political support for the project. He proudly recalled that "they have been my friends all my life." His first nurse was a Pima woman from Sacaton who taught him how to count in the Piman language. As a boy, he had met the great chief Antonio Azul. Hayden agreed that the Pimas needed an adequate water supply if they were to move into the twentieth century. Although he acknowledged the concerns of friends of the Indians—"principally artists and authors"—who regretted efforts to modernize Pima lifestyles, Hayden contended "that it is better for them to be prosperous than picturesque."[23]

Pimas themselves actively lobbied for the San Carlos Project, issuing pamphlets, public statements, and other information in support of Hayden's bill. The Pima First Presbyterian Church pointed out that Pimas "had been farming by irrigation when Columbus discovered America," and W.F. Haygood, agency superintendent at Sacaton and twenty-six-year veteran of the Indian Service, testified that "the Pimas are the best people I have ever worked with.... They pride themselves that they have few gratuitous appropriations and that they have supported themselves by their own efforts." Tribal leaders, in turn, expressed gratification and pleasure over Hayden's work in their behalf. Hayden and the rest of the Arizona delegation exploited to full advantage this much-publicized Indian support for the San Carlos Project.[24]

Moral and legal justification notwithstanding, the San Carlos Project faced an uphill political battle. Ironically, antagonism from other western states buttressed opposition from the East and Midwest. Representatives from Utah, Colorado, New Mexico, and Wyoming reminded Hayden that Arizona had already received more than its share of reclamation funds. More ominously, the emerging fight over Colorado River water threatened to draw behemoth California into San Carlos Project politics. Hayden feared that his bill would be submerged by larger regional issues.[25]

To counter opposition arguments, Hayden launched a vigorous education campaign. In sub-committee hearings and in public, the Arizona congressman pointed to the success of the Salt River Project as an argument in favor of building a similar project on the Gila. San Carlos Dam would join the two regions into "a single expanse that ...

Pima Indians at Coolidge Dam, 1930 (ASU: CP CTH 167).

will reach the million acre mark." Florence-Casa Grande valley farmers announced that they could contribute as much as their neighbors to the north to the progress and prosperity of Arizona. Hayden also cited Internal Revenue Service figures showing that because of reclamation the Salt River Valley had poured millions of dollars into the federal coffers. Stated simply, the San Carlos Project was well worth the investment.[26]

Hayden received strong support from a wide range of organizations within the state. Gila River Valley farmers formed a San Carlos Association and, in 1918, began holding annual "San Carlos Days," replete with bands, parades, speeches, and barbecues. Thousands of individuals joined civic groups, chambers of commerce, veterans organizations, and the University of Arizona in working for passage of the bill.[27] The Arizona Industrial Congress (AIC), comprised of businessmen and agricultural leaders dedicated to the promotion of the San Carlos Project, provided Hayden with useful economic information. AIC president and Gila River Valley resident P.G. Spilsbury corresponded regularly with Hayden, offering and receiving advice on how best to utilize the organization.[28]

Hayden also organized an extensive letter-writing campaign, beginning in 1915, in which Arizonans urged out-of-state acquaintances to press their congressmen to vote for the project. A Casa Grande druggist lobbied an old friend who had been recently named to the bench in southern California. "The purpose of this appropriation," the Arizonan explained, "is to build a dam to provide irrigation for about fifty thousand acres of land capable of supporting large numbers of people." He concluded by pointing out that even California stood to gain from the San Carlos Project—"As anything which benefits this portion of Arizona would benefit southern California and Los Angeles in particular." Vice-President Thomas Marshall, a frequent Arizona visitor, volunteered his help, writing letters to congressmen urging them to approve the project. Texas Democrat Sam Rayburn offered to help Arizona in its "just cause," and even California Republican Phil Swing pledged his support for Hayden's bill. Although tedious and time-consuming, the outpouring of letters added yet another important dimension to the effort and resulted in a broadening of support for the San Carlos Project.[29]

Even so, significant obstacles stood in the way. In particular, World War I delayed serious consideration of the bill. As early as October of 1915, Hayden complained that the "present demand for increased armament" had diverted attention from reclamation. In 1918, he explained to a frustrated constituent that the "great difficulty in obtaining bills for the development of new reclamation projects is that the time of the House and the Senate is so occupied with measures related directly to the war with Germany that it is very hard to obtain consideration for any other legislation." Besides forestalling action on the San Carlos Project, wartime emergencies delayed passage of a much-discussed National Reclamation Program.[30]

Inauguration of the fiscally conservative Harding administration in 1921, followed by the even more penurious Coolidge administration, caused reclamation proponents in the desert Southwest still greater concern. Harding's election, Hayden noted, boded ill for "any extensive scheme of reclamation," especially since the Republican administration expressed "little toleration for any increase in federal taxation." Fearing that "increased competition would further lower prices in the already depressed corn belt," midwestern congressmen renewed their attack on western reclamation.

Despite opposition, western congressmen elicited assurances from President Harding that he would "actively aid in the passing of a national reclamation program." As late as September of 1923, shortly before Harding's death, Hayden thought that the chief executive was "committed to enactment of legislation for the establishment of an enlarged reclamation policy as manifested in the Smith-McNary bill." Arizonans hoped that the San Carlos Project would be the first constructed under the proposed legislation.[31]

While the House and Senate versions of the Smith-McNary bill languished in committee, Hayden quietly pursued another method to force congressional action on the San Carlos Project. Working closely with his colorful Senate colleague Henry F. Ashurst, as early as 1916 Hayden had convinced Congress to insert the first $75,000 designated for "the San Carlos Irrigation Project," into the annual Indian Appropriation Act. With this initial outlay, work began on one of two proposed diversions downstream from the main reservoir site. Although World War I delayed construction, Arizonans took heart. In 1922, Indian service engineers completed the structure—the "largest Indian Weir Type Dam in the United States"—on the Gila River twelve miles east of Florence. Appropriately, Commissioner of Indian Affairs Charles Burke named it the Hayden-Ashurst Dam.[32]

For the dedication on May 10, the Arizona Eastern Railroad ran special trains from Phoenix as Native American and Anglo revelers enjoyed barbecue beef, beans, and dill pickles. The governors of neighboring New Mexico and Nevada attended the festivities, labeled "The Biggest Event in the History of Arizona." While Arizonans celebrated, Hayden dashed off a note to Judge Otis T. Baughn, president of the San Carlos Association, attempting to place the dedication ceremonies in their proper context. "The real reason why the dam was built," Hayden reminded Baughn, "was that it was an integral and essential part of the larger San Carlos Project concept."[33]

In subsequent years, Congress continued to fund the San Carlos Project through the Indian Affairs budget. Although piecemeal, the approach nevertheless produced results. The Indian Appropriations Act of March 2, 1917, included $125,000 for a diversion dam and bridge at Sacaton. The following year, Congress designated $50,000 for construction of the main canal and laterals. Supplemental appropriations followed in quick order. Prior to Harding's inauguration on March 4, 1921, Hayden and Ashurst had secured $1.670 million for construction of diversion dams and delivery systems for the San Carlos Project, this despite the lack of a full endorsement from either Congress or the president. Through innovative use of the federal bureaucracy and cooperation of the Indian service, the Arizona delegation had increased the chances of passing a San Carlos Project bill. The government, Hayden reasoned, would not squander its already substantial investment.[34]

Other factors contributed political momentum to the project. The appointment in 1923 of a Committee of Special Advisors on

Reclamation (also known as the "Fact Finders Committee") indicated that central Arizonans' flood-control and irrigation needs were being taken seriously. Secretary of the Interior Hubert Work, a Californian, appointed outgoing Arizona governor Thomas Campbell, a Republican well-steeped in the problems of reclamation, to chair the committee that included such luminaries as former Secretary of the Interior James Garfield and future head of the Bureau of Reclamation Elwood Mead. Moreover, the Republican landslide of 1920 swept Tombstone Democrat Marcus Smith from office and carried a Republican, Ralph Cameron, into the Senate. Although Cameron promised unrealistically prompt results on the San Carlos legislation and later proved an embarrassment to the Republican party, his election added an important bipartisan dimension to the Arizona congressional delegation.[35]

As the winds of politics shifted, Hayden pressed on, attempting to break down regional opposition. In June of 1920, he persuaded Chairman Homer Snyder of New York and eight other members of the House Committee on Indian Affairs to visit the proposed damsite. The inspection convinced them of the project's merit and, according to Hayden, "did more than any other one thing towards securing favorable report on the bill." In March of 1922, the Arizona congressman invited his friend and colleague, Louis C. Cramton of Michigan, to visit the San Carlos site. Cramton, chairman of the House sub-committee on appropriations, was so impressed with the project, and "with Hayden's presentation of the facts," that he increased the 1923 appropriation for canal construction from $150,000 to $250,000.[36]

Meanwhile, Hayden spearheaded negotiations to remove another obstacle—the Southern Pacific Railroad. The congressman convinced Southern Pacific directors Walter Douglas and Paul Shoup to drop their right-of-way claim through Box Canyon and negotiate with the government for an alternate route on their Phoenix-to-Safford line. Together, with the secretary of interior and the commissioner of Indian affairs, Hayden, Douglas, and Shoup hammered out an agreement whereby the government and the Southern Pacific shared the cost of removing track already laid on the San Carlos reservoir site. The final agreement saved Gila River valley landowners more than $1 million.[37]

Sensing that the most important obstacles to the San Carlos bill had been removed, in the fall of 1923 Hayden called together Ashurst, Cameron, and San Carlos Association representatives for a series of strategy meetings, most of which took place in Hayden's office. As a result, on December 11, Cameron—Arizona's lone Republican in Washington—introduced in the Republican controlled Senate a bill (S. 966) "to continue construction of the San Carlos Federal Irrigation Project." While Ashurst lobbied for support of "every Democrat in the Senate," Republicans—pleased to have one of their own from traditionally Democratic Arizona—fell in line behind Cameron. On April 23, 1924, the Senate, in a rare display of unanimity on a floor vote, passed the bill.[38]

Attention then shifted to Hayden in the House. During the spring of 1924, Arizona newspapers drummed a steady beat of hometown sentiment on the San Carlos bill. "For twelve years Hayden has been striving for what Arizonans hope is actual fact—the development of the San Carlos District." Partisan accounts placed responsibility for fulfilling the hope of Arizonans squarely on the shoulders of the state's Democratic congressman. An editorial entitled "Up to Carl Hayden" in the Republican *Tucson Citizen* darkly suggested that Hayden's political career would end if the bill did not pass at the present session of Congress. "Arizona as a unit is demanding passage of the San Carlos bill," the writer inveighed, "and we are anxious to ascertain the scope of influence of Arizona's congressman-at-large in the lower house." A political confidante warned Hayden: "The whole state is watching you on the San Carlos bill.... But oh boy, everyone, both Republicans and Democrats are watching you." Most newspaper editors, however, felt that Hayden had learned on the job and had adapted to the "Washington system."[39]

Statewide praise of Hayden's effectiveness translated into unprecedented political success. Including the special election of 1911, Arizona voters returned Hayden to seven consecutive terms in Congress. In 1916 the Republican-owned *Tombstone Prospector* lamented: "We wish the Arizona Republicans would sometime nominate a man for congress who would start the perspiration on Carl Hayden. Nothing they have produced yet has made the Arizona boy break into a trot." Even during the 1920s Republican ascendancy, Hayden ran stronger in Arizona than any other candidate, state or national. Although Calvin Coolidge won the electoral vote in the 1924 general elections, Arizonans split their ballots to give Hayden a huge margin of victory (40,329 to 8,628) over challenger W.J. Galbreath.[40]

More revealing perhaps, Hayden consistently outpolled his opponents in areas where reclamation was a pressing concern. In 1924, he defeated his opponent in Maricopa County, home of the Salt River Project, 12,774 to 690. In Pinal County, the potential beneficiary of the San Carlos Project, Hayden won 1,484 to 20. And in Yuma County, he outpolled the Republican candidate 1,608 to 72. Clearly, voters identified Hayden with the benefits of federal reclamation.[41]

Amid an atmosphere of heightened anticipation, Hayden worked calmly and purposefully to win House passage of the Senate bill. After two months of diligent lobbying, he confidently reported, "I do not believe that a single Democrat will vote against it.... I have made it my business to talk to all of them." Chairman Snyder recognized Hayden's contribution when he suggested that the Arizonan deliver the Indian Affairs Committee report. Hayden modestly declined the honor, explaining "I am not seeking credit out of this legislation." "You are the chairman," he reminded the New York congressman, "and your name on the report might give it more weight.... I will do all the work preparing it, but you sign it." Hayden, nevertheless, asked Snyder for one concession: a sentence stating that "The Committee of Indian Affairs is authorized to say that the President favors enactment of this bill." Snyder agreed, providing that Coolidge approved the addition.[42]

In late April, Hayden drove to the White House to discuss the San Carlos bill with President Coolidge. Although the president had heard about the measure, Coolidge professed not to know enough about its specific provisions to approve. He suggested that Hayden meet with the director of the budget. Unable to get a commitment from the frugal New Englander, Hayden decided that "the time had come to smoke Mr. Coolidge out." With Chairman Snyder's approval, he dispatched telegrams to newspapers in Florence, Casa Grande, Tucson, and Phoenix, informing them that he "had been to the White House and the President declined to commit himself in favor of the bill." "I have no doubt," Hayden recalled later, "that the backfire from the publicity had a very beneficial effect on Mr. Coolidge." Even so, the economy-minded president remained characteristically silent.[43]

In the meantime, Congress forced Coolidge's hand. On June 4, the House unanimously approved the San Carlos Project bill. Unfortunately, the House and Senate versions differed so drastically that Hayden was compelled to rewrite the entire bill.[44]

Hayden's revisions reflected the influence of recently appointed commissioner of the Bureau of Reclamation Elwood Mead and recommendations included in the Reclamation Fact Finder's Committee report. Mead viewed federal reclamation as a key to social reform, and his appointment demonstrated the increasingly important role that engineers played in public life. When Interior Secretary Hubert Work designated Mead to head a reorganized bureau, Hayden cheerfully acknowledged that "The reclamation sky is beginning to clear." In fact, the Arizona congressman had long admired the professor's work, especially his scholarly tracts promoting government assistance for land settlement proposals for adapting the Australian method of financing irrigation development in the American West. Not surprisingly, Hayden had conducted a hallway campaign for Mead's appointment to the reclamation post.

Although Hayden's bill granted Pimas first rights under the San Carlos project, the portion of the legislation that dealt with privately held lands (almost one-half of the total 80,000 acres to be brought under cultivation) embodied Mead's vision of reclamation as a tool for social reform. The San Carlos Project would be a community of small, self-sufficient farms—a twentieth-century reaffirmation of the American agrarian ideal. Lands held in private ownership were limited to 160 acres. Excess acreage would be returned to the federal government as homestead land for ex-servicemen. In a nutshell, Hayden saw in the San Carlos Project legislation "one of the best examples" of the original intent of the 1902 Newlands Reclamation Act.[45]

Despite his prominent role, Hayden thanked individuals and organizations who worked long and hard for the project. "The active assistance of the friends of the Pima Indians throughout the United States," he noted, "and the various churches, especially the Presbyterian and Catholic, were particularly helpful." Tens of thousands of Arizonans who wrote letters to their friends in the East also deserved much credit. Finally, he singled out the Arizona Industrial Congress, the Phoenix and Tucson chambers of commerce, the Southern Pacific Railroad, and many other organizations for their support. The effort, he concluded, "was one of splendid cooperation —there is glory in it for all."[46]

Predictably, Arizonans reacted enthusiastically to the bill's passage. Dwight Heard, editor of the influential *Arizona Republican* and Republican candidate for governor in 1924, announced that "the glorious news of the passage of the San Carlos bill brings joy to every citizen of Arizona." "The fight for the bill," he continued, "was one of the great epics of the West and is a story of courage, steadfastness, and cooperation." A Tucson reporter added that "The great reservoir soon to be created in the canyons of the Gila will not only bring the greatly needed relief to the long-suffering Pima Indians but also will bring into cultivation thousands of acres of privately owned land." Others predicted the lands downstream from the dam would develop into one of the most productive agricultural districts in the nation—a new Arizona inland empire.[47]

Rosy predictions notwithstanding, President Coolidge had yet to sign the legislation. The conference committee had completed its report and Congress had approved $5.5 million for construction of the dam and accouterments, but Coolidge complained that the project would place too heavy a burden on taxpayers. Hayden quickly arranged a meeting with Interior Secretary Work and Commissioner of Indian Affairs Burke, seeking their advice on how best to avoid a presidential veto. They suggested naming the structure "Coolidge Dam."

Hayden (sixth from left) with Indian Service engineers prior to completion of Coolidge Dam, 1930 (ASU: CP CTH 171).

Hayden liked the idea. Along with Ashurst, he met Coolidge at the White House and informed the president that the "marvelous structure" on the Gila River would bear his name. Evidently, the flattery worked; on June 7, 1924, Coolidge signed the San Carlos Project bill.[48]

Construction commenced promptly under the able direction of Indian service assistant chief engineer Charles R. Oldberg, who had previously designed Roosevelt Dam on the Salt River. Erection of the multiple-dome San Carlos structure created hundreds of jobs in the economically depressed Gila River valley. Pimas and neighboring San Carlos Apaches, bitter enemies historically, took full advantage of wage opportunities. The Pimas also looked forward to increased agricultural production once the dam was completed. The Apaches, facing inundation of the community of San Carlos by the waters stored behind the dam, were forced to move their agency headquarters north to Rice, renamed "new" San Carlos. Despite the inconvenience caused by the relocation, the tribe of modern-day cattle growers and timber producers discovered commercial opportunities catering to the growing number of weekend campers and fishermen on San Carlos Lake. When the dam was completed and water storage began in 1929,

Anglo and Native American farmers alike started annual planting and harvesting of corn, melons, wheat, and especially cotton, "King of the San Carlos Project." Although decidedly a secondary consideration, power development nevertheless played a role in the maintenance and operation of the project. In 1930, the Nevada Consolidated Copper Company's nearby Ray mines purchased all the electricity generated at the dam.[49]

On a sunny March 4, 1930, former President Coolidge and his wife, Grace, arrived in Arizona to dedicate the dam. State officials, Pima and Apache tribal leaders, and other dignitaries gathered for the event. As 10,000 spectators looked on, and two all-Indian bands played the "Star Spangled Banner," Coolidge smoked a peace pipe with the headmen of the Pimas and Apaches. Ironically, Congressman Hayden was unable to attend the festivities because of a scheduling conflict.

Later, at an outdoor luncheon atop Coolidge Dam, a parade of speakers lauded the virtues of the project. Humorist Will Rogers delivered the most entertaining of the day's speeches. Referring to the Colorado River controversy and Arizona's protests over construction of Boulder Dam, the honorary mayor of Beverly Hills, California, remarked: "I came here to see that California gets its pro-rata share of this dam." He also needled Congressman Hayden's use of Pima water rights to obtain funding for the San Carlos Project. "You folks got this dam built by using the Indians as an alibi," Rogers joked. "They won't use any of it after today for they'll go back to the reservation to live like they've always lived." Finally, the folksy humorist uttered the most memorable line of the day. Noticing a clump of weeds protruding above the water from behind the dam, Rogers quipped, "If this was my lake I'd mow it." The audience laughed and shouted as he left the lectern.[50]

The crowd quieted and thousands of Arizonans tuned into KTAR radio as Coolidge strode to the microphone and launched into a speech that was notable for its lack of diplomatic aplomb. The former president informed his audience that only a telegram from President Hoover had prompted him to come to Arizona. He compounded the insult by wondering aloud whether he was expected "to talk to the dam or the water." Finally, Coolidge referred to the struggle between California and Arizona for water and power rights to Colorado River resources and the soon-to-be completed Boulder Dam. He pleaded with Arizonans to "get along with thine enemy." "It seems to me," Coolidge concluded, "that we ought to dedicate this (dam) to the advancement of nations, to the benefits of education, to the making of better homes, and the making of a better country." He then broke a bottle of Gila River water against the dam. Forgetting for the moment that Coolidge had been a less than enthusiastic supporter of the San Carlos Project, the crowd roared its approval. Apart from the incongruous spectacle of New Englander Coolidge delivering a speech atop a dam in the rugged and remote southwestern desert, the former president's presence at the dedication ceremonies symbolized the significance Arizonans attached to reclamation.[51]

Beyond the political consequences for Hayden and the economic benefits for the Gila River valley communities, the San Carlos legislation affected the legal and political configuration of future reclamation development in the Southwest. In 1963 the Supreme Court ruled in *Arizona v. California* that Nevada would receive 300,000 acre-feet of mainstream water annually, California 4.4 million, and Arizona 2.8 million, plus "exclusive rights to the Gila River." California objected to the formula, contending that the approximately 1 million acre-feet of water put to use annually under the San Carlos Project should be considered part of Arizona's 2.8 million allocation. Instead, the court accepted Arizona's long-held contention that water put to beneficial use under the San Carlos Project gave Arizona prior and exclusive rights to the Gila River. As a result, Carl Hayden's "Indian Card" produced a federal reclamation project for Native American and Anglo landowners in central Arizona, while at the same time significantly altering the shape of water resource development in the Southwest in the second half of the twentieth century.[52]

IV

Origins of the Colorado River Controversy in the Southwest

Issues surrounding the use and distribution of the waters of the Colorado River occupied more of Hayden's time in public office than any other political issue. His direct involvement in Colorado River politics can be traced to its earliest emergence as a problem of national and international significance. His bill, H.R. 9421, presented in May 1919 during the first session of the Sixty-sixth Congress, was among the earliest legislative attempts "to authorize ... a Colorado River reclamation project" along the lower reaches of the river. Subsequently, he was involved in virtually every phase of Colorado River development—from the Colorado River Compact negotiations of 1922 to the passage of the Colorado River Basin Project Act of 1968, which authorized, among other things, construction of the Central Arizona Project (CAP). For Hayden, passage of the Colorado River Basin Project Act of 1968 was a personal victory—the capstone of his public career. "My efforts in behalf of the Central Arizona Project," he informed his constituents shortly before his retirement in 1968, "began while I was still a Congressman and I consider it ... the most significant accomplishment of my career." As Hayden indicated, the foundation for this legacy began during the 1920s when development of the Colorado River became an issue dominating the politics of the American Southwest.[1]

Compared to federal reclamation on the Gila River, development of the Colorado posed far more complicated political challenges for Hayden and other Arizona leaders. Unlike the San Carlos Project legislation, Hayden exercised little direct control over legislation concerning the Colorado during the same period. In addition to overcoming anticipated regional opposition that threatened most western reclamation projects, any Colorado River project contained the problem of dividing the river's resources among seven southwestern states and the Republic of Mexico.[2]

From its source in the Rocky Mountains, the Colorado River drains some of the most arid and beautiful country in the United States. Its 244,000 square miles of drainage area flows nearly 1400 miles in a southwesterly direction through deserts, canyons, and fertile valleys. Within the United States the river drains watersheds in Wyoming, Colorado, Utah, New Mexico, Nevada, Arizona, and California. Before emptying into the Gulf of California, the Colorado crosses the international border near Yuma, Arizona, and flows its last 100 miles through Mexico. Despite its large tributary system, which includes the Salt and Gila Rivers, the Colorado is not a heavy flowing stream. It ranks only sixth in volume among the country's rivers. Average precipitation in the basin amounts to only fifteen inches, and evaporation reduces runoff by ninety percent. Based on records kept since 1922 the remaining ten percent of runoff amounts to only 15.5 million acre feet annually, or one-twelfth the volume of the Columbia River. As a result of the demands placed upon the flow by the seven states and Mexico, the Colorado, according to historian Norris Hundley, Jr., has been the most litigated, regulated, politicized, and argued-about river in the world.[3]

The interstate and international stream possesses other noteworthy characteristics. It flows on a ridge above sea level and in ages past, it tore through its banks and poured into lower lying valleys. Important consequences of these intermittent floodings were the creation of a large lake of fresh water, the Salton Sea, and the depositing of rich alluvial soil that reached hundreds of feet deep. Also, the Colorado was one of the heaviest silt carriers in the world, carrying

Hayden poses with government surveyors and their wives at the rim of the Grand Canyon, 1922 (ASU: CP CTH 311).

five times that of the Rio Grande and seventeen times that of the Mississippi. Toward the delta, its speed decreased, dropping much of its load of silt, thereby causing the channel to rise above the surrounding countryside. By the twentieth century, these periodic floodings had created a rich delta in a climate conducive to year-round agricultural production.[4]

The origins of the Colorado River Basin Project Act cannot be precisely traced, but nineteenth century visionaries and dreamers contributed significantly to later developments. John Wesley Powell, undoubtedly, stimulated the imaginations of Americans when he argued for a more rational approach to problems posed by the arid West. In his "Report on the Lands of the Arid Regions of the United States," he predicted accurately that reservoirs would enable Americans to divert water to southern California's fertile lowlands. Though he failed to envisage the precise location of Hoover Dam, his ideas struck a responsive chord among his contemporaries. Richard Hinton, the widely read western journalist, carried Powell's arguments further. In uncompromising terms, Hinton urged massive federal spending for devising comprehensive irrigation works in the region. Famed scientist and army engineer Hiram Chittenden added that a "comprehensive reservoir system in the arid regions of the United States is absolutely essential." And with prescience, Hinton and Chittenden agreed that the federal government was the best agency to facilitate this development.[5]

Still others acted on the notion that the river was a source of potential livelihood. In 1849 Dr. Oliver Wozencraft, on his way to the California gold fields, first conceived of a plan to irrigate the Imperial Valley by gravity flow. Although Wozencraft spent the remaining years of a frustrated life in a vain attempt to fulfill his dream, he laid the groundwork for future efforts. In 1879, no less a promoter than John C. Frémont, then acting as territorial governor of Arizona, proposed a grandiose scheme that outraged his charges on the east bank of the river: the governor endorsed a plan to alter the climate of the Imperial Valley by flooding the Salton Sink with Colorado River water. Arizonans vigorously opposed the scheme, prefiguring later animosities over the dispensation and use of the Colorado. It took another nineteenth century pioneer, however, to realize Wozencraft's dream. In 1892, Charles Rockwood, while investigating the possibility of irrigating land along the border with Sonora, observed, as Wozencraft had earlier, that the Imperial Valley could be turned into a vast year-round garden if water could be placed upon the fertile soil. After several setbacks and false starts, Rockwood, in 1896, with substantial financial backing from American and European investors, created the Colorado Development Company. Enlisting the technical expertise of internationally known irrigation engineer George Chaffey, Rockwood succeeded in delivering water to the Imperial Valley on June 21, 1901.[6]

The introduction of water to the valley precipitated a major land rush. Thousands of settlers formed mutual water companies that purchased and distributed water from Rockwood's company. By 1909 over 15,000 people farmed approximately 160,000 acres in the area. Yet serious problems quickly besieged these pioneers. Of immediate concern was the water delivery system. Specifically, Chaffey, relying largely on Wozencraft's earlier designs, tapped the river just north of the international border and fed water into the Alamo Channel that skirted the California sand dunes through the Republic of Mexico for fifty miles, before turning north again into the United States. International legal problems, questions over control of the diversion route below the border, troubles related to the Mexican Revolution, and the presence of American speculators in Mexican lands, who often worked at cross-purposes to Imperial Valley interests, made life for Rockwood, the Colorado Development Company, and valley residents a series of crises.

Indeed Mexico sought to exact a high toll in water, money, and other concessions for the use of her territory. Revolutionary activity threatened the quality and quantity of the valley's water supply. Wealthy Americans caused Imperial Valley farmers further consternation. A group of Los Angeles businessmen, led by *Los Angeles Times* publisher Harry Chandler, were the largest landholders in the Mexican delta. By 1905, the Chandler syndicate owned more than 840,000 acres, most of which they leased to Mexican, Chinese, and Japanese tenants. These sets of circumstances created the atmosphere which prompted a movement for an "All-American" canal.[7]

A natural disaster further stimulated the movement for an All-American Canal. In February 1905 flood waters began rising, and within a matter of weeks the area known as the Salton Sink became the Salton Sea. The flood ruined Rockwood and forced his company into bankruptcy. He surrendered control of his corporation to the Southern Pacific Railroad in exchange for help in controlling the river. By 1907, after nearly two years of flooding, Southern Pacific work crews had the river back within its banks. Yet the consequences of the flood left valley residents with two masters over their water supply: the Southern Pacific Railroad and the Mexican corporation, Sociedad de Irrigacion y Terrenos de la Baja California, which controlled the water supply south of the border. In an effort to free themselves from two receivers and eliminate their water supply from Mexican control, Imperial Valley residents saw the need to establish public control over the irrigation works in the United States.

In 1911, Imperial Valley lawyer Phil Swing and promoter Mark Rose, led the valley in this direction by organizing the Imperial Irrigation District (IID). This agency gave settlers the ability to elect directors, issue bonds, levy assessments, condemn property, and most importantly, purchase and operate the valley's irrigation system. Legal complications, however, involving the two receivers and damage claims related to the flood delayed action for five years. Finally in 1916, the Southern Pacific, anxious to get out of the irrigation business, sold the assets of the Colorado Development Company for $3 million. The IID, thereafter, lobbied Congress for a water delivery system located wholly within the United States.[8]

If the great flood of 1905-7 contributed to the creation of the IID and the movement for an All-American Canal, it also served notice that there was a pressing need for flood control and storage along the river. Arthur Powell Davis of the newly created Reclamation Service in the Department of Interior emerged as the chief spokesman and most influential advocate of federally sponsored flood control and water storage on the Colorado. He not only championed the idea of flood control, but he also argued for comprehensive development of the river. By 1902 Davis had devised a plan for the "gradual comprehensive development of the Colorado River by a series of storage reservoirs." Soon thereafter, President Roosevelt, in response to the floods, called upon Congress "to enter upon a broad comprehensive scheme of development for all irrigable land" along the river. Davis, with the support of Congressman Hayden, convinced Interior Secretary Franklin Lane to earmark funds to launch an extensive investigation of the Colorado River. After 1914, Davis, as Director of the Reclamation Service, oversaw the survey. Not surprisingly, California, and especially the Imperial Valley, foresaw the development of comprehensive irrigation and flood control works as the result of the study.[9]

Proponents of comprehensive development received much publicized support from the League of the Southwest, a regional booster organization. Largely a California-sponsored group, the League, founded in November 1917, nevertheless claimed that it represented businesses and local governments dedicated to the commercial and social interest of the southwest quarter of the country. At its initial convention at the Hotel del Coronado in San Diego, California, representatives from the seven basin states, Oklahoma, and Texas joined envoys from Washington, D.C., and even Europe to discuss the future possibilities of the fast-growing region. Hayden and other Arizonans came away from the initial meeting pleased after University of Arizona President Rufus B. von Klein Smid was selected the League's first president. During 1917 and 1918 the group met at San Diego and Tucson where discussions based upon the development of the Colorado River centered on tourism, commercial development, and transportation. By 1920, the League of the Southwest became an organization with virtually one purpose, which was reflected on its newly adopted letterhead: "The League of the Southwest holds as axiomatic that the development of the resources of the Colorado River Basin fundamentally underlies all future progress and prosperity of the Southwest."[10]

Meanwhile, in November 1917 the IID had convinced Interior Secretary Lane to conduct a survey determining the feasibility of the proposed All-American Canal connecting the Imperial Valley with Laguna Dam, a diversion structure that supplied irrigation water to the Yuma Reclamation Project. The valley thereby could link up with an established reclamation project. Lane assented to the survey, but only if the IID paid for two-thirds of its cost. Residents quickly agreed to these terms and a committee of three engineers, called the All-American Canal Board, conducted a study that lasted through 1918. In December it issued a preliminary report, recommending the construction of a sixty-mile-long canal at an estimated cost of $30,000,000. Naturally, Harry Chandler and his partners opposed the findings. Imperial Valley residents, however, repudiated Chandler and the "Los Angeles Syndicate" in a January 1919 referendum that overwhelmingly endorsed the project. Armed with the report and the mandate from valley residents, IID attorney Phil Swing stepped up pressure for congressional support of a federally funded All-American Canal.[11]

For Hayden, however, flood control and storage took precedence over the canal. Along with Congressmen William Kettner and Charles Randall, both from California, he submitted flood control bills as well as a bill calling for the construction of the All-American Canal. Submitted between February and June 1919, during the third session of the sixty-fifth and first session of the sixty-sixth congresses, these earliest Colorado River reclamation bills attracted little support, but congressional hearings focused national attention on Colorado River issues. One of Kettner's bills, H.R. 6044, submitted on June 17, 1919, called for the construction of an All-American Canal without a storage dam further upstream. The House Committee on Irrigation of Arid Lands held extensive hearings on the bill, and Hayden, as a senior member of the committee, carefully scrutinized the proposed legislation.

Hayden opposed the move as did Reclamation Director Davis. Davis reasoned that Californians were trying to put the cart before the horse. If additional land was put under cultivation, the director pointed out, "it will threaten the water supply of the whole valley." Furthermore, premature construction would increase the danger of flood. Hayden agreed with Davis, for uppermost in his mind was the safety of Arizona's Yuma Project. "There must be reservoir construction," he argued, and in addition the Imperial Valley "should pay some equitable part of the cost of water storage." The Arizona congressman broadened the issue at hand. He told Californians that "you are now coming to Congress asking that an extraordinary thing be done by the passage of this legislation and Congress must look to the development not only of the Imperial Valley, but the Colorado River valley as a whole, and that can only be fully developed by storage." In effect, Hayden served notice that he opposed California gaining prior right to Colorado River water with the aid of the federal government.[12]

Indeed he viewed the Kettner bill with great suspicion as did various local Arizona leaders. One Yuma Project spokesman, Colonel B.F. Fly, feared that "Yuma would be wiped off the map without storage." "I think it a crime to even talk of constructing the All-American Canal until ample provision for storing the headwaters have been carried out," he wrote Hayden. Fly offered some choice observations: "The people over in Imperial Valley don't care a rap for us. One bunch over there wants all the water for the present cultivated lands, while the other bunch wants the All-American Canal constructed purely for speculative purposes—to sell lands they have claimed through bogus desert claims." Colonel Epes Randolph, Tucson resident and consulting engineer, agreed with Fly's overall assessment of the situation. "The Imperial Valley is in a precarious situation and should receive help, but the remedy...is not an All-American Canal.... The danger is in the Colorado River itself, which at the moment overhangs the Imperial Valley and the Yuma Valley like a sword of Damocles."[13]

In seeking to protect Arizona interests, Hayden proposed legislation of his own. H.R. 9421, "a distinct improvement over the Kettner bill," according to Interior Secretary Lane, which provided for a storage reservoir, an All-American Canal, and preferential treatment for returning World War I veterans. In September 1919 Hayden informed a Yuma Project resident, "My idea is that when the bill is perfected it should be reintroduced under Mr. Kettner's name because he represents the larger interests affected and I am interested in securing good results rather than personal credit in the matter." Hayden's bill addressed the difficult dual problems of protecting his constituents' interests, while simultaneously reconciling those interests with the needs of the region.[14]

While hearings on the Kettner All-American Canal bill exposed sharp differences on how to approach Colorado River development, they also revealed broad areas of agreement. As Hayden's flood control bill attested, Arizonans too wanted to conserve and develop the river's resources. Moreover, Arizona business and political leaders had long supported river development. In the mid-1890s, for example, territorial governor Nathan Oakes Murphy proposed a rudimentary version of the modern-day Central Arizona Project, when he called for damming the river near the Grand Canyon and irrigating the land between there and Phoenix. Murphy, a Republican appointee in a Democratic territory, suffered much editorial abuse for his "chimerical schemes." Yet one of his most outspoken critics, Anson Smith, editor of Kingman's *Mohave County Miner* and a prominent state legislator from that northwestern Arizona county, soon became an ardent proponent of Colorado River development. Storage, Smith later editorialized, would provide electricity for Arizona's mines and water for agriculture, thus turning Arizona into a "Garden of Eden." The Kingman resident, like many other Arizonans, spent a considerable portion of the remainder of his public career campaigning for multiple use of the river.[15]

Yet the rapid growth of the Imperial Valley and the aggressiveness of Californians to utilize the river tempered Arizona's enthusiasm for immediate action. Imprudent California water diversion practices especially concerned Hayden, causing him to publicly rebuke the Californians. Their small weir dam, Hanlon Heading, which raised water high enough to permit diversion, repeatedly caused flooding on valuable Arizona farm lands abutting the river. In 1916 this practice flooded the entire town of Yuma. Hayden's curt, pointed reference to the Imperial Valley during hearings on the Kettner bill revealed his displeasure. A related situation concerned him as well. Most observers knew that preliminary engineering studies confirmed the long-held notion that the only adequate storage sites on the lower reaches of the river lay in Arizona. Many Arizonans, therefore, believed California possessed grand designs to benefit from the use of Arizona's resources. Still others saw sinister motivations in any California-supported measure. George Maxwell, foremost reclamationist articulated these sentiments, and at the same time helped revitalize his stagnating career, when, in January 1919, he informed a special joint session of the Arizona legislature: "Don't sell your birthright for a mess of pottage. Arizona is in danger, and unless you become alive to the situation, you will wake up one of these days to find Arizona on the dry side of the river." Maxwell's pronouncements were not based on scientific studies, but he nevertheless assured his audience that Arizona was entitled to half the floodwaters. "Vast enterprises are afoot in California which could use to good advantage all the floodwaters," he warned. "It is up to Arizona to show that it has the available acreage for its half and then to organize to protect its rights." Unfortunately the more extreme sentiments inherent in these statements found fertile political soil among Arizonans, and for Hayden, at least, the fight with California over the Colorado had begun.

Meanwhile the Arizona congressman had little trouble convincing chairman of the House Irrigation Committee, Moses Kincaid of Nebraska, to table the Kettner bill. Citing testimony of Reclamation Director Davis, objections from the Department of State and Treasury, and statements from noted irrigation specialist Elwood Mead, he sealed the bill's fate. Secretary of State Robert Lansing objected to the measure because, he ventured, an All-American Canal should be built only after a treaty had been negotiated with Mexico. "Equity and comity" entitled Mexico to some of the river's flow, Lansing suggested, citing a treaty drafted in 1906 that awarded Mexico 60,000 acre-feet annually from the Rio Grande. Treasury Secretary Carter Glass criticized the bill in harsher terms, finding the financial features of the bill "untenable." He objected vigorously to the feature that compelled the federal government to underwrite the project by guaranteeing IID bonds. "If the project is meritous," he snapped, "it should be funded with a direct appropriation of a specific amount for the purpose." Mead, Chairman of the California Land Settlement Board, added his objections. Veterans, he avowed, should receive preferential treatment and landholders should be limited to 160-acre single-family farms.[16]

In January 1920, against Hayden's advice, Kettner tried once again, submitting a bill which incorporated criticisms of his previous measure. This latter bill provided for a canal, storage, preferential treatment of veterans, and provisions that proved palatable to secretaries Lansing and Glass. By this time, however, Congress realized that Colorado River development posed problems of enormous legal, engineering, political, diplomatic, and economic complexity. Reclamation Director Davis also emphasized the need for further scientific studies. "The most feasible point for storage," he testified, "is in Boulder Canyon" in Arizona, but the Reclamation Service required more investigations. "We have made surveys there for a high dam," he added, but high water and the exhaustion of funds curtailed these studies. In May 1920 Congress tabled Kettner's bill, heeded Davis's advice, and approved the Kincaid Act—a compromise measure—named after the House committee chairman, which authorized the Secretary of Interior to complete ongoing surveys, with special attention paid to the needs of the Imperial Valley.[17]

The Kincaid Act provided Hayden with a welcome respite, yet he watched carefully the growth of an informal, not always agreeable, but powerful alliance between the IID and the Reclamation Service. This alliance not only alarmed Hayden, but also leaders throughout the Colorado River Basin. Hayden understood and accepted the visceral fear of upper basin leaders that the lower basin would develop more rapidly and then lay claim by prescription and prior appropriation an inequitable amount of Colorado River water. To add to these growing fears, the city of Los Angeles joined the Colorado River sweepstakes, making known its desire to secure power and water for its rapidly expanding population. Similarly, upper basin states saw southern California urban and agricultural water users as threatening their future development, since California projects would put a large share of the river's flow to prior use.[18]

As the engineering investigations continued, upper basin fears crystallized at a meeting of the League of the Southwest in Denver, Colorado. At this August 1920 meeting, just four months after a harmonious gathering in Los Angeles, upper basin representatives raised serious questions about California and its motives concerning the Colorado River. Colorado Governor Oliver Shoup sounded the clarion call: "It is not time for the western states holding the headwaters to lose any of the rights for any reason whatever." His state engineer, A.J. McCune, echoed these remarks and added, "Our main fear is that Los Angeles and the people of the Imperial Valley will get the government committed to a policy that will interfere with our development." Furthermore, he warned that construction of the reservoir and beneficial use of the water would give California prior rights over upper basin states. Like Arizona, the upper basin expressed great trepidation regarding California and called for some form of protection.[19]

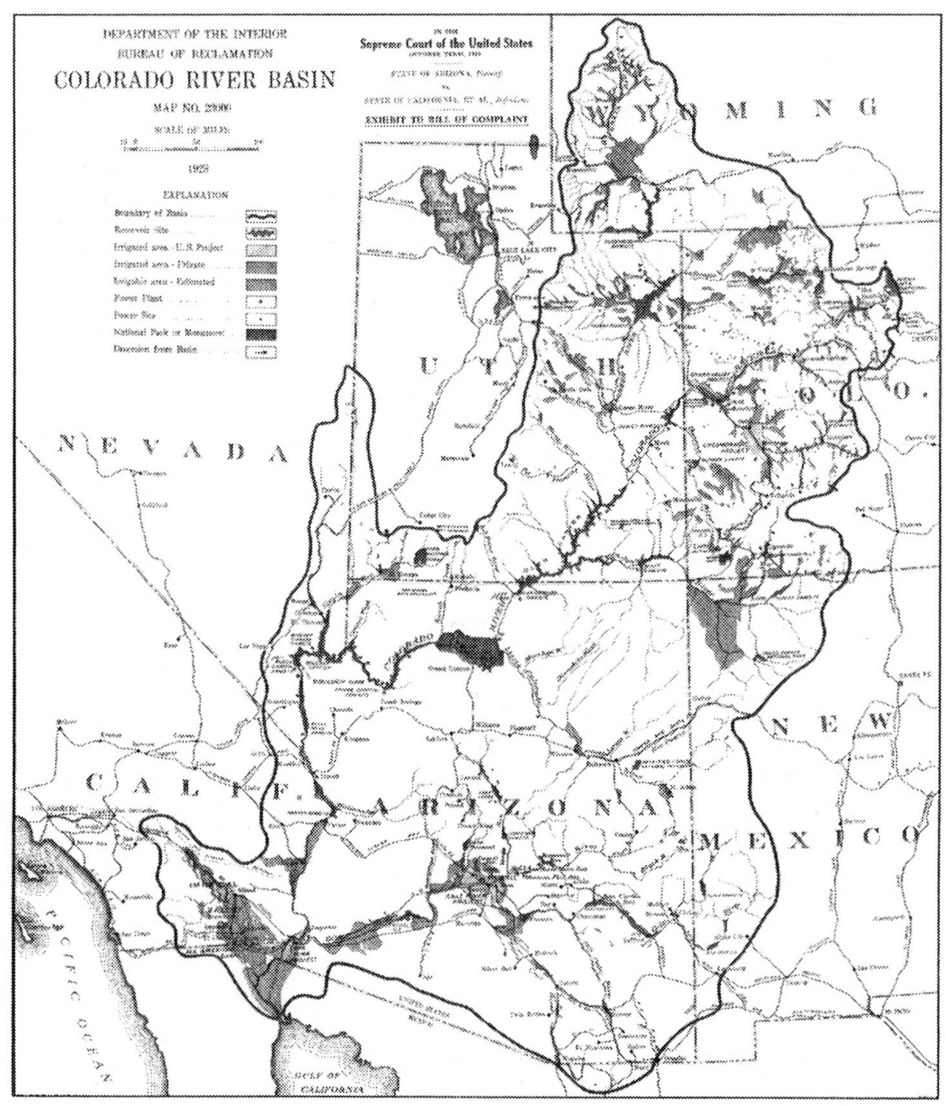

The Colorado River basin as drawn in 1935 for the Bureau of Reclamation (author's collection).

Governor Shoup's legal advisor, Delph Carpenter, offered a recommendation to address upper basin fears. His proposal led ultimately to the creation of the Colorado River Commission and the Colorado River Compact negotiations. At the time of this portentous League of the Southwest meeting, Carpenter served as a member of the defense counsel in the eight-year old *Wyoming v. Colorado* (1922) Supreme Court case. The suit centered on rights to the waters of the Laramie River, which rose in Colorado and flowed northward into Wyoming. Hoping to spare the seven states that shared the Colorado River the cost, turmoil, and often unsatisfactory results of a Supreme Court decision, Carpenter found an audience receptive to ideas he first outlined in 1912. He advocated action under little-used Article Six of the U.S. Constitution, which allowed states, once receiving permission from Congress, to negotiate treaties among themselves. Such a compact, Carpenter reasoned, could assure slower-developing states that they would receive protection, while at the same time, the Colorado River could be put to beneficial use as quickly as possible. Carpenter firmly believed that an agreement among the states could incorporate both a lower basin dam and a provision for upper basin protection. In response to his admonition, the Denver delegates adopted a resolution, calling for a compact to determine present and future rights of the states who claimed interest in the Colorado River. Furthermore, the resolution suggested the seven states authorize the appointment of commissioners for the purpose of entering into an agreement and for the subsequent ratification by the state legislatures and Congress.[20]

Inexorably the movement for compact negotiations moved forward. By spring 1921 the basin state legislatures had taken a formal first step in the direction of a Colorado River Compact. On May 10, 1921, Arizona Governor Thomas Campbell joined six other basin state governors in Denver and issued a request to President Harding to support negotiations. In June, with the support of the new administration, House majority leader Franklin Mondell introduced legislation calling for a Colorado River Commission, comprised of representatives from each of the states and a federal representative. On August 19, 1921, President Harding signed the Mondell bill into law, and shortly thereafter named a surprise appointee to represent the federal government in the negotiations, Secretary of Commerce Herbert Hoover. Although Californian Hoover had not been the most obvious candidate for the assignment, none questioned his honesty, integrity, and sterling international reputation.[21]

While Hayden took satisfaction in the Mondell legislation he maintained keen interest in the contents of the engineering report authorized under the Kincaid Act. For the Arizona congressman, the Fall-Davis Report, named after Interior Secretary Albert Fall and Reclamation Director A.P. Davis, contained few major surprises. At a public hearing in San Diego on December 8-9, 1921, Davis presented the results, recommending construction of an All-American Canal and a high dam capable of generating power at or near Boulder Canyon. He told his listeners, "In the northwestern corner of Arizona there is a profound and very deep narrow canyon, where it would be feasible to build a dam 700 feet high." This site, moreover, held other advantages, most important among them was that the damsite was closest to the power markets in the areas where year-round irrigated agriculture took place. In addition, a high dam would create a reservoir that controlled flooding, regulated flow, and allowed silt to settle, eliminating that problem without destroying storage capacity.[22]

Notably, hydroelectric power generation, previously an incidental byproduct of reclamation endeavors, suddenly emerged as one of the most emotional, bitterly contested, and complicated issues of the entire program. Davis, in a preliminary version of the report, left open the possibility that a private, municipal, or state agency might build the dam and sell power. Almost immediately private power companies, like Southern Sierras Power and Southern California Edison, saw the potential for enormous profits, and quickly filed applications with the recently created Federal Power Commission (FPC). Likewise, the city of Los Angeles, seizing upon public sentiment that private power companies were charging unfair rates and eager to secure affordable power for a rapidly increasing population, also applied to build a power-generating dam at the proposed site. The subsequent conflict over the merits of private versus municipally operated power raged for months, polarizing contending interests, and resulting in the dissolution of the League of the Southwest. Secretary Fall, however, closed this portion of the power debate and ended preliminary speculation over who would build and operate power plants when, at the public hearing in San Diego, he announced that the U.S. government possessed the ultimate authority to deal with the issue.[23]

Hayden observed with great interest this phase of the Colorado River debate. He wrote Arizona Governor Campbell that power needs in the state were not as immediate as those in southern California, but projected that Arizona's requirements would mushroom in the near future. Hydroelectric power would be needed for groundwater pumping, expanding Arizona's world-renowned copper industry, and meeting increasing domestic demand. Moreover, power was needed for the dream of pumping water from the Colorado to the central portion of the state. As one state official described the still-nebulous scheme: a high dam at either Black or Boulder Canyon would generate power, pumping Arizona's share of the river to the central portion of the state in a "highline canal" to "the Gila Basin and other places."[24]

Early in 1922, as federal officials prepared the final draft of the Fall-Davis Report and the Colorado River Commission commenced negotiations, Hayden continued his policy of "watchful waiting," while refining his ideas on river basin development. He believed that Colorado River development was too large an undertaking for any other agency except the federal government. "It is certain to my mind," he wrote University of Arizona Professor G.E.P. Smith, the noted irrigation engineer, "that the construction of necessary dams will never be undertaken by private enterprise." In addition, he agreed with the conclusions of the Fall-Davis Report which asserted that the federal government alone should construct and operate any power plant on the river. Yet, like most western political leaders at the time, he sought to protect the just prerogatives of the states in determining policies of preservation, conservation, and utilization of natural resources within their borders. In spite of having formed these general conclusions on river development policy, Hayden strove to remain "open-minded, absolutely unbiased ... and perfectly free to weigh without prejudice" the expected variety of programs and proposals from interest groups with conflicting claims to the river. The Arizona congressman placed his faith in the Colorado River Commission and their widely publicized negotiations and in doing so mirrored the hopes of most responsible western political and business leaders.[25]

On January 26, 1922, the Colorado River Commission began hearings in Washington, D.C., and after intermittent meetings throughout the West during that year, concluded its negotiations with the drafting and signing of the compact on November 24, 1922, at Bishop's Lodge in Santa Fe, New Mexico. Hayden made a noteworthy contribution to the negotiations when he urged that the final phase of the hearings, all seventeen of which took place in Santa Fe, be held after the November 1922 elections. "The chances for agreement among the seven states," he reasoned, "will be greatly improved if the meetings are held after the elections thus reducing the temptation to demagogue in certain quarters." His suggestion related to political events taking shape in Arizona. Colorful three-time former governor G.W.P. Hunt, a Democrat, was challenging two-term Republican incumbent Thomas Campbell in the general elections of 1922. Both candidates forced the compact to the forefront of the campaign. Campbell, naturally, favored the commission's deliberations. Hunt opposed them, suggesting to Arizona voters that William S. Norviel, Campbell's appointee to the commission, was "selling out" Arizona's interests and that only he, Hunt, could "save" the Colorado for Arizona.[26]

While Hayden favored Norviel's approach throughout the course of the negotiations, the Arizona congressman also believed that Hunt failed to consider that Norviel and other representatives, in order to arrive at an agreement, necessarily compromised their claims to the river. The Colorado River Compact's provisions have been widely discussed and analyzed. Its chief innovation, the brainchild of Colorado's representative Delph Carpenter, divided the Colorado River watershed into two basins, with the division point at Lee's Ferry located in the rugged canyonlands of northern Arizona near the Utah border. The commissioners, in forging an accord, allotted the upper basin—Wyoming, Colorado, Utah, and New Mexico—7.5 million acre-feet

Governor Thomas Campbell, supporter of federal reclamation and Colorado River development, 1922 (Sharlot Hall Museum, Prescott, Arizona).

of water annually. The lower basin, comprised of Nevada, Arizona, and California, received 7.5 million acre-feet of mainstream water per year, plus a million acre-feet annually, plus an additional one million acre-feet under the vaguely worded and controversial Article III (b): "In addition to the apportionment ... the Lower Basin is hereby given the right to increase its beneficial consumptive use of such waters by one million acre-feet per annum."[27]

Article III (b) reflected Arizona's interests in the beneficial consumptive use of the waters of the Gila River, the Colorado River tributary whose watershed lay almost entirely within Arizona borders. Moreover, Hayden and the Arizona delegation were working assiduously to put the Gila to beneficial use under the terms of the San Carlos Project legislation. Arizona Commissioner Norviel, who, according to one interpreter of the compact, "played a major role in shaping the treaty that was eventually drafted," compromised significantly on the one million acre-feet figure, for Arizona's "tributaries," the Gila system, according to some contemporary estimates, produced between two and three million acre-feet of annual surface runoff. Norviel explained to Hayden, "it was understood though not expressed, that the one million acre-feet from the Gila would practically take care of or offset all the water produced" in Arizona. Since the commission agreed to apportion water to basins rather than states, such an understanding, implied or otherwise, could not be expressly written into the pact. Chairman Hoover lent unofficial credence to Arizona's claim when, after the signing of the compact, he gave an autographed picture of himself to Norviel that carried the inscription: "To the best fighter on the commission. Arizona should erect a monument to you and entitle it one million acre-feet!"[28]

Hayden paid special attention to Article IV, which like Article III (b), dealt with an issue crucial to Arizona hydroelectric power generation. Agriculture and domestic uses for water, according to commissioners, took precedent over power development. Hayden agreed in principle with the article, yet quickly noted that he intended to address hydroelectric power in separate legislation.[29]

The Arizona congressman scrutinized several other aspects of the pact. He expressed concern over provisions that made states' rights superior to those of the the federal government. He agreed with an upper basin initiative which foiled attempts by California to include a storage provision in the agreement. As a result of this latter omission, flood protection on the lower reaches of the river had to await congressional action. He noted that Native American rights to Colorado River water were disposed of in curious fashion. Article VII of the compact, dubiously referred to as "Hoover's Wild Indian Article," was in reality a non-article. It postponed addressing Indian water rights. "Nothing in this Compact," it stated, "shall be construed as affecting the obligations of the United States of America to Indian tribes." Future generations have wrestled with this costly, but not surprising omission.

Likewise, the commissioners ignored Mexican rights on the river. If the United States recognized the right of Mexico to use of the Colorado, Article III (c) stipulated that both basins share the obligation in equal proportion. Hayden agreed with the commission's silence on this point. In the summer of 1922, while the commission recessed, he informed the House Committee on the Irrigation of Arid Lands, "I do not want to ... See ... any treaty with Mexico until we have settled our own troubles in the United States." "I shall oppose any kind of Mexican right in the Colorado River," he continued, "until it is definitely and fully determined that there is a surplus of water in that stream for which there is no possible use in the United States." Hayden believed that the Mexican issue was a problem for the State Department and Congress, not the Colorado River Commission.[30]

Although close observers of the Colorado River Compact negotiations were well aware of the document's limitations, omissions, and ambiguities, they were soon calling it the "Law of the River." The sobriquet carried the implication that the agreement would keep the river out of the courts. Ottamar Hamale, solicitor for the Reclamation Service, Hoover's legal advisor at the compact deliberations, and a leading voice for federal control over unappropriated waters in western streams, expressed such optimism. "This settlement was reached within a year," he wrote Hayden, "while the settlement in court of the Wyoming-Colorado case required about eleven years and is unsatisfactory to both sides involved." "The compact was not intended to be a complete settlement," Hamale added, but "a big step in the right direction and as big a one as can be made at this time."

Other basin leaders expressed similar optimism. Delph Carpenter placed the compact signing in broader perspective when he wrote Hayden: "This is the first exemplification of interstate diplomacy on so large a scale." Fellow Colorado water law expert L. Ward Bannister called the pact "a great document ... a product of two years of labor by the best minds the states and nation had to give." In Arizona, newspaper editor, businessman, and politician Dwight Heard hailed the compact as a broad and necessary foundation for the erection of machinery that would ultimately determine the rights of the basin states and expedite development of the river. Hayden, however, sensing the political storm gathering force in Arizona with the recent decisive election of fellow Democrat G.W.P. Hunt, a critic of the compact deliberations, reserved an assessment of the pact deliberations for later.[31]

The congressman had several questions about the compact that remained unanswered, yet he hoped the Arizona state legislature would ratify the agreement. While Hayden supported the concept of a Colorado River Compact, California actions in Congress during the course of the negotiations caused him great worry. He opposed outright the introduction of the first of several Swing-Johnson bills, which, like earlier bills, provided "for the protection and development of the Lower Colorado River Basin." H.R. 11449, introduced in the House of Representatives on April 25, 1922, contained provisions for storage, power production, and an All-American Canal. Hayden registered his opposition to the bill not only for the poor timing of its introduction, but also because its content "was purely for the benefit of California." As a senior member of the House Committee on the Irrigation of Arid Lands, he used his considerable influence to bottle up the objectionable bill for the remainder of the congressional session.[32]

Just as he opposed what he considered California's premature legislative actions, Hayden fought similar initiatives emanating from private interests within Arizona. James P. Girand, a respected former Arizona state engineer and businessman had filed, revised, and refiled applications with various state and federal agencies for the right to produce hydroelectric power at a site on the river in northern Arizona. Significantly, Girand acted in behalf of the state's powerful copper interests, which, after the creation of the FPC in 1921, pressed the application to that agency. In response to the introduction of the first Swing-Johnson bill, Girand and his backers pursued their application with great vigilance. Hayden opposed this effort, especially against the backdrop of the Colorado River Commission hearings. Of course, the upper basin and California notified Hayden of their opposition to the Girand Project. Reclamation Director Davis also argued against the application, claiming that the development of power at Diamond Creek, Girand's proposed power site, would supply a market for power which otherwise might be supplied by Boulder Canyon Dam. Such an untoward intrusion into ongoing federal-state negotiations, Hayden counseled Girand and his backers, jeopardized Arizona's long-range interests in the river. Federally dependent

Arizona did not need a short-sighted response to the ill-advised introduction of the Swing-Johnson-bill.[33]

While encouraging compromise, Hayden presented his views on reclamation and Colorado River development to the House Committee on Irrigation of Arid Lands in June, 1922. To the surprise of committee members, an uncharacteristically loquacious Hayden held the floor for long periods. He began, "An irrigator is entitled to receive water as cheaply as possible." "That," he argued, "is in the public interest." It was also in the public interest for the United States to sell power "as cheaply as it could be sold and still reimburse the government," for cheap power would stimulate "mining and every other industry tributary to power development." Hayden reiterated his opposition to private power development on the river and concluded his statements with a call for the federal government to act responsibly: "The government should not seek to obtain a greater revenue out of the development of power over and above that needed to recoup itself."[34]

Besides outlining his philosophy of reclamation for the Southwest, Hayden presented Arizona concerns to the committee. The Fall-Davis Report, he told Irrigation Committee members, specified ten suitable damsites along the river. One of these sites in particular interested Arizonans. Glen Canyon, located in northern Arizona near the border with Utah, was an ideal site, and Hayden called upon the Reclamation Service for detailed studies of it. At Glen Canyon, a site wholly within Arizona, the state would not have to share any potential royalties or tax revenues derived from power generation with any other state. In contrast to Glen Canyon, Arizona shared the Boulder Canyon site with Nevada and any benefits would have to be shared between the two states. Glen Canyon, although well-suited for storage, lay two hundred miles further away than Boulder Canyon from vast power markets in southern California. Well aware of this disadvantage, Hayden, nevertheless dutifully presented the Glen Canyon alternative to the committee.[35]

The Arizona congressman continued pressing his state's water and power concerns. "The people of my state," he informed the committee, "are immensely interested in power development on the Colorado River." Since the Salt River Project could not yet produce enough electricity to meet all demands within the state, and, at that time, Arizona possessed neither oil nor coal, the state was compelled to import fuel oil from California and Texas and coal from New Mexico and Colorado. Therefore, operating costs for Arizona's primary industrial activity, copper mining, were extremely high. Arizona copper mines, he informed his listeners, "would be consumers of large quantities of cheaper hydroelectric power." Also, groundwater pumping for the irrigation of lands provided a secondary market for power. Hayden concluded: "The people of Arizona have an immediate interest in the power question ... and are anxious to have cheap power as soon as possible."[36]

Hydroelectric power, the key to expanding Arizona's agricultural and industrial economies, was also viewed as the savior of "ghost cities." Tombstone, once one of the most active silver mining centers in the Southwest, limped into the twentieth century because of the prohibitive cost of power to operate water pumps in the mines. Affordable power from the Colorado River offered new hope to the fabled mining town. One local businessman wrote Hayden that "the development of cheap power will make it possible to operate the huge pumps at small expense and the development of the mines will again be possible!" Tombstone's dreams exemplified yet another of the innumerable potential uses Arizonans could find for power generated from a high dam on the Colorado.[37]

Perhaps the grandest scheme concerning hydroelectric power generation involved the dream of pumping water from the Colorado to the fertile central valleys through a "highline canal." Hayden injected this idea, widely discussed in Arizona, into the committee debates on the Swing-Johnson bill: "There has been some discussion of a highline canal following about the 1200-1300 foot contour below Boulder Canyon, which would cover an immense area of land in Arizona." In fact, during the summer of 1922, prominent Arizona water leaders formed an organization dedicated to a state-owned, state-operated highline canal. The Arizona Highline Reclamation Association, founded by Apache County State Senator and one-time gubernatorial candidate Fred T. Colter, with the aid of the ubiquitous George Maxwell, promoted the "development of Arizona with Arizona resources." In time, the highliners emerged as a powerful political voice with which Hayden had to contend and yet represent.[38]

By January 1923, Hayden announced to his constituents that he favored ratification of the compact. He arrived at his decision in typical fashion—after careful detailed study. In December 1922, he prepared several lists of elaborate questions for "those best qualified to speak" on the pact; Herbert Hoover, Arthur Powell Davis, and Ottamar Hamale. Their answers clarified his lingering legal, political, and engineering questions. Davis' responses convinced him that the basin produced enough water for the irrigation of all Arizona land "that might be served by the Arizona Highline Canal." Hayden then turned this "vital information" over to the Arizona state legislature for consideration. When the Arizona legislature began discussing reservations and amendments to the agreement, he sent them a sharp message: "Acceptance of this compact with reservations is in fact no approval at all." His endorsement prompted a flood of critical mail to which he responded with a single lengthy sentence: "Any fair-minded person must conclude that Arizona alone can not undertake the development of the great river without the consent of the United States, and without an understanding with the other states of the Colorado River Basin, all of which leads to the conclusion that sooner or later the Colorado River Compact must be approved by the State of Arizona."[39]

In supporting the pact, Hayden disavowed that portion of the 1922 state Democratic party platform advocating a states' rights approach to Colorado River development. His opposition more closely resembled the Republican platform which called for "a return to that Republican policy, reclamation, inaugurated under the administration of President Roosevelt." The Republican platform emphasized the goal of greater federal involvement in western reclamation in order to facilitate growth and development, and concluded with a ringing endorsement of the $350,000,000 Smith-McNary legislation:

"We strongly urge the enactment of the Smith-McNary reclamation bill as being one of the most comprehensive measures from a state and national standpoint." At least in the realm of federal reclamation policy and the Colorado River Compact, Hayden found common ground with Arizona Republicans.[40]

Framers of the 1922 Democratic party plank contended that Arizona's rights to the river were "superior and natural." Benefits derived from river development should be preserved for the people and not for "selfish private interests." Furthermore, reclamation and flood control were the prime objectives in any development program. Power, although "tremendously important," was a secondary consideration. The Salt River Valley Water Users Association, doubtlessly influenced the relegation of power production in the majority party's platform. Competition from a power-producing dam at either Glen Canyon or Boulder Canyon would eliminate the association's monopoly on power within the Salt River Valley.

The overall content of the Democratic party platform, sprinkled with old-time populist rhetoric, held great appeal to the voters of Arizona in the general elections of 1922. Voters not only elected Hunt for the fourth of his seven two-year terms, but also they chose an overwhelmingly Democratic state legislature. When the sixth legislature convened in Phoenix on January 8, 1923, eighteen Democrats and one Republican comprised the Senate, while forty-one Democrats and six Republicans sat in the House of Representatives. Arizona, to outside observers, appeared to be a one-party state.[41]

More than any other Arizona politician, Hunt, who served as governor from 1922 to 1932 with only one interruption, dramatized Arizona's struggle against the pact. The rotund former mining camp waiter, who paid scant attention to the rules of grammar in his speeches, railed unremittingly against the aggressor state, California. The self-proclaimed savior of the Colorado River issued hundreds of proclamations and messages and made scores of speeches, all of which centered on one theme—opposition to the Colorado River Compact. The governor summed up his views and those of the "anti-pacters" in one circular issued in 1923: "The Colorado River is our greatest resource, and unless we conserve it and get the maximum benefit from it, we can depend upon becoming a sort of vermiform appendix to Los Angeles," adding "I am not at all ambitious toward building up Los Angeles with Arizona resources." Hunt knew that Arizona businessmen, workers, miners, and farmers found intolerable the notion of being considered a colonial offshoot of the booming southern California economy. Indeed, in uncanny fashion, he parlayed Arizonans' obvious inferiority complex, and their great distaste for neocolonial status in the Southwest, into a politically attractive and potent issue.[42]

As the sixth legislature met, political pundits foresaw that the compact faced stiff challenges. Hayden and Hunt had proclaimed their divergent positions concerning the agreement. The congressman urged federal development of the Colorado River under the terms of the seven-state pact, because to Hayden, the interstate stream was a regional resource. The governor maintained the proprietary position that Arizona possessed ultimate authority over the river within her borders. The debates in Arizona's legislature over the issue illustrated this philosophical contradiction and tested the sensitive strands of American federalism.[43]

V

The Battle Within

Throughout 1923 Hayden campaigned for ratification of the compact, spending extended periods of time in Arizona speaking to audiences throughout the state. Governor Hunt, the outspoken anti-pacter, provided formidable opposition and as they each maneuvered for position, Arizonans witnessed the beginning of an epic political struggle that preoccupied the state for the next forty years. As Hayden recalled much later, "the period 1922-23 was one of the most politically charged periods in Arizona in my memory."[1]

Even before the convocation of Arizona's Sixth Legislature, Hunt revealed his intransigence concerning the pact. His resolve perplexed some because he had only recently returned to the U.S. from his two-year stint as ambassador to Siam, and therefore was not fully versed on the complex events that led up to the compact negotiations. When commission chairman Hoover invited the governor-elect to attend the last session of the hearings in Santa Fe during November 1922, Hunt curtly informed Hoover he would not attend. Arizona lacked the necessary information on irrigable acreage, Hunt wrote, and thus he could not consider signing the pact for at least two years. Instead he offered to send highline canal activist George Maxwell, who in recent months had emerged as Hunt's chief advisor on Colorado River matters. Hoover, who had previous dealings with the reclamation propagandist, considered Maxwell a "crackpot" and a "demagogue" and refused the offer.

The governor knew well the stir he was creating. His diary entry for November 28, 1922—four days after the signing of the compact—indicated a keen awareness that basin leaders watched his every action: "My attitude on the Colorado pact seems to worry a good many people." And when Hunt learned that Chairman Hoover planned a trip to Arizona to lobby for pact ratification, the governor confided to his diary, "Herbert Hoover will run up against a brick wall—the plot thickens!"[2]

In an effort to influence public opinion and at the same time stem the growing popularity of Hunt's state's rights challenge, Hayden convinced Hoover to take his case to Arizona. On December 8, 1922, the commerce secretary arrived in Phoenix for the hastily organized Friday night address at the elegantly appointed Columbia Theater. After an introduction by outgoing pro-pact governor Thomas Campbell, Hoover began on a safe note, apprising the attentive overflow audience of 1500 that an immediate need existed for flood control on the lower reaches of the river. He reminded his listeners of "the great floods of some twelve or fourteen years ago," and emphasized that flood control was a primary concern for federal officials. Yuma County residents were among the 80,000 citizens of southern Arizona and California that stood to benefit from flood control.

Playing to his Arizona audience, Hoover suggested that the government might construct a dam at Glen Canyon, a site that had gained favorable statewide attention preceding his visit. "Together," he counseled the audience in calm, measured tones, "Boulder Canyon and Glen Canyon possess an incomparable volume of storage. It is possible to create two large reservoirs on the river, which, between them, would hold more than two years of continuous flow of the river." Indeed, these opening remarks seemed prudent and diplomatic.[3]

The commerce secretary then attempted to raise the level of discussion, appealing to the "pioneering spirit" of Arizonans, urging them to think first of their progeny. "We have reached a new crisis in our national development. The problems our fathers faced have been solved; new and greater problems have risen, tasks more difficult which require the same courage and determination of the pioneers who went before us." "The Colorado River project," the commerce secretary averred, "which has reached the stage of ratification or rejection by the legislatures of the seven states, unquestionably involves the single greatest asset in undeveloped resources in America." If work began immediately, Hoover prophesied, "in three or four generations to come" there would be such storage in the river that "every drop of its annual flood could be retained by the hand of man for his betterment." And he confided to his audience that he would take great pride if he could help secure "even a few years advancement in the development of this work." He ended this portion of his remarks with a call for the cooperative development of the river under the wise and benevolent stewardship of the federal government. In effect, Hoover advocated, as one critic called it, "socialism in the Southwest."[4]

Hoover's speech took a distinctly different tack, however, beginning with a criticism of Hunt's state's rights argument. An "Arizona only" approach, he declared, "would create endless litigation, and unless the opportunity is taken to settle the issue peaceably and fairly, it will take its place as the subject of controversy and conflict between the states for the next twenty-five years." Moreover, endless litigation would postpone the expected quadrupling of population and the "addition of a million homes" in the region. He feared that Arizona, philosophically, was taking the same stance that South Carolina had in 1861—"the right of one state in relation to other states." "There will be no Civil War over this issue," he warned, "but it will be a fine field for demogogue's oratory."[5]

At this point, the commerce secretary irritated anti-pact elements in the audience when he said, "there has never been a document in the history of mankind which has not been the subject of destructive criticism—the problem today is not to destroy but to build up." He accused "selfish interests" in Arizona that tried to undermine the pact for their own purposes. These people, he suggested, were interested only in "power, property, and politics." Jealousy, moreover, played a crucial part in anti-pact sentiment in Arizona, or as the commerce secretary put it: "A simple unwillingness to allow credit for such a great achievement as an early settlement to go to men who labored so long and hard to bring it about."

Hoover's finger-pointing ended with a veiled insult. "When you talk to your friends and neighbors, you will hear many arguments against it based on a variety of grounds, but I want you to do this—listen carefully, and then consider whether the person who opposes the pact has the same, clear-visioned unselfish motives as the men who framed it." Everyone in attendance knew Hoover's comments were aimed at Hunt and Maxwell. Although Hayden agreed with these sentiments he knew that Hoover's statements gave anti-pact leaders significant political ammunition in their fight against ratification.[6]

Hayden watched Hoover's blunder knowing it played into Hunt's hand. During the weeks following the address, Hunt pandered to a largely sympathetic press that portrayed him as the object of unjustified federal oppression. At this juncture, moreover, the governor moved into an even more inflexible position concerning the pact. Hunt used a variety of methods to undermine support for the river agreement. Perhaps his most successful ploy was sending his chief lieutenant, George Maxwell, on a speaking tour throughout the state in December 1922 and January 1923 urging rejection of the compact. In addition to Hunt and Maxwell, Apache County Senator Fred Colter, a new and potent force in Arizona water development politics, embraced the anti-pact message and entered the political fray. Congressman Hayden knew he had a serious challenges ahead in Arizona.[7]

Some of Maxwell's claims stretched the imagination. Warren Harding's administration, he contended, had concocted a conspiracy to deprive Arizona of its rightful share of the river. Audiences heard his standard xenophobic rambling about the compact making possible an "Asiatic Colony" on the Colorado River delta. The presence of the foreigners, he asserted, would eventually lead to a conflict with China and Japan in which "Arizona and California would be the shock country as was Belgium in the world war." Maxwell, in addition, told listeners from Flagstaff to Clifton to Yuma that Colorado Commission Chairman Herbert Hoover had misled the public in stating that the agreement was equitable. He further frightened water users in the Salt River Valley by claiming that the compact guaranteed Mexico water from the Roosevelt reservoir that served the valley. Journalists statewide lavished attention on Maxwell, uncritically reporting his litany of claims and helping spread his message beyond his immediate reach.[8]

Hayden had difficulty gauging the degree of Maxwell's influence within Arizona. Like A.P. Davis, Hoover, and others who received unsolicited material from Maxwell, Hayden considered him a nuisance. But Hayden had to contend directly with Maxwell. First, the congressman attempted to gather as much information on Maxwell in order to assess and define accurately "the problem." As reports filtered back to Washington, Hayden concluded that ratification faced "a tough road in Arizona." Within the state, the Hunt-Maxwell-Colter anti-pact coalition was gathering force and as the Arizona congressman confided to his administrative assistant, Jack Gavin, "Maxwell could not be dismissed." W.S. Norviel, Arizona's Colorado River Commissioner, sustained this view and wrote Hayden, "Mr. George Maxwell is using his best endeavors here to prevent ratification of the ... compact.... Mr. Maxwell assumed the attitude of an opponent a year or so ago and he has been somewhat bitter at times in his attacks upon those who were interested in procuring an agreement among the states."[9]

At first Hayden had trouble gauging Maxwell's influence on the Arizona public, but he learned at the outset that Maxwell had great influence on the governor. In January 1923, M.C. McCalla, a member of the state Democratic party central committee, informed Hayden that Hunt was "entirely ignorant about the Colorado River," and that virtually all of his public statements were written by Maxwell. Furthermore, McCalla believed Maxwell had swayed public opinion in his favor, and if a vote on the compact were to be taken in Maricopa County, "it would fail by a big majority." B.F. Fly, director of the Yuma Valley Water Users Association, corroborated McCalla's assessment: "Maxwell is the only fly in the ointment.... Just why Governor Hunt relies so wholly on Maxwell is a puzzle to me."[10]

Nevertheless Hayden sought more information on Maxwell and his plan for an Arizona Highline Canal. He contacted two of the federal government's top engineering officers, G. Otis Smith of the U.S. Geological Survey, and A.P. Davis of the Reclamation Service. Both agreed that the highline canal was an "extravagant absurdity." Smith reported that "I will not knowingly spend federal appropriations on investigations that do not give reasonable promise of yielding valuable results, nor give aid or standing to an investigation by a State, even by the loan of men, which does not give such promise." Davis saw political chicanery in Maxwell's program: "The highline canal scheme, which Mr. Maxwell changes from time to time is ... entirely impractical, and is apparently advocated for the main purpose of preventing the development of the Colorado by the United States. Besides, this plan would be prohibitive in cost and for maintenance after built." Upon receipt of these opinions Hayden confided to his administrative assistant that the Colorado River controversy was growing more complicated by the day and he wondered how to reconcile highliners' aims with federal priorities as embodied in the Colorado River Compact.[11]

Finally Maxwell confronted Hayden in early 1923, wiring a lengthy telegram to the congressman expressing his outrage and shock that one of the West's most informed and knowledgeable representatives on reclamation would ally himself "with the enemies of Arizona." "The water power trust and every interest allied with Wall Street were for the pact," Maxwell asserted. Worse still, the Japanese, who were conspiring to construct an "Asiatic Aeroplane base in America," were for the pact. "Wait until you know all the facts," Maxwell ironically inveighed, "and hold fast for Arizona." Hayden's response scarcely disguised his exasperation. "A careful reading of your 294-word telegram," he wrote, "convinces me that your purpose was to let me know that you are opposed to the Colorado River Compact." The congressman chided Maxwell for his inconsistent approach to federal reclamation and he questioned the wisdom of attacking the pact from "the safety of generalities." The congressman urged Maxwell to consider it "possible that you may be mistaken." The exchange suggested just one dimension of the philosophical divisions over Colorado River development in Arizona. These differences sharpened when, between January and March 1923, the Sixth Legislature of the State of Arizona met to debate ratification of the Colorado River Compact.[12]

At 2:00 P.M., January 8, 1923, Governor Hunt addressed a joint session of the legislature. He held the floor for sixty-six minutes, covering thirty-four different topics. He devoted the last fifteen minutes of his talk to "the most important problem ever to come before this legislature." The future prosperity of every interest in Arizona, Hunt told Arizona lawmakers, depended upon proper solution of the problems surrounding the future development of the Colorado River. Arizona, he warned, "can not afford to give up her greatest natural resource," water, "with millions of acres awaiting development, and she can not afford to plunge blindly into a contract that may be unfair to her." The governor worded his message in such a way as to not call specifically for its rejection. Instead, he advised "cautious delay." "We must know how much water can be used in Arizona, how many acres can be irrigated and what steps are necessary to secure the quantity needed for adequate development of our state." Hunt concluded this portion of his speech with a rejoinder to Hoover's Phoenix address one month earlier, with a declaration: "The agreement is too important to be rushed into without a more thorough investigation."[13]

Despite claiming a lack of sufficient information Hunt felt knowledgeable enough to comment on several aspects of its provisions that he thought inimical to the state's interest. The allocation of 7.5 million acre-feet to the upper basin, the governor charged, would waste potential power resources in the lower basin. Hunt took another swipe at State Water Commissioner Norviel, criticizing his handling of the Gila River question in the negotiations. Mexico also benefited at the expense of Arizona according to the governor. He incorrectly informed the legislature that the pact provided for an estimated 6 million acre-feet of water for Mexico "capable of irrigating over 6 million acres of land." His final claim reflected the unmistakable influence of Maxwell. "I think it well to call your attention to the fact that Arizona land speculators are seeking to reap huge profits from Japanese financiers interested in land in Lower California." Hunt, pleased with the applause that greeted his remarks, noted in his diary that evening, "My message ... was very well received."[14]

During the two month regular session of the state legislature, Hayden carefully monitored events in Arizona from his Washington offices. He knew that Maxwell's arguments, factual or not, provided compact opponents with substantial political ammunition. Arizona lawmakers debated, sometimes bitterly, the pros and cons of compact ratification. The house introduced eleven ratification bills and the senate thirteen, ranging from outright rejection to conditional approval with reservations and finally to unconditional acceptance, though only one branch of the legislature agreed to accept unconditionally the pact. As for the reservations, Hayden continued to vigorously oppose them, insisting they "would throw open the whole subject to further changes by the other six legislatures" and leave Arizona badly exposed. The other six states could argue, perhaps justifiably, that the Gila River basin's flow and the water put to beneficial use under the San Carlos Project should not be included in Arizona's allotment. "Would not the Colorado legislature," Hayden theorized, "have the same right to insist that the tributaries in that state be likewise eliminated from the Compact?"[15]

Legislators from Yuma and Mohave counties, especially, shared Hayden's view that the pact should be ratified immediately and without reservation. Mohave County, location of the probable damsite, provided strong support for the congressman's pro-pact stand. To residents of that northwestern Arizona county, immediate ratification meant that Kingman, the county seat, would become one of the chief supply points for labor and material. Local residents also anticipated increased land values, industrial development, and tourist dollars if the nation's largest flood control and power dam were built in the vicinity. The election returns of 1924 reflected the degree to which Mohave County looked toward prompt development of the river. Pro-pacter Hayden outpolled his Republican opponent in the county 1,162 to 297. Hunt, on the other hand, in his reelection bid, had severe problems in Mohave County, where Democrats outnumbered Republicans by almost 6 to 1. Residents there gave Dwight Heard, the pro-pact Republican nominee for governor, 1,069 votes while only 91 people voted for the Democratic incumbent. Clearly, Hunt's calls for delay in ratifying the compact led to his overwhelming defeat in Mohave County, while Hayden's large majority was attributable to his calls for immediate and unconditional ratification.[16]

Yuma County also favored ratification, but for different reasons than her sister county to the north. Flood control and irrigation, rather than the promise of future employment and tourist income, attracted Yuma County leaders to unconditional ratification. On January 15, 1923, Yuma Representative William Wisener, submitted the first house bill for unconditional ratification. While Yuma leaders worked the Arizona legislature, they also maintained constant contact with Hayden's office in Washington, informing the congressman about local events. During the critical months from January to March 1923, several prominent leaders from that county asked Hayden to intervene directly and to address the legislature, but Hayden, realizing such entreaties might harm the pact's chances, rejected these suggestions.

Yuma County's Mulford Winsor, Senate president, illustrated the importance with which his county viewed the issue. Up to the time of commission deliberations, he had aligned himself with Governor Hunt's wing of the Democratic party. The governor's opposition to immediate unconditional ratification, however, forced Winsor into Congressman Hayden's camp. Winsor, one of Hayden's primary opponents in the special election of 1911, had long maintained polite, professional relations with his former rival. Now he fervently embraced Hayden and his support of the compact. From December 1922 onward the powerful Yuma politician kept Hayden informed of events within his county as well as within the legislature. "This Colorado River question is a tremendous one, Carl," he wrote his new ally, "The effects of the Colorado River deliberations will be apparent long after we who are here now are gone.... We must not cause the memory of us to be blackened by having taken a narrow, selfish position."[17]

As a result of his position on the pact, Hayden grew more popular than ever in the southwestern portion of the state. His past careful attention to Yuma's reclamation issues coupled with his pro-pact stance played a major role in his winning more than ninety percent of the county vote in the general elections of 1924. Since statehood Hayden and Yuma County had maintained a mutually beneficial relationship. With an uncanny degree of prescience, B.F. Fly perhaps best stated the county's strong affinity for Hayden in an effort to coax its congressman southward to deliver a talk. "I hope you can find the time to come down to Yuma to make us a speech so we can show you how much we think of you. When we elect another U.S. Senator his name will be Carl Hayden and we will keep him in the Senate for as long as he wants to stay there. Mark my words."[18]

Despite such support for Hayden from the counties abutting the Colorado, the legislature, after two months of intense political activity, refused to approve the compact. Three bills, two in the house and one in the senate, came close to passage. On February 15, 1923, the house by a vote of 28 to 17 passed a bill, promoted by Yavapai County Representative Lewis Douglas, ratifying the pact with three amendments: a $5 per unit royalty tax on hydroelectricity, a limitation on Mexico's water use; and a provision excluding the Gila River from Colorado River system computations. On the same day that the Douglas bill passed, William Wisener of Yuma County submitted legislation calling for unconditional ratification. On March 8, 1923, the last day of the legislative session, the Wisener measure fell one vote short of passage. A senate bill, which passed 10 to 9, advocated ratification with one proviso: "The full unrestricted right of taxation by way of the imposition of the royalty upon electrical power generated within the state." The senate bill, unlike the house version, did not specify the royalty amount. The house bill died in the senate and the senate bill died in the house. Governor Hunt and his backers had prevented ratification.[19]

The success of Hunt had been due at least in part to support from the most powerful institutions in the state. Large agricultural interests, powerful mining corporations, private utilities, and even the Salt River Valley Water Users Association (SRVWUA)—a creation of federal reclamation—had come out against the pact.[20]

To Hayden's chagrin, Arizona agricultural interests, especially cotton growers and cattlemen, while not calling for outright rejection of the compact, pressed the state legislature for "ratification with reservations." They worried most about limiting Mexico's use of Colorado River water, one of George Maxwell's major concerns. One bill submitted to the House sought to "limit" Mexico to 2 million acre-feet annually; in retrospect a generous allocation. Fear spread through Maricopa and Pinal counties that cheap labor in Mexico would result in an abundance of cheap produce, thereby "stealing American profits." Pinal County, which had emerged as the principal cotton growing area in the state, was especially apprehensive about potential competition from Mexican cotton producers. Both central Arizona counties also pointed to "wealthy American interests in Mexico," especially California newspaperman and land speculator Harry Chandler, who were accused of employing "cheap and inferior asiatic labor."

These same agricultural interests expressed concerns over the status of the Gila River and the San Carlos Project. Representatives from these areas of the state sought to amend the pact in order to give Arizona sole right to the Gila. Article III (b) needed clarification, they contended, so that "the waters of the Gila system should not be considered as including the waters of the Colorado allocated by the pact." Pinal County Representative A.T. Kilcrease, local leader in the movement for the San Carlos Project, sponsored legislation that included a reservation to the compact excluding the Gila from the lower basin allocation. The reservation, he told his fellow lawmakers, "was for the purpose of safeguarding the perfected rights of the waters of the Gila River upon which Arizona cotton growers, Indians and whites alike, were dependent in large measure." These amendments and reservations submitted to the Arizona legislature, a consequence of the pact's vague wording, revealed that central Arizona farmers wanted a precise statement concerning their water rights in the lower basin, both in amount and priority of usage.[21]

Much to Hayden's consternation, the Salt River Valley Water Users Association, with which he had strong political ties, had joined the movement against ratification. The association, one of the state's most powerful pressure groups, had devised plans to meet increasing demand for hydroelectric power in the Southwest and wanted no competition from a federally constructed power plant on the Colorado River. Fearful that cheap power would lower prices and usurp the market, in 1917 (after SRVWUA became a public agency) it embarked on a $10 million expansion program that by 1927 included five dams and three power plants. To help pay the costs, association officials planned to sell hydroelectric power to local mining corporations. The SRVWUA's attitude about competition from the federal government mirrored the apprehension that characterized the nation's private utilities toward public power.[22]

The most significant opposition that Hayden and his pro-pact supporters faced were the mining corporations, many of which were tied to eastern corporate capital. At the time of the ratification fight, Arizona mining interests paid half of the total taxes collected by the state. It would be to their benefit, therefore, for Arizona to encourage private power development because the state could then levy taxes on those utilities and lower the assessment on mining. When the Arizona legislature met, this reasoning dominated among lawmakers from copper-producing counties who introduced measures to levy taxes "in perpetuity" on every unit of electricity generated on the Colorado River in Arizona whether produced by federal, private, or state agencies.[23]

Agriculture, the utilities, and the mining companies each had distinct reasons for opposing ratification, and they found an umbrella organization willing to publicize their interests in the Arizona Highline Reclamation Association. Under the direction of Apache

County Senator Fred Colter, the association published its opposition in *The Highline*, which was mailed to each voter in the state.[24]

Colter proved a prodigious worker for his cause, writing, editing, and soliciting materials for the magazine. During the height of the ratification debate he wrote a persuasive essay entitled, "Growth and Prosperity Without the Pact," in which he argued that the defeat of the agreement opened the way "to file on and develop in Arizona the Glen Canyon-Colorado Gila Highline and Reclamation Power Project, the largest in the World." According to Colter, the pact did not give Arizona its rightful share of water and power, therefore increasing the chance for protracted litigation.[25]

To Hayden, opponents of the compact had made two incorrect assumptions: their belief that the development of the Colorado could be prevented by the refusal of only one of the seven basin states to approve the compact and their expectation that irrigation and power development could be local and gradual. The compact, Hayden felt, represented a radical departure from such a narrow, proprietary view.[26]

Hayden knew that the indecision in the Arizona legislature displeased officials in the Warren Harding administration. Federal officials told Governor Hunt in early 1923 that no development on the Colorado, by the state of Arizona or any other agency, would be tolerated until all concerned parties had reached an agreement. In a move calculated to appear constructive, Hunt, on short notice, called for a Colorado River Conference to devise an "Arizona Plan" for development. Forty state leaders, including the congressional delegation, huddled and agreed that Hayden, then touring the Colorado River Basin with twenty-two other congressmen, should return to Phoenix and attend the conference. Of the thirty-six people at the meeting, only four—including Hayden—supported the compact. Conspicuous by his absence was senate President Mulford Winsor of Yuma, who apparently stayed away because he felt the meeting would not be productive. He made his position clear to the governor, however, in a fifteen-page letter. "I believe Arizona's highest interest lies in the ratification, as speedily as possible, of the Colorado River

Compact.... It is a genuine deep-seated belief that the treaty is equitable and practical and essential to the early development of the Colorado River, essential to the early development ... and industrial progress vital to Arizona...." Winsor sent a copy of this letter to the *Arizona Republican* where it was reprinted in its entirety and circulated among the delegates.[27]

Hayden listened patiently, yet skeptically, as the delegates considered proposals to supplant the compact. The governor's "Arizona Plan," designed to replace the compact, called for a bond issue of between $25 and $100 million to finance a dam and hydroelectric plant inside Arizona at Glen Canyon. Former State Engineer Thomas Maddock, a prominent Tucson Republican, outlined a plan that differed significantly from Hunt's proposal. He condemned the "Arizona Plan," claiming that it would merely provide flood control for California. Maddock argued that the compact stopped short of securing Arizona its share of the river and suggested an agreement among Arizona, California, and Nevada as a prerequisite for Arizona ratification. John C. Greenway, a highly respected mine developer from southern Arizona and an ex-Roughrider, suggested yet another alternative. He urged ratification of the pact with the provision that private enterprise be allowed to develop irrigation works and hydroelectric power plants. At the end of the first session, the *Arizona Republican* offered that the day's discussion was "aimless, uninforming, and not well-informed."[28]

On May 8, 1923, the second day of the conference, Hayden addressed the delegates, telling the overwhelmingly anti-pact audience that "it would be extremely difficult to present an agreeable substitute for the pact." "The chief purpose of the basin-states agreement was to remove the danger of litigation," he stated, "and the main reason for the allocation of water between basins had been made to quiet the fears of the northern states, especially Colorado." Inherent in his plea for ratification was Hayden's wish to avoid the time and cost of an unsatisfying Supreme Court case like *Kansas v. Colorado* (1907) or *Wyoming v. Colorado* (1922). Moreover, if Arizona attempted to go it alone, as Governor Hunt advocated, it would doubtlessly encounter resistance from Congress and the Harding administration, which, Hayden ventured, "would almost certainly be effective." He reiterated his familiar message that nothing could be done on the Colorado River without an understanding among the states.[29] The result of the two day conference was further delay. Hunt appointed a "Committee of Nine" to draft a new plan for submission to the next session of the legislature.[30]

Hayden remained in Arizona to campaign for unconditional ratification of the compact. In mid-May he started a summer-long speaking tour that reached all areas of the state. The congressman shaped the content and detail of these sometimes lengthy orations to fit the composition of the audience. Residents of Yuma heard more about flood control and reclamation than the miners of Clifton-Morenci, who were primarily concerned with hydroelectric power generation. Hayden became the leading pro-pact spokesman in the state during the congressional recess that lasted through November.[31]

Hayden's message was clear. Arizonans had to understand that the federal government was a senior partner in Colorado River development and that the compact was "the foundation upon which a superstructure of progress may be erected." He also counseled that federal and state administrators faced insurmountable obstacles in coming to an agreement on water rights based upon the existing doctrine of prior appropriation. Moreover, congressional testimony revealed that various engineers and technicians could produce conflicting statistics on the amount of irrigable acreage each state purportedly possessed. On May 16, 1923, scarcely one week after the inconclusive Colorado River Conference, Hayden delivered his first major address concerning the controversy. The Hotel Adams in downtown Phoenix, the political epicenter of Arizona, hosted the Chamber of Commerce-sponsored event. For two hours Hayden detailed weaknesses in the proposed state-owned and operated reclamation program. He began by analyzing the Arizona Highline Reclamation Association's favorite damsite, Glen Canyon. Besides mixed reviews from federal engineers, Glen Canyon posed vexing legal problems for state and federal authorities. "By an irrevocable ordinance which is part of the Constitution of Arizona," Hayden pointed out, "the people of this state have agreed forever to disclaim any right and title to the public lands or to any Indian Reservation within its boundaries." Half of the Glen Canyon site lay on public domain while the other half was on the Navajo Indian Reservation. Besides, the secretary of interior had already withdrawn a strip of land one-quarter mile wide and reserved it for a federal power site. If state leaders hoped to construct an Arizona-owned dam at Glen Canyon, the state must amend its constitution, convince the secretary of interior to repeal his withdrawal of the public domain, and then negotiate with the Federal Power Commission for a permit to the site. Indeed, this appeared unrealistic considering the morass of bureaucratic detail and time required in such an undertaking.

He continued his analysis of the problems inherent in the "Arizona Plan." Even if Arizona amended the state constitution and somehow persuaded the interior secretary to change his mind, state leaders would find tough going when applying for a license from the FPC. In addition to satisfying several tedious engineering and legal conditions, Arizona and the federal government had to answer affirmatively the question, "Is it in the interest of all people affected that the State of Arizona construct a dam for power and irrigation at Glen Canyon?" In view of existing upper basin protests already on file against the Girand application at Diamond Creek further downstream, Hayden informed his listeners, he doubted the success of a state-supported application. "The states of Wyoming, Utah, Colorado, and New Mexico," he averred, "will be as prompt in making their desires known as Arizona would be in protesting against the granting of a license to the City of Los Angeles to construct the Boulder Canyon Dam."

The congressman concluded his presentation with an analysis of the advantages of entering into the basin-state agreement and the disadvantages of remaining wedded to a program doomed to failure. Ratification would gain the assent of all southwestern states to any plan of utilization of the waters of the Colorado River within Arizona. Failure to ratify the pact blocked development not only for Arizona but also for the other six states. Until Arizona ratified the agreement the other states would vigorously oppose any move made by Arizona to develop hydroelectric power, to construct flood control dams, or build water storage reservoirs intended to facilitate irrigation projects.[32]

At Prescott on August 2, 1923, Hayden delivered his most comprehensive pro-pact speech of the campaign. Cowboys, miners, ranchers, and businessmen gathered at the local high-school gymnasium to listen to the message. After the familiar statistics and calls for basin-wide cooperation, Hayden discussed the hydroelectric power issue. He painted a broad, optimistic picture of the unlimited potential in development of "white coal." Within Arizona, he announced, the Colorado produced more power than in any other basin state because the river dropped more than 2,000 feet between the Arizona-Utah line and the point where the state began to share the stream with Nevada. The United States controlled the power rights to the river, but distribution rights were open for discussion. "Should Arizona," Hayden asked his listeners, "stand in the way of other states if we can not immediately use the river?"[33]

In crafting an answer to his question, the congressman posed several others. Californiaphobes in the audience probably cringed when Hayden asked, "Suppose that cheap power doubles the population of Los Angeles, making that great city a manufacturing center, how will Arizona be injured?" "Will there not be mouths to feed and backs to clothe and will not that create a demand for the products from Arizona's farms and stock ranges?" "How can Arizonans fail to share in the prosperity of so close a neighbor?" Hayden ended with the bold declaration: "There can be no cause for jealousy but upon the contrary we should rejoice at the prospect thus presented, for anything that promotes the welfare of the great Southwest, of which we are an integral part, is bound to redound to our benefit." In effect, Hayden invoked the idea of a common regional destiny predicated on the development of the interstate stream under the terms of the Colorado River Compact.[34]

Hayden discussed two other concepts. First, since the power sites were within or partly within Arizona, and the principle power markets were in California, he believed that "a power royalty, or tax" was just and reasonable. He reemphasized, however, that Arizona must ratify the pact. Secondly, the congressman pressed for a tri-state or lower basin agreement, an idea proposed in the legislature that had gained broad support among Arizona residents during the summer. By the fall of 1923, Hayden, with increasing regularity, touted the benefits of a supplemental, tristate agreement, "as long as it ... accomplished results and brought about immediate development." Carl Hayden became the voice of moderation and compromise, emphasizing the regional and national implications of Colorado River development.[35]

In spite of predictable criticisms from opponents of the compact, Hayden's round of speeches attracted much favorable attention within Arizona and throughout the basin. "I can assure you," declared state Senator Hugh Campbell of Flagstaff, "that the stand you have taken is one of the best things you have done in your life.... We may not be able to ratify the compact, but it is not because the rank and file voters are against it." Upper basin leaders, anxious to secure an agreement, also praised the Arizona congressman. "You are certainly doing a fine piece of work in Arizona and doing it in such a way which does not excite enmity on the part of those who are opposed to the compact," wrote Colorado water attorney L. Ward Bannister. Added Delph Carpenter (also of Colorado): "You have done great work in a magnificent manner." Another major player in basin water politics, California congressman Phil Swing, was equally congratulatory: "The people of Arizona are bound to come over to your point of view.... I have no doubt. I think you gave it to your people in a straight and diplomatic manner."[36]

Meanwhile a much-awaited state-sponsored engineering study, conducted under the auspices of the Arizona Engineering Commission, was completed. This study, commissioned by outgoing Governor Campbell and the second of its kind in as many years, reflected Arizona leaders' calls for more scientific information concerning the amount of irrigable land in Arizona. Directed by E.C. La Rue, famed USGS hydraulic engineer and Colorado River authority, the three-man commission entered the field in October 1922 and submitted their report to Governor Hunt on July 5, 1923. The La Rue

Survey focused on two issues crucial to Arizonans: the amount of land irrigable in the state from the Colorado River and the feasibility of a highline canal from the Glen Canyon damsite.[37]

The conclusions of the survey echoed the findings of a previous preliminary study drafted by former USGS engineer and University of Arizona irrigation professor Harry F. Blake in 1921. Blake, in his hastily conducted reconnaissance, appraised the feasibility of an Arizona highline canal that originated at the Boulder Canyon damsite. While finding the canal an engineering possibility, Blake questioned its prudence: "Directing and carrying water across a hot, arid country without crossing any large bodies of irrigable land until 470 miles south of its diversion ... would be a precarious undertaking." La Rue, like Blake, studied the feasibility of an Arizona highline canal, but from Glen Canyon rather than Boulder Canyon. Two million acres of Arizona land was irrigable from the Colorado River, and a gravity flow canal from Glen Canyon to the Salt River Valley was possible. Construction, operation, and maintenance of the massive undertaking, however, would cost beneficiaries at least $225 per acre at a time when farmers on other western reclamation projects complained to government officials about charges that approached $70 per acre. Thus the canal possessed some engineering merit, but, according to LaRue, was economically impractical.[38]

La Rue submitted a chilling supplemental section to the study. He harbored doubts about the amount of annual runoff in the Colorado, suggesting that it carried only 9 to 10 million acre-feet annually instead of the often-cited 16 million acre-feet figure. Some observers, including Hayden, attributed the skeptical tone of LaRue's attachment to his strong personal differences with U.S. Reclamation Service chief A.P. Davis. Indeed, Davis had ignored LaRue during the course of the compact deliberations, and the USGS engineer had "no great love" for the man he felt had slighted him.

The vendetta notwithstanding, La Rue's addendum to the Arizona Engineering Commission Report added another vexing variable to the already complicated issue. It locked Hunt more firmly into his inflexible position. If the Colorado carried even less water than originally estimated, the governor reasoned, then Arizona must take more strident measures to protect her share of the river's resources.[39]

Hayden considered the LaRue report as part of the process of information gathering—not a call for a state-owned and operated reclamation project. On July 26, 1923, two weeks after the report became public, he told a Flagstaff audience that the commission report confirmed the need for Arizona to enter into the compact. It also revealed, according to Hayden, several distinct possibilities for irrigation in the western portion of the state. With a dam above Parker, for example, canals could be constructed on each side of the river, irrigating 764,000 acres in Arizona, 310,000 acres in California's Palo Verde and Chuckawalla irrigation districts, and 164,000 acres on the Colorado River Indian Reservation.

The cost for the proposed Arizona highline canal ($225 per acre), however, was too expensive. "As a member of the Committee of Irrigation of Arid Lands I have listened to testimony of water users from all of the reclamation projects," he told his northern Arizona listeners, "and when charges reach above $70 per acre the farmers complain bitterly." Besides noting the unrealistically high costs for the canal, the LaRue Survey raised the specter of future water supply shortfalls. Hayden told his audience that the commission suggested "the water may not be sufficient to reclaim the lands which may be found to be commercially feasible."[40]

Thus Hayden counseled against ill-planned, hastily conceived water projects. Arizona leaders should not react, but instead organize a rational, orderly approach to river development in concert with neighboring states and the federal government. "That visionary and impractical projects are being proposed in New Mexico, Utah, Colorado, and Wyoming does not justify us in insisting upon reservation for water in equally visionary and impractical projects," he declared. Furthermore, nothing in the report of the Arizona Engineering Commission added anything to the rights that the people of Arizona had to the river. Nor did the report alter the rights that the United States or other basin states had to the river. To the people of Flagstaff and the surrounding area, he reiterated his now familiar axiom: "For prompt development and progress, Arizona must approve the Colorado River Compact as written at Santa Fe."[41]

Governor Hunt and the anti-pact coalition took steps to neutralize the congressman's impact. First, he refused to call a special session of the legislature, thus leaving pact ratification in limbo. Then, in late September 1923, Hunt and the Committee of Nine traveled to Washington for a hearing before the Federal Power Commission (FPC). The FPC, formed as a result of the Federal Water Power Act of 1920, was an agency comprised of the Secretaries of War, Interior, and Agriculture. Its primary function was to issue licenses for power development on navigable rivers or on public land. The process included hearings held in conjunction with the issuance of such licenses.[42]

As Congressman Hayden watched from the gallery, the governor began defiantly, informing the commissioners that Arizona "would never consent to the Santa Fe Compact." Instead he proposed a "state-owned, operated and controlled enterprise" which would "cooperate with the FPC." Hunt envisioned the creation of a new Arizona bureaucracy—the Arizona State Power Commission—which would oversee the construction and operation of hydroelectric power plants in the state. After outlining the benefits of Glen Canyon as the best site for a state-owned project, Hunt, incredibly, told the commission that he also supported the privately-financed Girand proposal at Diamond Creek.

George Maxwell testified shortly after the governor and further obfuscated the issue by stating that he opposed the Girand Project. He included in his testimony another of his jingoistic tirades: "Forty per cent of the water released in the electrical generating process would go to Mexico and would spawn an Asiatic wedge that would be driven into the heart of America and a war with Asia, otherwise avoidable, would become inevitable." After the first day of testimony, Hunt sensed the effect of Arizona's conflicting and confused presentations, confiding to his diary that evening, "I can't help but feel our mission is going to be a fruitless one."[43] Naturally, the upper basin states and California registered their strong opposition to the Arizona Plan and the FPC, in quick order, rejected the Arizona application.

Shortly after the Arizona delegation returned from the fiasco in Washington, Hayden ally, Dwight Heard, through personal and editorial prodding, proposed that Arizona issue invitations to the governors of California and Nevada for a tri-state conference. Such a meeting, Hayden reasoned, could perhaps lead to a supplemental lower basin agreement. While Nevada governor and former Colorado River Commissioner James G. Scrugham agreed to meet, California Governor Friend Richardson rejected the idea, informing Governor Hunt on one occasion, "Former correspondence gives reasons why I do not deem it wise to take part in a limited conference." Richardson's highly publicized rebuke, gave Hunt and his forces further cause to rail against haughty California. Thus the governor diverted attention away from his administration's recent series of setbacks on the river. Most notable among these failures was the lack of the development of a coherent or constructive Colorado River policy.[44]

As Arizona's leadership groped for a unified approach to Colorado River issues, Hayden prepared for the next round of battles in the upcoming congressional session. He realized that Richardson's rebuff of Hunt and the tri-state conference proposal indicated that California leaders, anxious to commence development, had devised alternative plans to circumvent Arizona's foot-dragging on the compact. "California," Hayden wrote *Arizona Republican* editor Dwight Heard, "is marshaling her forces for a protracted fight in Congress in order to pass the Swing-Johnson legislation." While California organized, Arizonans appeared as deeply divided as ever. Hunt refused to abandon his program of state-controlled water resource development. Hayden remained firm in his commitment to the compact and federal reclamation. With little hope of quick settlement of the issue in Arizona, Hayden turned his attention to Congress and another dimension of the Colorado River controversy, the Swing-Johnson Bill. Unlike the compact, the Swing-Johnson Bill (proposed by Californians Phil Swing in the House of Representatives and Hiram Johnson in the U.S. Senate) was unfair, Hayden believed. As he put it, "its provisions were entirely for the benefit of California." He informed the chairman of the House Irrigation and Reclamation Committee: "I intend to use any and every legitimate means to prevent action on the bill."[45]

VI

Leader of the Opposition

In November 1924 Governor Hunt won reelection and Congressman Hayden realized little or no hope existed for Arizona joining the seven state agreement. Hayden's vision for southwestern regional cooperation, however, did not include the Swing-Johnson Bill. The proposed legislation held important and lasting implications for Hayden and Arizona's Colorado River policy. Congressional consideration of the bill forced dissenting factions within the state to suppress their differences over the pact, close ranks, and unite in an effort to delay or defeat the California-sponsored legislation. Notably, Hayden, a voice of moderation and regional compromise during the ratification fight, became Arizona's most visible and outspoken opponent of the Swing-Johnson legislation. The *New York Times*, which covered the protracted controversy, labeled Hayden "the westerner in the forefront of opposition to the proposed legislation." Indeed during this period Hayden demonstrated his considerable skill as interstate diplomat, intrastate conciliator, regional spokesman, and, concerning the struggle with California, leader of the opposition.[1]

This transition signaled the beginning of Hayden's leadership in state and regional reclamation issues. From the outset of the Colorado River controversy, with few exceptions, Hayden's voice became Arizona's when water resource development issues were discussed. This continuity of leadership in water policy, which had its roots in the political ferment of the Swing-Johnson debates of the 1920s, lasted through the late 1960s when Hayden retired from the Senate.[2]

The Swing-Johnson debates provide a detailed lesson in the complexities of legislative compromise. And Hayden, while facing a difficult battle in Congress, had to contend with a governor and legislature often at cross-purposes with him on the compact. The governor and his supporters failed to negotiate seriously with the other states for a lower basin agreement and they steadfastly refused to enter into the seven-state agreement. Still, Hayden tried to influence the political process within Arizona. He demonstrated his muscle in intraparty affairs in 1924 when he succeeded, over the vigorous objections of Governor Hunt and his allies, in preventing any denunciation of the Colorado River Compact in the state Democratic party platform.[3]

Nevertheless, Hayden watched with exasperation as Arizona's leadership remained deeply divided over Colorado River policy. For example, pro-pacters in the Seventh Legislature passed House Concurrent Resolution No. 1, a measure ratifying the Colorado River Compact, "conditional upon a separate agreement between Arizona, California, and Nevada." The resolution did not require the governor's signature to become effective. Compact supporters believed they could circumvent the governor because the seven-state agreement would become effective when it "was approved by the legislature of each of the signatory states." Hunt moved quickly and effectively to quash the insurrection. He vetoed the measure, curtly informing the legislature that its action was "void, worthless, and of no effect." Besides exceeding its constitutional powers in trying to ratify the compact without his approval, the governor inveighed, a resolution was "only the will or pleasure of the legislature, not law, and does not emanate from the people of the state." He concluded his lecture to the legislature: "I have done what was possible ... to conserve the interests of the state in the Colorado River, and I intend to continue my efforts. If there be any who entertain the idea that Arizona can be compelled to accept the Colorado River Compact as written, they shall find me resolute and determined as ever to resist to the utmost any such attempt."[4]

Hayden saw mixed results in the deliberations of the Seventh Legislature. He expressed disappointment at the "politics of inaction," but nevertheless expressed satisfaction with the manifestation of pro-pact sentiment. One pact supporter, Mohave County Senator Kean St. Charles counseled the defeated forces: "We must not forget that we have only two senators and one representative against twelve senators and nineteen representatives of the other six interested states ... the real fight will be in Congress and we can see what our chances will be with such an alignment." Hayden took solace that some members of Arizona's legislature acknowledged the critical challenge he faced in Washington.[5]

In early 1927 Hayden finally began receiving support from his state's executive and legislative branches of government. Significantly, members of the Eighth Legislature focused their attention not on the Colorado River Compact, but rather on the pending Swing-Johnson legislation. Governor Hunt even called a special session of the legislature to deal with the threat posed by the bill. In the special and regular sessions Hunt sought appropriations for money and manpower to support Arizona's congressional delegation. Indeed Hunt's inflexible state's rights approach to the river now seemed almost anachronistic in light of the Swing-Johnson bill which, if passed, would nullify all existing water laws in the Colorado River Basin, diminish drastically state control over the river, and place the administration and appropriation of water under the direct control of the secretary of the interior. For Hunt, the Swing-Johnson bill was a threat, an outrage, and a violation of state sovereignty. Thus, with the governor's support, the Eighth Legislature created an Arizona Colorado River Commission, dedicated to support Arizona's congressional delegation in its opposition to the Swing-Johnson legislation.

Hayden welcomed the support but lamented that the Eighth Legislature had not introduced a bill to approve the Colorado River Compact. As long as Hunt served as governor, Arizona lawmakers looked for ways to circumvent or abrogate the interstate agreement. Outside of the newly created commission and strongest indications that the state held serious reservations about any federally supported program for Colorado River development, Hayden received little constructive support or direction from either the governor's office or the state legislature during the debates on the Swing-Johnson bill.[6]

Hayden contended with another important variable in the controversy—notably the tri-state conferences which began in August 1925 and lasted through the signing into law of the Boulder Canyon Project Act. From Phoenix to San Francisco to Reno, lower basin water leaders met, sometimes peacefully, often acrimoniously, in several attempts to fashion a supplemental agreement to the Colorado River Compact. Hayden supported these efforts and adapted relevant information to arguments he presented to Congress.[7]

He attended the first of these tri-state conferences, held in Phoenix on a blazing-hot August 17, 1925. As within Arizona, sharp differences divided the lower basin states. Characteristically, Governor Hunt's introductory statements to the California and Nevada delegations were more like "wild war cries" than welcoming remarks. "You gentlemen did not come here for charity," he began. "If we have something you want and can utilize, economic justice dictates that it be paid for." He then enumerated the pact's errors and inequities, asserted Arizona's right to tax hydroelectric power generated within the state, argued for the need to allocate water to the states rather than arbitrary divisions, and pronounced the supremacy of state's rights. Thomas Maddock, a member of Arizona's delegation, followed Hunt's remarks with a trenchant comment concerning the Swing-Johnson legislation: "We are not willing to let the sheep of flood protection cover up the wolf of power and water greed."[8]

Not surprisingly, California and Nevada found little room to negotiate. Chairman of the California delegation, Ralph Swing, elder brother of California congressman Phil Swing, responded to Hunt's opening diatribe: "We came over here for the purpose of arriving at something ... and were confronted the very first thing with the statement of your governor.... I think it is a waste of time to negotiate any further." Charles Squires, chairman of the Nevada delegation, followed Swing to the podium. Much to the chagrin of Arizona's representatives Squires told the delegates that Nevada supported

California: "The basis of all negotiations must be the recognition of the immediate necessity for a dam at or near Boulder Canyon on the Colorado River. That, gentlemen, is the position Nevada takes in the matter." Hayden noted that this first attempt at lower basin diplomacy was a dismal failure, confiding to his administrative assistant that Hunt's remarks resulted in an unproductive meeting.[9]

In mid-December 1925, the three state commissions met again in Phoenix to attempt negotiating a lower basin agreement. In order to avoid the contention of the abbreviated first meeting, California submitted its proposal to Hayden two weeks before the conference so he could present it to Arizona's legal and engineering teams. The congressman noticed at once that the "California Plan" contained significant concessions to Arizona. For the first time California supported the right of Arizona and Nevada to collect power royalties. Part five of the proposal stated: "When a dam creating a reservoir of twenty million acre-feet or more was constructed, at which hydroelectric power would be generated, the agency generating such power would pay one dollar per horsepower annually as compensation to the states of Nevada and Arizona for loss of tax revenues." Moreover, Hayden was pleased to note that California also conceded the Gila River's entire flow to Arizona. California's proposed water allocation formula, however, which allotted the Golden State two-thirds of the mainstream flow after Nevada received 300,000 acre-feet, posed serious problems for Hayden. Nevertheless, he came away from the December conference with two important issues to introduce into the Swing-Johnson debates: an Arizona power royalty and exclusive rights to the Gila.[10]

Congressman Hayden's frustrations continued in spite of recent progress made at the tri-state conferences. At Los Angeles in January 1927, the California delegation, after two weeks of constructive negotiations, abruptly terminated the discussions. Just as the commissioners were about to reach an agreement on the power royalty issue "a prominent Californian not a member of the commission," ordered a walkout. Hayden soon learned that Secretary of Commerce Herbert Hoover, who at the time was laying the groundwork for his campaign for the presidency, objected to the "federal government giving a tax revenue or its equivalent to Arizona." The commerce secretary was not only California's most influential politician, but also he needed his adopted state's support in the upcoming presidential election. Hoover wanted to minimize chances that Colorado River issues could cost him California's substantial electoral vote in the 1928 general elections.[11]

If Hoover's political aspirations frustrated Hayden, so too did Nevada's vascillation during the course of the tri-state conferences. Nevada, which at times wholeheartedly backed California, on other occasions assisted Arizona. Her senator, Key Pittman, for example, helped Arizona gain recognition of the right to a power royalty, while simultaneously supporting California's calls for a dam at Boulder Canyon. As much as each side coaxed the Nevadans to their respective positions both Arizona and California viewed the state as a "thorn in the side."[12]

Nevada, however, played an integral role in perhaps the most significant interstate meeting that took place within the broader context of the Swing-Johnson debates. The Denver Conference, actually two separate conferences spanning from August 22 to October 4, 1927, helped shape Hayden's arguments before various congressional committees. Upper basin frustration at the lower basin's inability to arrive at an agreement prompted the governors of Colorado, Utah, New Mexico, and Wyoming to issue a joint call for a meeting with their lower basin counterparts. Also, the possible consequences of a six-state compact becoming law played a prominent role, prompting calls for an interbasin parlay. The upper states, especially Utah, now feared that California could obtain the Boulder Canyon Project and the All-American Canal, therefore establishing uses to nearly all the lower basin's water. In that event, Arizona, a noncompact state, would be free to encroach upon the upper basin's allocation and establish prior uses that the Supreme Court might recognize as prior perfected rights.[13]

Hayden attended most sessions of the Denver Conference and watched as Utah Governor George Dern, the conference chairman, set the tone for the meeting. Dern, who later became President Franklin Roosevelt's Secretary of War, sounded little like a New

Dealer when, in his opening remarks, he stressed the need for western states to maintain their sovereignty against the encroachments of the federal government. Concerning the West's rivers he announced: "We hold that the western states have absolute jurisdiction over their streams and unless invited to do so, the federal government has no authority on our rivers except to regulate navigation." Utah had already shaken the foundations of basin state negotiations in January 1927 when the state legislature repealed its approval of the Colorado River Compact, and then one month later passed legislation asserting the state's rights to the river bed. Most observers believed that Utah had adopted this strident state's rights attitude because of its desire to exploit hydroelectric power sites and oil deposits in the channel of the Colorado near Moab, Utah. Dern offered still other reasons for his state's attitude. The Swing-Johnson legislation threatened the sovereign rights of Utah just as it threatened the rights of Arizona. The federal government could not come in, he avowed, and build a dam in one of the states without its consent. In some instances, Dern told his audience, "the interests of Utah and Arizona are common."[14]

Hayden considered carefully Dern's comments and the resolution of Key Pittman, Nevada's Democratic senator. In the only significant accomplishment of the meeting, Pittman fashioned Dern's ideas into a resolution: "The states could demand and receive compensation for the use of their lands and waters whereby the state or states upon whose land a dam is built ... are entitled to a preferred right to acquire energy." The upper states, Nevada, and Arizona enthusiastically approved the Pittman Resolution. California opposed it because it threatened passage of the Swing-Johnson bill, opened the way for higher power rates, and jeopardized availability of electrical current. Hayden viewed the resolution as a source of political ammunition in his case against the Swing-Johnson legislation, and described it as "the last basin-wide ideological assertion of state's rights" in the whole history of the controversy. When necessary or expedient he invoked the Pittman Resolution into the Swing-Johnson debates.[15]

Ultimately the other states and the federal government engineered an end to the political logjam created by Arizona. Shortly after

Arizona's Sixth Legislature failed to ratify the compact in 1923, Delph Carpenter, who had originally proposed the idea, suggested to Herbert Hoover and other federal officials that the agreement be allowed to become effective after six states had agreed to its provisions. Despite protests from Arizonans, by mid-1925 the legislatures of the upper states and Nevada had approved the six-state formula. California threw a wrinkle into the plan when it made ratification contingent upon executive or legislative approval of a lower basin dam. This reservation, introduced by Assemblyman A.C. Finney of Brawley, Imperial County, California, stated that the compact would not become binding until the President of the United States "had authorized the construction of a storage dam" at or below Boulder Canyon. When the Finney Reservation caused upper basin leaders to balk at the six-state proposal, Californians devised another way to secure a Boulder Canyon dam. Representative Swing and Senator Johnson, when they reintroduced their bill to Congress for the third time on February 26, 1926, included a provision that had not been seen in their two previous measures. Passage of this version of the Swing-Johnson bill made the Colorado River Compact effective with a six-state ratification.

Hayden opposed vigorously this California maneuver: "Congress has no right," he told his fellow lawmakers, "to force adherence to ... the compact without the full concurrence of the states that would be effected thereby." While Hayden favored the compact, supported the concept of a lower basin agreement, and touted the advantages of regional cooperation, he opposed California and the federal government imposing the compact on Arizona.[16]

Hayden devoted his full energies to blocking the Swing-Johnson bill. He drew upon years of experience, writing letters, calling in debts for old political favors, and working long nights. When the bill reached the House Committee on Irrigation and Reclamation, he kept Colorado's Delph Carpenter "on the stand for several days in an effort to kill time in an intelligent manner." He also advised witnesses opposed to the measure. Four days before Dwight Heard appeared to testify, Hayden suggested, "it would be very helpful if you urge approval of a change in the bill to provide that the location of the dam be left to a board of competent engineers, thus making the determination an engineering rather than a political question." He also told Heard to ask that "the bill be not reported at this session so that additional time could be allowed for a supplemental compact." To supporters of Arizona's position, these moves appeared prudent, constructive, and reasonable.[17]

Hayden found several additional ways to hold the bill in committee. He pointed to the House's crowded calendar and also emphasized how a delay would assist the U.S. State Department in its negotiations with Mexico to limit that country's use of Colorado River water. When, on April 23, 1926, the Senate Irrigation Committee, by a vote of 13-2, issued a favorable report on the Swing-Johnson Bill, Hayden's struggle in the House intensified. In a "confidential" note to Tucson newspaper editor R.E. Ellinwood, he relayed some "inside information" so that there would be no confusion when "the news wires started crackling." "The truth is that all manner of pressure is being brought to bear upon the House Irrigation and Reclamation Committee to secure a favorable report on the Swing-Johnson Bill." President Calvin Coolidge reportedly approved of the legislation as had prominent California Democrats William McAdoo and Isadore Dockweiler. Hayden analyzed his chances for success: "The committee consists of nine Republicans and eight Democrats and my constant effort has been to hold the members of our own party in line. That they are my friends is the best asset I have." Thus far three Republicans—from New York, Illinois, and Utah—had supported Hayden. The Utahan claimed the supremacy of state's rights and private power; the others disdained large federal handouts for western water projects. Hayden now sought firm commitments from the three Republicans.[18]

On May 22 Hayden appeared before Committee Chairman Addison Smith of Idaho and moved to postpone consideration of the bill. Smith who supported the measure, tried to rule his longtime friend out of order on a technicality, but failed. "By a vote of nine to six," Hayden wrote Arizona newspaper editors that afternoon, "The House Irrigation and Reclamation Committee adopted my motion to postpone consideration of the Swing-Johnson bill." The three Republicans and all the Democrats held for Hayden. Texas Democrat C.B. Hudspeth, who favored the legislation, voted to postpone because he "owed Hayden favors and promised to help in this fight." The Arizonan had accurately assessed the situation.[19]

Hayden completed his work on the third Swing-Johnson bill with a flourish. On May 24, 1926, two days after his victory, he wrote August F. Duclos, Navajo trader and longtime friend, for a special favor. "My Dear Duke," he began, "I am under great obligation to the nine members of the Committee on Irrigation and Reclamation who voted with me to postpone consideration of the Swing-Johnson bill and have decided to send each one of them a Navajo blanket as evidence of my appreciation of their loyal support at a time when the welfare of the state of Arizona was at stake." Duclos quickly sent the blankets to the delighted congressmen who supported Hayden in committee.[21]

The issue was not dead, however, and from 1926 to 1929 Hayden devoted much of his time to delaying what he called "'A Force Bill' which seeks to compel the State of Arizona to conform to the will of other states, particularly California." Hayden's role in resisting the Boulder Canyon measure had important political consequences for the seven-term representative. Early in 1926 he announced his intention to run for the U.S. Senate against incumbent Ralph Cameron. As in Hayden's election of 1922 and 1924, the Colorado River controversy was the main issue of the campaign. Rather than defending Arizona water rights, however, Republican Cameron had spent most of his single term defending himself against allegations of bribery, misuse of public funds, and land fraud that embarrassed the Harding and Coolidge administrations. Coolidge was rumored to favor a Hayden victory. In an election marked by its predictable outcome, native Arizonan Carl Hayden advanced to the U.S. Senate.[22]

The election of 1926 served as a referendum on Hayden's fourteen-year performance in the House of Representatives. During that time he had won the respect and admiration of his colleagues. "For years," one fellow member wrote, "Carl Hayden has been recognized as one of the outstanding leaders of the House" and "after all is said

Who Stopped the Swing-Johnson Bill in Congress? The Californians Know!

These headlines from California Newspapers record the skill and courage of Arizona's ablest defender in her hour of need.

The San Francisco Daily News

HAYDEN WINS DAM BATTLE

Defeat of Boulder Bill Personal Victory For Him

BY RUTH FINNEY
Daily News Washington Bureau

WASHINGTON, May 24.—"It was a personal victory for Carl Hayden," said Rep. Phil Swing today of the 9 to 6 vote by which the House irrigation committee postponed action on the Boulder dam bill until next session.

"Hayden's power was shown by the loyal support he received from all Democrats of the committee.

The Calexico Chronicle

OUTLOOK FOR RIVER BILL GLOOMY

Attorney Childers Back From Washington; Is Not Optimistic

HAYDEN IS BLAMED

The Swing-Johnson bill has only a doubtful chance of passage at the present session of Congress according to the statement of Attorney Charles Childers, who returned yesterday from Washington.

The Anaheim Bulletin

BOULDER DAM HAS NEW FOE

Arizona Representative Declares He Will Fight To Finish

WASHINGTON, Feb. 5.—The revised Swing-Johnson Boulder dam bill, embodying changes proposed by Secretary of Interior Work, encountered material opposition when presented to the house irrigation committee today for the first time.

Representative Hayden, Arizona Democrat, charged that the new bill "ignored" his state and announced that he "would fight it to a finish."

The Los Angeles Times

COMMITTEE LEAVES RIVER DAM-SITE ISSUE IN DOUBT

Arizona Representative Argues for Latitude in Selection of Project Location

(EXCLUSIVE DISPATCH)

WASHINGTON, May 12.—After two hours of debate in executive session the House Committee on Irrigation today adopted an amendment to the Swing-Johnson bill, the effect of which is to leave in doubt the location at which the Colorado River Dam shall be built.

The Visalia Times

BOULDER DAM BILL ONCE MORE DELAYED

Arizona Representative Is After Information From State Department

The Calexico Chronicle

RIVER BILL IS ENDANGERED IN CLASH

Hayden of Arizona Moves To Have Measure Tabled By House Committee

Swing Criticized for Plan To Withhold Measure From Action on Floor

WASHINGTON, May 6.—Consideration of the Swing-Johnson bill in the House Irrigation and Reclamation committee was continued to a later date yesterday.

The Monrovia News

NEW DELAY FOR BOULDER DAM BILL MAY PREVENT ACTION THIS SESSION

Arizona Representative Demands Statement of Plans for Mexico to Obtain Water

WASHINGTON, May 1.—(U.P.)—The Swing-Johnson Boulder dam bill met further delay today in the House irrigation and reclamation committee. The committee expected to close hearings and consider the bill in executive session, but Representative Hayden, Democrat, Arizona, asked for another meeting Wednesday. Hayden wants officials of the state department to explain the status of their negotiations with Mexico over the use of waters of the Colorado.

The Riverside Press

HAYDEN IS DELAYING THE GAME

Arizona Man Secures Another Meeting On Boulder Dam Bill

SWING OPPOSES THIS

The Santa Ana Register

HEARINGS ON BOULDER DAM PROJECT ARE TO CONTINUE

Grant Request By Representative Hayden, Arizona, For Another Meeting

TIME GROWING SHORT

Doubt Expressed Whether Scores Of Changes Can Be Voted On At Session

(By United Press)

The Indio Date Palm

HAYDEN OF ARIZONA URGES AGREEMENT

WASHINGTON, April 26.—Representative Hayden today declared that Yuma valley flood protection would be delayed by the passage of the Swing-Johnson bill and telegraphed the Yuma County Water Users association that flood control would be possible only after long litigation.

He urged instead that an interstate agreement be reached between Arizona, Nevada and California.

CARL HAYDEN

Democratic Candidate For United States Senator

Hayden's campaign poster in his initial—and successful—campaign for the U.S. Senate, 1926 (author's files).

and done probably the biggest work that Carl Hayden has done in Congress has been his intelligent and consistent struggle to safeguard the great natural resources of the United States." Speaker of the House Champ Clark, just before he died, insisted that Hayden was one of the ablest men in the House of Representatives: "He has ability and courage plus sanity, he is progressive but he is responsible, he never tears down the old structure until he is prepared to put something better in its place." Senator Thomas Walsh of Montana, famous for uncovering the oil scandals at Teapot Dome and Elk Hills, added, "He has already made friends in the Senate particularly among members from the West, who will welcome him and be glad to secure for him committee assignments that will best enable him to be of service to his state." Arizona voters doubtlessly took pride in such glowing accounts of their newly elected senator's past work.

In addition to his reputation on Capitol Hill, Hayden's critical role in the Colorado River controversy assured his advancement to the Senate. Even those few Arizonans who favored positive action on the Swing-Johnson legislation, like Yuma resident C.W. Ingram, favored Hayden. "You certainly have made a record for a great single-handed fight," Ingram wrote the Senator-elect, "and as we see it here in Yuma, Carl Hayden can probably do more than any other man to ameliorate the bitterness on the Arizona side." Henry D. Ross, chief justice of the Arizona Supreme Court, penned a congratulatory letter to Hayden and commented, "I think you are making a remarkable case in the Colorado River question.... I am especially impressed with the legal aspects you present. I think you are doing great work." Thus, with fourteen years experience in the House of Representatives and a solid political foundation in Arizona, Hayden began his unprecedented forty-two year career in the U.S. Senate.[23]

Upon entry into the Senate, Hayden, as Senator Thomas Walsh had predicted, received "choice committee assignments." Notably, his appointment to the Appropriations Committee during his first term had implications that reached far beyond Arizona's water and power future. Tucson's *Arizona Daily Star* wrote proudly of this accomplishment: "An exceptional preferment was granted to Carl Hayden by his election to membership on the powerful committee on appropriations. Membership to this great committee is highly coveted and is very unusual for a senator to be chosen at the very beginning of his term of service." Hayden not only had a role in tightening and loosening the federal purse strings, but also, with continued reelection and seniority, he became chairman of the Senate's most powerful committee. Hayden, through his position on the Appropriations Committee, gave Arizona and the West significant leverage in federal affairs.[24]

On the heels of his win in November, he returned to Washington and once again faced the Swing-Johnson bill. Also at this time Hayden, recognizing that Governor Hunt and other pact opponents in the state legislature would never modify their position, determined to act independently in Colorado River politics. He now believed that passage of the Swing-Johnson bill was inevitable, but he hoped to secure provisions in the measure that would safeguard Arizona's water and power future. He drafted a "Minority Report" to accompany the Boulder Canyon Project bill, detailing his objections and offering an alternative approach to Colorado River development.[25]

On January 21, 1927, less than one month after he submitted his report, Hayden pled publicly for compromises in nearly four hours of testimony before the House Rules Committee. While the legislation provided not one dollar for reclamation in Arizona, he emphasized, it gave California $31,000,000 for a water delivery system (the All-American Canal) and provided a federally subsidized hydroelectric power plant to generate cheap electricity to stimulate the growth of Los Angeles and the southern California coastal plain. The requirements of Los Angeles and other California cities, Hayden avowed, did not justify passage of such legislation at the expense of Arizona. The Swing-Johnson bill, he argued, "was purely and selfishly a California measure."[26]

Under the terms of the bill Arizona received no protection from the possibility of Mexico gaining a prior right to Colorado River water. In the absence of an international treaty with that nation, Mexican landholders or American speculators, with a regulated flow of water obtained at no cost, and with cheap labor, could produce crops and claim "prior right" to water that might otherwise be dedicated to Arizona farmland. The legislation, Hayden insisted, should include a provision that reserved mainstream water stored in an American-built reservoir for reclamation of lands in the United States.[27]

Hayden next addressed the issue of federal versus state control of the river. The Swing-Johnson legislation gave the federal government unprecedented control over the interstate stream. He reminded his listeners of the 1902 Reclamation Act and its recognition of the exclusive jurisdiction of the several states over the appropriation, use, and distribution of water. Neither Congress nor the six states, he argued, have the right to apportion the waters of the river in which seven states were interested. Hayden reiterated his contention that the basin should agree upon a seven-state compact, a far better alternative than either state or federal control of the river.[28]

From Hayden the Rules Committee also heard testimony concerning Arizona's demand for a power royalty. The senator presented evidence demonstrating that the Colorado River fell more than 2,350 feet within Arizona's borders. Numerous power sites along the river, he argued, should be treated as natural assets belonging to the state. In any agreement with California or Nevada, Arizona was entitled to a reasonable tax return on the potential value of its assets. California had already agreed in principle to the royalty, Hayden told members of the committee, and he now requested a sum equal to the taxes that private enterprise would pay if they owned and developed the same site.[29]

Hayden concluded with a brief discussion of federal reclamation in the West and Arizona policy concerning the Swing-Johnson bill. "The utilization of the now wasted resources of the Colorado River," he noted, "is a project of such magnitude and of such importance to the entire nation that at least the initial development should be undertaken for the combined purposes of flood control, irrigation, and power under public rather than private development." He pressed for an equal division of the lower basin's mainstream water and stressed that Arizona was unified in its opposition to the Swing-Johnson bill. Enactment of the legislation could only result in "protracted interstate litigation over

Colorado River water rights." "Arizona," Hayden warned, "would be compelled to file a suit in the U.S. Supreme Court to restrain the construction of Boulder or Black Canyon Dam until the water rights of Arizona in and to the Colorado River are determined." [30]

On February 27, 1927, after a three week delay in the House Rules Committee, Swing succeeded in having his legislation reported to the House. Meanwhile, Senator Hiram Johnson moved his bill through committee hearings to the Senate floor. In response to the Californians' legislative maneuvers, Arizona Senator Ashurst began a filibuster that, with the help of loyal friends, lasted to the end of the session. Thus, Arizona again prevented action on the bill.[31]

Beginning in the spring of 1927, support for the Boulder Canyon Project grew. Disastrous spring floods on the Mississippi generated calls for the project in order to prevent a similar catastrophe in the West. The floods, which cost taxpayers millions of dollars in repair costs, prompted powerful Nebraska Senator George Norris to call for passage of the Boulder Canyon legislation to "save the Imperial Valley" from flooding. While Norris acknowledged that the project would produce crops that would compete with midwestern products, he nevertheless saw flood control on the Colorado as more important than regional competition.[32]

During consideration of the fourth Swing-Johnson bill, several developments dimmed Hayden's chances for further delaying the legislation. In the spring of 1928, the Federal Trade Commission (FTC) disclosed findings of a two-year investigation into the activities of the private power lobby. Not surprisingly, private power firms closely monitored federal reclamation legislation like Boulder Canyon and Muscle Shoals. The commission focused its investigations on the National Utility Association (NUA) and the National Electric Light Association (NELA), two organizations that lobbied heavily against Muscle Shoals and Boulder Dam. The NELA, for example, spent 1 million dollars each year attempting to influence public opinion toward private ownership of utilities. The commission also revealed that $400,000 above the annual 1 million dollars had been raised specifically to defeat the Boulder Canyon Project Act. Names like

Merritt C. Mecham, former governor of New Mexico, and James G. Scrugham, ex-governor of Nevada and a member of the Colorado River Commission, appeared on the NELA payroll. Further revelations, and the resulting public outcry and denunciation of the "power trust," helped accelerate passage of the Swing-Johnson bill. Representative Swing later wrote a friend, "The biggest benefit was exposition of Federal Trade Commission on power company propaganda." Senator Johnson concurred in a letter to Harold Ickes: "The biggest thing since I have been in public life is the investigation by the FTC of the power trust. It was a victory for me." While Hayden deplored the private power lobby and praised the investigations of the commission, he knew the political damage done to Arizona's cause.[33]

Solid support for the legislation also came from Congress, when, in December 1928, it received the "Sibert Report," a technical study conducted by a group of engineers and geologists under the directorship of Major General William L. Sibert. In May 1928 Hayden played a major role in gaining congressional support for the study of the Colorado River Basin and its relation to the features of the Swing-Johnson bill. The board investigated questions raised by Arizona about the project's engineering and economic features. In the end, the Colorado River Board, as it was also known, not only strongly endorsed the Boulder Canyon Project, but also observed that because of poor gauging equipment at Yuma, and data gathered after 1905 when the river flow was unusually heavy, water supply estimates "were exceedingly uncertain." The Sibert Report also recommended construction of the dam at Black Canyon, twenty miles downstream from Boulder Canyon. In spite of the suggestion, the legislation continued to carry the Boulder Canyon label.[34]

Although public opinion and scientific justification aided Boulder Canyon Project supporters, Hayden found further ways to delay action. On May 15, 1928, the House Rules Committee voted again to send the bill to the House. There, Representative Lewis Douglas, Hayden's successor in the House, and Elmer Leatherwood of Utah led the opposition. On May 25, 1928, Douglas filed a motion to recommit the bill to the Irrigation and Reclamation Committee, but the motion failed on a roll call vote 219-139. On the same day and by the same margin, the Boulder Canyon Project Act passed the House of Representatives. The Senate, which at the time was debating the bill, now became the focus of nationwide attention.[35]

On May 28, 1928, Senator Hayden participated in one of the most celebrated events in the history of the legislation. Together with his Arizona colleague Henry Ashurst, Hayden conducted a filibuster of the bill. With only two days left in the session, the two Arizona senators attempted to talk the bill to death. Senator Johnson forced a vote to require the Senate to stay in session all night. The gallery gasped as the vote ended in a 40-40 tie, but broke into cheers when Vice-President Charles Dawes broke the deadlock in favor of his fellow Republican's motion.

In his maiden speech on the floor of the Senate, Hayden, the "Silent Senator," spoke nine hours to a mostly empty chamber. When Ashurst took over, Johnson moved to extend the session to June 5 in an effort to wait out the Arizonans. The motion lost, however, 39-41. Accusations and threats of fist fights filled the chamber as the Senate adjourned in "wild disorder" on May 29, 1928. One observer noted that an executive session during the final hour "deprived the gallery of one of the wildest and emotional scenes since war days." An exhausted Hayden confided to a friend after his filibuster: "It is true that if brought to a vote the Swing-Johnson Bill would have passed both houses.... I sincerely doubt it will be possible to prevent its passage in the next Congress."[36]

The Seventieth Congress began its second session on December 5, 1928. Despite Hayden's vigorous opposition in the Senate, on December 16, it passed the Boulder Canyon Project Act by a vote of 64-11. Two days later the House approved the Senate version 167-122. President Coolidge signed the legislation into law three days later thus ending one phase of the Colorado River controversy, yet signaling the beginning of an era of unprecedented development in the basin.[37]

Few measures have had a greater impact on the Pacific Southwest than the congressional action that in 1928 authorized Hoover Dam and approved construction of an All-American Canal that would supply water to California's Imperial Valley at the expense of farmers in northwestern Mexico. It was a move that in 1944 spurred a controversial water treaty between the United States and Mexico. It also precipitated a long series of Arizona-generated actions in the Supreme Court that culminated in 1963-64. In addition, the act repealed the law of prior appropriation as it applied between the upper and lower basins, and much to the chagrin of the majority of Arizonans, the terms of the Colorado River Compact became effective with the passage of the Boulder Canyon legislation. At the time of its passage, the Boulder Canyon Project Act was viewed by Arizonans as giving California everything and Arizona nothing.[38]

Concessions to Hayden and his constituents were evident, however, and testified to the Arizonan's resourcefulness. California, in winning support for passage, agreed to limit itself to a specific amount of the 7.5 million acre-feet allocated to the lower basin in Article III (a) of the compact. The act also contained the Pittman Amendment, named for the Nevada senator who introduced a compromise that outlined the Hayden-supported concept of a lower-basin tristate agreement. Under its terms, Nevada would receive 300,000 acre-feet of water annually, California 4.4 million, and Arizona 2.8 million plus "exclusive rights to the Gila River." This aspect of the Pittman Amendment, as interpreted later in *Arizona v. California* (1963), represented a clear victory for Hayden, who had long fought for the exclusion of that river from any mainstream water computation. Finally, under the terms of the Pittman proposal, Arizona and California would divide equally any surplus mainstream water.[39]

Other Arizona contentions were included in the law. The construction, repayment, and maintenance of the All-American Canal were separated from the dam and the power plant. Hayden had suggested the arrangement as early as 1922 during hearings on the first Swing-Johnson bill, and had consistently pressed for its separate financial status. Moreover, the bill recognized the principle of a power royalty or tax on power. Arizona and Nevada were each to receive 18.75 percent of the surplus profits of power revenues. Hayden and Arizona, although they had lost the first major battle over the

Colorado River, could point to several skirmishes along the way that, in some cases, made California's victory far from complete.[40]

While grappling with the subtleties and complexities of the politics of water in the Southwest, Hayden never lost sight of his vision of a common regional destiny. In 1926, during the debates on the Boulder Canyon legislation, he had pronounced this "regionalist view." "The West is an entity," he told the other members of the Arizona congressional delegation, "and there is a growing homogeneity among its people, an identity of interest which makes the region a reality geographically, commercially, industrially, and economically." Injury could not be done to one western state without affecting the others. "If the West is to maintain its identity and become a destined factor in the increased wealth, population, and strength of the nation," he concluded, "it will be because the large communities and states of the West continue to recognize the necessity for mutual consideration of the problems peculiar to the West." Unfortunately for the ideal of southwestern regional cooperation, however, the Swing-Johnson formula for developing the lower basin's water resources proved a major obstacle to Hayden's vision.[41]

Arizona played a distinct, and some have argued, contentious role in this chapter of the Colorado River controversy. In its quest for a share of water and power from the river, Arizona showed little philosophical consistency in its approach. One of the most ardent proponents of state's rights at the outset of the controversy, Arizona, when events turned against it, looked quickly to the central government and the Supreme Court. As the struggle wore on, the river became a fixation in the Arizona body politic. As one popular writer described the apparently unresolvable conflict and its impact on Arizonans: "The river has had a traumatic influence in Arizona history: whole careers, even lives have been shaped by it. It has become Arizona's characteristic obsession."[42]

VII

Adversity and Opportunity

Congressional approval of the Boulder Canyon Project Act activated neither the compact nor the act itself. In fact, at the time of congressional passage of the Swing-Johnson bill, only four states had agreed to the pact. By early March, however, Utah and California again ratified the compact thus creating the six-state agreement. On June 25, 1929, newly elected President Herbert Hoover, after waiting six months, declared the act effective. Meanwhile, Arizona gave notice of its next course of action. On January 15, 1929, as Hayden had warned, the Arizona Colorado River Commission authorized Attorney General K. Berry Peterson to file suit in the U.S. Supreme Court. Arizona thus initiated another phase in the controversy.[1]

While Arizona commenced court action, representatives from Arizona, California, and Nevada met once again at Santa Fe, New Mexico, in an attempt to reconcile lower basin differences. These meetings, which took place in February and March 1929, like so many tri-state meetings before them, adjourned amidst feelings of bitterness and confusion. In the meantime, President Hoover's secretary of interior, Ray Lyman Wilbur, a Californian, secured power and water delivery contracts with the City of Los Angeles and Southern Sierras Power Company under the terms and provisions of the Colorado River Compact and the Boulder Canyon Project Act. When the contracts were finally approved—over Arizona's vigorous protests—Arizona acted on its threat and filed the first of several Supreme Court actions.[2]

Oddly, Arizona looked outside the state for legal expertise and hired Idaho lawyer John Pinkham Gray, reputedly "one of the outstanding lawyers in the West," to assist its stable of attorneys. On October 30, 1930, Arizona petitioned the Supreme Court "to enjoin the construction of Boulder Dam and the All-American Canal and to enjoin performance of the water delivery contracts between the Secretary of Interior and other California water users." Arizona declared that the Boulder Canyon Project Act, the Colorado River Compact, and the water and power contracts were unconstitutional. Attorney Gray vowed that "California and the federal government were not going to override roughshod on Arizona's sovereign rights." On May 13, 1931, however, in an 8-1 decision the Court rejected Arizona's suit without prejudice, asserting that the Boulder Canyon Project Act "represented a valid exercise of congressional power." One month later, physical proof of that power became evident as workers began excavating the diversion tunnels for the dam at Black Canyon, which, after more congressional wrangling, was called Hoover Dam.[3]

As Arizona's energies shifted from the legislative to the judicial branch, Hayden continued the politics of delay in Congress, arguing against the first $10,600,000 appropriation for construction of the dam. Of course Hayden and Arizona lost in this half-hearted effort and construction of the project continued apace. The underdog fight, nevertheless, won Hayden solid political support at home. His efforts against the Swing-Johnson bill gave Arizona the appearance of maintaining a unified water policy during the critical years from 1926 to 1929.[4]

In spite of these series of setbacks for Arizona, Hayden continued to assert his state's claims to Colorado River water and power in Congress. Yet a host of unresolved problems frustrated his efforts in behalf of Arizona. The confusion and factionalism that characterized Arizona water policy during the 1920s continued through the 1930s and the New Deal era. Several powerful political and agricultural organizations, including Fred Colter's Arizona Highline Association, continued to excoriate California's water and power greed while at the same time reaffirming their commitment to state-owned and operated reclamation programs. Similarly, state's rights Democrats, for the most part, dominated Arizona's political affairs during the period, promising to "save" the Colorado for Arizona, yet offering little new or progressive in water resource development policy. Aging Governor George Hunt, who served his last term between 1930 and 1932, and his successors in the thirties, Dr. Benjamin B. Moeur, (1932-36), Rawleigh C. Stanford (1936-38), and Robert T. Jones (1938-40)—all Democrats—maintained proprietary views concerning the Colorado and opposed Arizona entering into the Colorado River Compact. As Hayden assessed the situation from Washington, Arizona experienced the expansion and benefits of federal reclamation during the New Deal in theory only, not in practice.[5]

Hayden, George W.P. Hunt, and Franklin Roosevelt campaign in Arizona, 1932. (ASU: CP CTH 1367).

Hayden expressed frustration over the lack of progress at other levels of state government. He maintained close ties to Arizona's Colorado River Commission, and in one missive, A.H. Favour, Salt River Valley water leader and a veteran of several commissions, informed Hayden of that agency's lack of effectiveness: "We haven't formulated any definite policy pertaining to the Colorado." In 1935 the editor of Tucson's *Arizona Daily Star* noted that for over a dozen years "factional disputes within the state have cost it a pretty price." And in 1939, Favour, briefing newly elected governor Robert T. Jones, again commented that "Arizona has gone through various administrations since 1922 with no very definite water policy." Thus, the Arizona Colorado River Commission, often inefficient, usually unprofessional, and with little political power, further reflected the state's problems within the context of evolving federal reclamation policy.[6]

Meanwhile, the Depression and drought of the 1930s forced the Roosevelt administration to take action with a host of New Deal initiatives. In the wake of economic and environmental catastrophe, proponents of federal reclamation found seeds of opportunity. Fortunately for the arid West in the Depression, President Roosevelt, Secretary of the Interior Harold Ickes, and Commissioner of Reclamation Elwood Mead found the expansion of the federal reclamation program consistent with the goals of the New Deal. They provided strong political support and, more importantly, money. Throughout the New Deal years, the government spent an average of 52 million dollars per year on federal reclamation projects; over five times the average annual amount spent during the previous decade.[7]

Other noteworthy developments marked the expansion of federal reclamation during the New Deal. Projects begun and completed, for example, reflected a multi-purpose approach; planners combined hydroelectric power generation with water for irrigation, as well as drainage, flood control, and recreation. Also, Congress passed laws further modifying a variety of financial aspects of the reclamation program, thereby stimulating the expansion of water resource development in the West. Hayden gave unwavering support to the growth and modification of federal reclamation in the western states during the New Deal.[8]

In many ways, the Bureau of Reclamation reflected the spirit of the New Deal. Between 1933 and 1941 the Bureau began several monumental water projects in the West. Construction of the Grand Coulee Dam, the chief structure of the Columbia River Basin Project, began in 1934. Work on the Shasta Dam, key to the success of California's Central Valley Project, commenced in 1937. Roosevelt administration representatives, when touring the West, rarely missed a chance to marvel at Grand Coulee, Shasta, or Boulder Dams. Together with the quickened pace of the reclamation program, the emergence of hydroelectric power as the chief benefit of these multiple-use projects, marked the New Deal years. According to one leading scholar of federal reclamation during this era, "Revenues from the sale of electricity, and the availability of inexpensive power had an enormous influence in the economy of the West, attracting industry and benefiting millions of consumers." As residents of northern California and the Pacific Northwest knew, Senator Hayden of Arizona, Chairman of the Subcommittee of the Senate Committee on Appropriations, played a crucial role in the expansion of federal reclamation in their regions.[9]

In addition to supporting projects throughout the West, Hayden played a major part in other, less glamorous, but equally important developments in New Deal water policy. In fashioning the Interior Department Appropriation bill for 1939, for example, Hayden and Senator Joseph C. O'Mahoney of Wyoming sponsored an amendment that bore enormous implications for the future of federal reclamation. The Hayden-O'Mahoney Amendment provided that 52.5 percent of accumulated revenues from the sale of naval petroleum reserves be transferred to the Bureau of Reclamation for use in construction work and other activities. Also, the senators worked out a repayment formula, which, in effect, lessened the cost burden on individual water users. Finally, general funds were made available to the reclamation program thus lending stability to the Bureau. This fiscal reorganization, according to one prominent Arizona agricultural journal, "was the most vital legislation affecting the reclamation program since the Reclamation Law of 1902." It passed with little fanfare, not only reflecting Hayden's legislative style, but also underscoring his broader commitment to federal reclamation in the West.[10]

During these years California began enjoying the benefits of the Boulder Canyon Project Act. Although slowed by the Depression, construction of Hoover Dam was completed in 1935. The following year, hydroelectric power reached the southern California coastal plain. Beginning in 1939 the Metropolitan Water District of Southern California, much to the alarm of Arizonans, commenced delivery of Colorado River water to its customers. Imperial Valley residents, in 1942, saw water delivered by the All-American Canal. As a result of these developments, southern California and the Imperial Valley prospered, attracting millions of newcomers in subsequent decades. Not surprisingly, Arizonans looked warily to their west and vented their frustration in a variety of ways.[11]

Energy spent expressing this unfettered envy, Hayden ventured, was costly and pointless. Nevertheless, twice more during the 1930s Arizona sought legal solutions to its claims to the river. In February 1934, in its second petition to the U.S. Supreme Court, Governor Benjamin B. Moeur and his administration asked to perpetuate testimony intended for use in future legal action. In this unusual legal maneuver, the Arizonans, once again, hoped to gain what they had lost in their opposition to the Colorado River Compact and the Boulder Canyon Project Act. State officials wanted a specific amount of mainstream water for future use and exclusive rights to Gila River water. Ironically, Arizona based its longstanding claims on testimony given during negotiations surrounding the drafting of the compact. Hayden, although not an attorney, predicted accurately the outcome of the suit. Since Arizona had not ratified the Colorado River Compact, he reasoned, it could not base its claims on that document. Indeed, in a unanimous ruling on May 21, 1934, the U.S. Supreme Court rejected Arizona's claim, ruling that the introduction of the proposed testimony was not relevant because Arizona had refused to ratify the compact.[12]

The Supreme Court ruling of May 1936 demonstrated not only Arizona's prolonged frustration, but also provided another vivid illustration of the increasing role the federal government played in basin state water politics. The Court contended that the rights of the United States government were superior, and therefore, a determination of the rights of the seven states could not be made without also determining the rights of the federal government. The justices reasoned that since the U.S. government had not been made party to the suit and had not agreed to be sued, they could not act on Arizona's petition. The Court also pointed out that Arizona had to demonstrate that its rights were being violated and its uses restricted. Since millions of acre feet of unused water flowed to the Gulf of Mexico, Arizona had not been harmed by ongoing developments.[13]

In Congress Hayden attempted to minimize the impact of Arizona's legal setbacks and at the same time dispel the state's growing image of non-cooperation. In cloakroom discussions, private talks, and committee hearings he distanced himself from state officials and their policies. During hearings on the Interior Department appropriation bill for 1938, for example, he expressed his views on Arizona's efforts at adjudication of the dispute. Before the Senate Subcommittee of the Committee on Appropriations, of which he was a member, he stated: "I did not advise the filing of any of the suits in the Supreme Court." Arizona's actions, he announced to the subcommittee, were misguided and he felt confident that the Court would take no action.[14]

The senator based this assessment on what he perceived were incorrect legal assumptions. The theory upon which the Arizona suits were filed, he told members of the subcommittee, was that the Supreme Court had the power to divide water between states. Hayden believed, however, that the sum and substance of the Court's decision pertaining to interstate water rights was that "it did not decide hypothetical cases." He told his fellow senators that in each of the three cases filed by Arizona, "the Court refused to make any attempt to divide the waters of the Colorado River or to assign any portion of such waters to Arizona." As Hayden interpreted these and other rulings concerning interstate streams, including *Kansas v. Nebraska* (1922), he concluded that the Supreme Court would make a decision only when there arose an actual conflict of right. Given that legal framework, Hayden believed that Arizona had asked the Court to pass upon a moot question. The implications of the Arizona senator's statements, official and unofficial, were not lost on other members of Congress. In short, Hayden did not support the actions of his state.[15]

Arizona leaders during the 1930s took other steps to express their outrage, some of them bordering on the dramatic. In 1932 the Department of Interior announced that it intended to contract with the Metropolitan Water District (MWD) of Southern California for the construction of a water storage and power dam near Parker, Arizona. When the news reached Arizona, Governor Moeur informed federal officials that he opposed further development on the river until Arizona's rights were clearly defined. In February 1933 he wrote outgoing Secretary of the Interior Ray Lyman Wilbur, stating flatly that the proposed diversion dams could not be placed on the river without Arizona's consent, and advised that the state would take action in opposition to the construction of the dams.[16]

Despite this warning and others, the Interior Department entered into a contract with MWD for the construction of Parker Dam. Late in the fall of 1934, as MWD employees began constructing a bridge between Arizona and California, Governor Moeur acted on his threat "to repel any invasion or threatened invasion of the sovereignty of the State of Arizona." On November 10, 1934, Moeur declared marshal law on the construction site and ordered a unit of the Arizona National Guard to occupy the area. In addition to the 101 men sent to Parker, an "Arizona Navy," comprised of the river boats Julia B and Nellie Jo, joined the guardsmen in the "war" with California. Offering to diffuse the highly charged situation, an unhappy Secretary of the Interior Harold Ickes ordered work suspended until the dispute had been resolved. After months of fruitless negotiation, the federal government, on June 14, 1935, filed suit in the Supreme Court to enjoin Arizona from interfering with the construction of Parker Dam. The Court, however, ruled against the federal government and held that the consent of Congress was necessary before the dam could be constructed. In effect, the Court asserted that the U.S. government had failed to show that construction had been authorized and therefore no grounds existed for granting the injunction. Arizona leaders had little time to rejoice. The Seventy-fourth Congress, shortly after the ruling, authorized construction of Parker Dam.[17]

Hayden again found himself at odds with state leaders. He questioned Governor Moeur's "dogmatic adherence" to state's rights water policy and disagreed with the calling out of Arizona National Guardsmen. Such tactics, although colorful, helped Arizona's congressmen little in gaining favorable compromises in federal legislation concerning the river. Moreover, in the context of the nation's economic crisis, Hayden believed the expenditure of state funds for the purpose of halting the construction of Parker Dam was wasteful. While the celebrated miniature war with California made exciting press, sold newspapers, and focused Arizonans' attention on their

Arizona Governor B.B. Moeur (1932-1936) who ordered the Arizona National Guard to the Colorado River in an effort to stop construction of Parker Dam (ASU: CP MLCP Moeur, B.B.-5).

perceived aggressors, the foolhardy fight further illustrated to Hayden the growing need for alternative approaches to Arizona Colorado River policy.[18]

During these years of recalcitrance and resistance, hints of a shift toward moderation and conciliation surfaced among some state leaders. In 1933, for example, the Moeur administration attempted to meet with Interior Department officials to discuss the formation of a lower basin compact. Extreme state's rights proponents, however, rallied behind Senator Fred Colter and the Arizona Highline Association and successfully doomed this effort. In the following year, as Governor Moeur tried to obstruct water delivery to California's coastal cities, members of his administration and the Arizona congressional delegation entered into detailed discussions with Interior Secretary Ickes in an attempt to secure a water delivery contract. Not surprisingly, as news of these talks spread throughout the basin, the other six states registered their protest. Arizona had not signed the Colorado River Compact, they complained. Still other actions revealed a slight shift toward moderation. In 1938 the state legislature authorized the Arizona Colorado Commission to file an application with the Federal Power Commission for preliminary permission to construct a dam on the Colorado River at Bridge Canyon. One year later, Arizona proposed to the Interior Department another water delivery contract, with water to be delivered to Arizona from Lake Mead, behind Boulder Dam. Taken together, these actions indicated that Arizona leaders recognized, albeit indirectly, federal authority on the river. Thus, while the 1930s could be accurately described as an era of confusion, conflict, and recalcitrance in Arizona water policy, the decade also contained an undercurrent of progress, conciliation, and moderation.[19]

Hayden finally received much-welcomed help in his efforts to secure a share of Colorado River water with the election of fellow Democrat Sidney P. Osborn as governor in 1940. Shortly after assuming office Osborn led a water policy revolution at the state level. Once a state's rights advocate and ardent opponent of the regionalism inherent in the Colorado River Compact, Osborn quickly informed the electorate that he now favored the interstate agreement. He told

Arizona Governor Sidney P. Osborn who championed the ratification of the Colorado River Compact in Arizona (ASU: CP SPC 28:1).

Arizona lawmakers that with the enactment of the Boulder Canyon Project Act in 1929 the era of philosophizing and theorizing about the river had ended: "Whatever our previous opinions about the best place or plan, we can only recognize that decisions have been made and the dam constructed."[20]

Over the years Hayden had tried to convince his old friend that Arizona might lose any hope for gaining a right to mainstream water if state leaders remained intransigent. Moreover, the series of legal calamities and a massive drought in the late 1930s and early 1940s similar in intensity to that which ravaged the Great Plains, created a water-and power-shortage crisis in the state. In addition, the pending water treaty with Mexico and California's announced plans to increase annual use of mainstream water to 2 million acre-feet, posed serious and immediate threats to future Arizona water supplies. Thus in a special session called specifically to deal with the Colorado River, the legislature, on February 9, 1944, first passed a bill authorizing a water delivery contract with the secretary of interior providing the annual delivery of 2.8 million acre-feet of mainstream water, plus one-half of "any excess or surplus ... to the extent for use in Arizona ... under the compact." Soon thereafter, on February 24, 1944, Osborn signed the bill which ratified the compact, thereby ending over two decades of controversy within Arizona. Importantly for Hayden, these actions enabled him to fight Arizona's reclamation battles in Congress within rather than outside federally approved guidelines.[21]

Other forces impelled Arizona leaders to reevaluate their previous positions. An unprecedented population influx taxed diminishing water resources. In the two decades preceding 1940, for example, Arizona's population had grown 67 percent to approximately 500,000. By 1945, 200,000 more people had moved to the state. Significantly, most of this growth was concentrated in and around Phoenix and Tucson, prefiguring the urban nature of Arizona's growth in subsequent decades. By the outbreak of World War II state leaders realized that they faced the possibility of water and power shortages if current demographic trends continued. These factors provided yet another impetus for a reconsideration of state water policy.[22]

The final major factor which convinced Arizonans that they must revise their positions concerned the resolution of Mexican rights to Colorado River water. Hayden had long hoped that Arizona could reach an accord with her neighbors before addressing the international question. On February 3, 1944, however, State Department officials completed arduous, complex negotiations with their Mexican counterparts culminating in an agreement which promised delivery to Mexico of 1.5 million acre-feet of water annually from the Colorado River. For once, it seemed, Arizona and California agreed on an issue concerning the Colorado River. Both states believed the amount excessive. U.S. negotiators, nevertheless, motivated by the Good Neighbor Policy and the recent close cooperation between the two countries in the global conflict, favored the generous allocation. The Roosevelt administration, Hayden informed his constituents, in view of the pressing international situation, hesitated to force Mexico to accept a lesser amount of water.[23]

The implications of the Mexican Treaty were abundantly clear to Arizona's senior senator. Unless Arizona took steps to put mainstream water to beneficial use within the state, California and Mexico could gain prior right to Arizona's claimed share. Bureau of Reclamation engineers, during hearings on the Mexican treaty, underscored this point when they reported that water supply figures were significantly

Senator Hayden's campaign portrait, 1944 (ASU: CP CTH 525).

less than previously believed. The recent water supply and power crisis, the Mexican treaty, and congressional testimony confirming fears of decreasing stream flow, prompted Hayden to immediate action.[24]

Hayden had laid the groundwork for such action nearly two years earlier. On October 17, 1941, in Phoenix, he addressed the tenth annual convention of the National Reclamation Association. Although his speech—the featured address of the convention—centered on federal reclamation policy and the mobilization effort, it contained another specific suggestion. "Instead of unity there has been discord in Arizona," he told his audience, then turning to Governor Osborn he continued, "I must urge that whatever differences of opinion that may exist be buried for the common good." He noted that Arizona would soon receive the initial installments of payments in lieu of taxes which Congress provided should be made from revenues derived from power produced at Boulder Dam. He suggested that these funds should be used for studies to determine how Arizona could put the Colorado to beneficial use within the state. "That step," he allowed, "should be taken promptly so the state and the Bureau of Reclamation can start the work whenever the demands for national defense slacken and a genuine cry arises that jobs must be found for those in need of employment." Keeping in mind the regional makeup of the convention, Hayden concluded his speech on a less provincial note, announcing: "What we must do here in Arizona should likewise be done everywhere in the West where additional water can be put to beneficial use."[25]

In October 1943, Hayden, in his role as Chairman of the Subcommittee on Roads and Reclamation of the Senate Committee on Post-War Planning, seized the opportunity. He called upon the Bureau of Reclamation for an inventory of irrigation and multiple-use projects which could be made ready for construction when servicemen and civilian workers returned from World War II. Capitol Hill observers, preoccupied with the war against the Axis, hardly noticed the apparently insignificant congressional measure. Indeed Hayden had spent his already lengthy congressional career supporting the Bureau's activities in the American West and few questioned his judgment in reclamation affairs. Yet after two decades of struggle with California and the federal government over rights to the use and distribution of Colorado River water, Arizona's new-found cooperative stance represented a dramatic shift in policy. Beyond the apparent rapproachment with Washington and the other basin states, the inventory held profound significance for Arizona during the second half of the twentieth century, for it marked the first meaningful step in Arizona's decades-long quest for diverting its claimed share of Colorado River water to the central portions of the state.[26]

By the early 1920s, with California rapidly asserting prior rights to increasing amounts of mainstream water, the Colorado River diversion concept—promoted by dreamers and schemers at the turn of the century—not only had taken on a greater degree of sophistication and urgency, but also had emerged as a widely discussed and politically potent issue within Arizona. In June 1922, for example, then-congressman Hayden injected the idea of a central Arizona diversion plan into the Swing-Johnson bill hearings before the House Committee on Arid Lands. With hydroelectric power generation, Hayden told the committee, mainstream Colorado River water could be pumped to the fertile central valleys of the state.[27]

Therefore, when Bureau of Reclamation officials announced the results of their inventory in June 1944, Hayden felt no small sense of accomplishment. Bureau engineers found Paradise Valley, north of Phoenix, and the Gila Valley, east of Yuma, as two likely areas eligible for post-war reclamation projects. They also recommended the construction of a water storage and power dam at Bridge Canyon, above Boulder Dam near the southern boundary of the Grand Canyon National Park. Viewed as the key structure in the Bureau's plans for Arizona, Bridge Canyon Dam would provide silt control on the river plus an additional 750,000 kilowatts of power. Although cast in the most general terms, this post-war "working paper," as reclamation officials called it, gave hope to those who dreamed of putting the Colorado to beneficial use in Arizona.[28]

Hayden quickly took advantage of the new political climate, convincing the Senate Committee on Irrigation and Reclamation to

Hayden urges members of the Senate Appropriations Committee to support Colorado River Basin development in the late 1940s (ASU: CP CTH 10).

make a complete study of the need for development of irrigation and hydroelectric power in Arizona. On July 31, 1944, a Senate Sub-committee on Irrigation and Reclamation began five days of hearings in Arizona to discuss the recently completed preliminary reports on importing Colorado River water to Arizona and to survey the needs of the state's irrigation interests. As fellow Arizona Senator Ernest McFarland, a member of the subcommittee, put it at the outset of the hearings: "The information gained ... will be the basis for legislation for the future development in Arizona."[29]

During the hearings, E.B. Debler, Director of Project Planning for the Bureau of Reclamation, presented various plans for what he called the "Central Arizona Diversion." The investigations commissioned by Hayden's committee on post-war planning, Debler informed the sub-committee, revealed three possible routes for the proposed diversion. The Marble Gorge Dam Plan, the most expensive and technically complex route, would take seven years to construct at an estimated

$487 million. The Bridge Canyon Dam Plan would take six years to construct at an estimated cost of $325 million. The third and least expensive plan, the Parker Pump Plan, would take three years to complete at a comparatively modest $134 million. Debler also discussed the engineering features of the various routes with the senators and informed them that the plans assumed an annual diversion of two million acre-feet of water.[30]

Another noteworthy feature of the Arizona hearings was the introduction of Tucson and Pima County into the emerging concept. During the third day of testimony Tucson City Manager Phil Martin announced that Tucson and Pima County were interested in obtaining a share of Arizona's allotment of Colorado River water. He presented petitions from the City of Tucson, Pima County, and Cortaro Farms Company to the subcommittee, requesting an allocation of 70,000 acre-feet annually for domestic and agricultural uses. Thus residents of the Old Pueblo and surrounding area signaled their intentions of sharing in the benefits of the Colorado River.[31]

Hayden remained active behind the scenes, using his committee assignments—especially his position on the powerful Committee on Appropriations—and good personal relationships with Interior Department officials, to Arizona's advantage. Shortly after the conclusion of the Arizona hearings he helped direct funds to the Bureau of Reclamation for the purpose of commencing "full-scale" feasibility studies for a central Arizona water delivery system. In the context of post-war planning and reconversion to a peacetime economy, he quietly funneled funds to the Bureau for what its engineers now called the "Central Arizona Project" or "CAP."[32]

These feasibility studies provided federal officials with the first detailed information concerning the proposed project. The earliest CAP planning studies focused on choosing the proper diversion route. In September 1945, E.A. Moritz, Southwest Regional Director for the Bureau of Reclamation, issued a report entitled "Comparison of Diversion Routes, Central Arizona Project, Arizona," which narrowed consideration to two routes; the Bridge Canyon Gravity Route and the Parker Pump Plan Route. A subsequent study, "Report of

Feasibility, Bridge Canyon Route, Central Arizona Project," issued in draft form to Hayden in February 1947, contained supplemental material on the Parker Pump Route, and a comparison of the two routes. From this information, Bureau engineers concluded that the Parker Pump Plan, the most economical and practical from an engineering standpoint, was the superior route. With surprisingly little controversy, federal and state officials agreed on the Parker Pump Plan for diverting Colorado River water to central Arizona.[33]

In July 1947, Senator Eugene Milliken of Colorado, Chairman of the Irrigation and Reclamation Subcommittee of the Senate Public Lands Committee, directed the Department of Interior to "prepare and submit as expeditiously as possible" a comprehensive feasibility report on CAP. The Bureau, drawing heavily from research completed in previous investigations, completed the study in mid-December 1947. On February 8, 1948, Secretary of the Interior J.A. Krug signed the report, and in accordance with provisions of Section 1 of the Flood Control Act of 1944, he sent it to the governors of the seven Colorado River Basin states for their comments. Significantly, the Bureau found the proposed project feasible from an engineering and financial standpoint.[34]

Secretary Krug offered several more noteworthy arguments to justify the construction of CAP. Essentially, CAP was a rescue project designed to eliminate serious disruptions in the state's predominantly agricultural economy. Arizona also had another more localized, but nevertheless serious water supply problem in connection with the Tucson metropolitan area. "That city," Krug reported, "obtains its water from an overdeveloped and rapidly shrinking groundwater basin," and additional surface supplies were an absolute necessity. Moreover, due to the rapid increase in population after the war, there existed an urgent need for additional hydroelectric power in Arizona, southern California, southern Utah, and southern Nevada. With CAP the Colorado would become a truly multipurpose natural resource: it could replace groundwater, provide hydroelectric power, provide supplemental water to lands currently in production but not adequately irrigated, and increase the domestic water supply of Tucson. The interior secretary, citing the varied and pressing need for additional water in Arizona, concluded: "I recommend ... the Central Arizona Project be authorized for construction, operation, and maintenance by the Secretary of Interior under the general plan set forth herein."[35]

The secretary, however, qualified his recommendation, suggesting that state leaders address three issues that could affect the prompt construction of CAP. The lingering water allocation question between Arizona and California required a final answer. California contended that the annual flow of the Gila River, estimated at one million acre-feet, should be included in Arizona's allotment. Arizona, of course, countered that the Gila and the water put to beneficial use under the San Carlos Reclamation Project and Coolidge Dam, was exempt, citing the Colorado River Compact and the Boulder Canyon Project Act as proof of that contention. If the controversy were resolved in favor of Arizona, Krug noted, the Department of Interior could move quickly in its plans for CAP. If decided in favor of California, he hinted that there would not be enough water to justify construction.[36]

In addition to resolving this longstanding dispute, Secretary Krug made it clear that Arizona had to adopt a groundwater control law. The legislation would have to limit effectively the average annual withdrawal from groundwater basins within and reasonably tributary to the areas served by the project. Finally, Arizona needed an improvement district to help repay construction costs and to oversee the local management of the project.[37]

Meanwhile, Arizona's senators, Hayden and McFarland, initiated legislative action on CAP. On June 18, 1946, McFarland introduced S 2346, the Bridge Canyon Project Bill, to the Seventy-ninth Congress. Drafted and introduced before the completion of the comprehensive feasibility study, Congress refused to take action, citing a lack of sufficient technical data to conduct hearings. At the beginning of the Eightieth Congress, on January 29, 1947, Hayden and McFarland introduced an identical bill (S 433), although it met the same fate as its predecessor. These early versions of the CAP bill, nevertheless, signaled Arizona's legislative intentions.[38]

Later in the Eightieth Congress, Hayden and McFarland submitted a revised version of the bill (S 1175), incorporating the Bureau's recommendations of the Parker Pump diversion route. The Subcommittee on Irrigation and Reclamation of the Public Lands Committee scheduled hearings beginning on June 23, 1947. In preparation for the hearings, and reflecting the importance with which they were viewed, Hayden contacted each senator by formal letter, asking for their support. He requested their attendance to the "fullest possible extent permitted by other obligations," and allowed that the purpose of the bill was to "bring water from the Colorado River to central Arizona to supplement our inadequate water supply." Additional water was absolutely vital to Arizona in order to sustain its economy, to prevent productive lands from reverting to the desert, and , to forestall the exodus of people. Included with the letter were copies of two magazines: the February 1947 issue of *Arizona Highways* and a slick colorful magazine entitled *The Central Arizona Project*, which outlined the nature and background of Arizona's water problems. This traditional method of garnering support for legislation, Hayden reasoned, also helped educate eastern and midwestern senators unfamiliar with federal reclamation in the arid West.[39]

Hayden led the parade of thirty-one witnesses who appeared at the CAP hearings between June 23 and July 3, 1947. "This legislation is based on sheer necessity," he told the subcommittee, and "it is absolutely essential a supplementary water supply be obtained and that source is the Colorado River." Anticipating California's principal objection to the bill, Hayden added: "We will demonstrate we have a perfect right to the water from the mainstream of the Colorado River which will be sufficient to meet our needs." The proposed project, moreover, rested on sound fiscal policy. Other federal reclamation projects in Arizona—like the Salt River Project and the Yuma Project—Hayden told the subcommittee, had produced dramatic results, creating wealth and broadening the tax base. Hayden testified further: "We have returned to the Federal Treasury many times every dollar that has been expended in reclamation by taxation, taxes we pay into the Treasury. This will maintain a source of federal taxation that is of great value, and without the water we can not do it." With that introductory testimony, Hayden commenced in earnest his long legislative quest for CAP.[40]

California gave prompt notice of its intentions concerning the legislation. On July 3, 1947, the final day of scheduled hearings on the bill and while Hayden and McFarland attended the hearings in a committee room down the hall from the Senate floor, Senators Pat McCarran of Nevada and Sheridan Downey of California introduced SJR 145, seeking congressional consent to a suit by California in the U.S. Supreme Court to obtain final determination of allocations of water among the basin states. Downey explained that there was not enough water for all state projects and furthermore he would resist to the end any report favorable on CAP until there had been a court determination of the competitive state water demands. McCarran and Downey sought to refer the bill to the Judiciary Committee, not the Public Lands Committee, in an attempt to postpone consideration of CAP, while at the same time raising legal questions about claims to the river that would further delay legislative action.[41]

Upon hearing of the introduction of the McCarran-Downey Resolution, Hayden and McFarland terminated the CAP hearings and rushed to the Senate floor. The Senate, at the end of a weary day of "unanimous consent" votes and preparing to leave for the July 4 holiday, halted the proceedings as Hayden and McFarland entered the chamber. The Arizonans arrived just in time to watch president pro-tempore of the Senate, Arthur Vandenburg, refer SJR 145 to the Judiciary Committee. Hayden, in an unusual action, approached the chair and appealed the ruling, asking that it be delayed for several days so he could organize and prepare opposition arguments. After a half hour of parliamentary debate, the matter was postponed until July 8, when the entire Senate could discuss the issue.[42]

Late in the afternoon of July 8, 1947, Hayden took the floor seeking to have the McCarran-Downey Resolution referred to the Public Lands Committee. Public Lands, he argued, maintained authority to consider questions of water rights between states. After California's rebuttal, Hayden concluded the debate by walking to the center of the floor and asking that "the full Senate now hold that the ruling of the chair is not the ruling of the full Senate." Then, by a vote of 41-35 the Senate agreed with Hayden to override its president pro-tempore; the resolution went to Public Lands where Hayden could control it."[43]

Arizonans hailed the vote as cause for celebration. The *Arizona Republic* proclaimed the vote a personal victory for Hayden, while another Phoenix-based daily commented that the Arizonan won the admiration of the entire Senate by the shrewd manner in which he conducted the fight to override the chair. Hayden and the rest of the Arizona congressional delegation, however, kept the minor victory in perspective, for in the legislative jousting over the resolution, they sensed the intensity of California's resolve to keep water out of central Arizona. Moreover, CAP held important political implications within the Golden State. California congressman Norris Poulson, for example, who sponsored one of the companion measures of the McCarran-Downey Resolution in the House shed light on this aspect of CAP legislation when he imprudently told reporters that California's position would be unremitting opposition to the Arizona project because "that's the way to get reelected in California." Indeed the irony of this position was not lost on Hayden. Just as Arizona had sought to delay California from putting the Colorado to use under the Boulder Canyon legislation in the late 1920s and early 1930s, California endeavored to obstruct Arizona from putting water to use twenty years later.[44]

Hayden knew that a major share of California's anti-CAP pressure stemmed from the utilities, especially the Metropolitan Water District (MWD) of Southern California. In 1932 that agency, which represented urban southern California water users, had entered into the seven-party agreement with the secretary of interior which established priorities among those users of Colorado River water. Significantly, the MWD stood in an inferior position. In fact, if California were forced to reduce deliveries, MWD would be the first party to forego its share. Yet the district was burdened with an enormous responsibility to its customers. In 1931, for example, the MWD bonded itself for $220 million to build the Colorado River

Aqueduct. Therefore, the district, with a duty to serve its urban and industrial water users, emerged as one of the chief opponents of Colorado River water diversion to Arizona. Postponing CAP in any way benefited MWD and its rapidly growing service area. Thus Arizona's victory in the skirmish over the McCarran-Downey Resolution alarmed MWD officials.[45]

In Arizona, meanwhile, Governor Osborn continued his efforts at water policy reform and institutional reorganization. He created two new agencies of government; the Arizona Power Authority (APA) and the Arizona Interstate Stream Commission (AISC). The APA, became the agency with authority to bargain for, take, and receive electric power from the waters of the mainstream of the Colorado River. Its five members were appointed by the governor with advice and consent of the Senate. Similarly, with the ratification of the compact, the Arizona Colorado River Commission passed out of existence. In its place, Osborn formed the AISC to protect the state's interest and prosecute its claims to Colorado River water before Congress and the courts. Its seven members, like those of the APA, were appointed by the governor with advice and consent of the Senate. Significantly, from the date of its formation, the AISC focused its energies at gaining congressional approval of the CAP.

In the context of the effort to gain CAP authorization, local business leaders formed a private, non-profit association, the Central Arizona Project Association (CAPA) to support the efforts of the state's congressmen. Organized on July 1, 1946, the CAPA was comprised of agricultural, business, professional, and industrial people who saw diversion of Colorado River water as fundamental to the future of Arizona's economy. The association raised money, provided research and legal assistance, lobbied for, and publicized the project. It also aided the congressional delegation in innumerable ways. Senator Hayden, for example, called upon CAPA in 1947 to provide witnesses for the hearings on S 1175, the CAP authorization bill. Moreover, CAPA worked closely with the AISC, lending its services and personnel. Finally, CAPA provided links among federal government, state government, and private sector individuals involved in issues pertaining to CAP. Indeed, in ensuing years Hayden viewed the association as an indispensable resource.[46]

Despite the progress and modest legislative gains made since Hayden secured funding for the initial post-war study in 1943, over the next few years CAP met strong and effective resistance. Indeed the struggle over the McCarran-Downey Resolution set the tone for the entire legislative history of the bill. During the second Truman administration (1948-1952), Arizona tried unsuccessfully, to secure passage of a bill to divert Colorado River water to central Arizona. An analysis of the hearings and votes in the Eightieth, Eighty-first, and Eighty-second Congresses reveals that Hayden and McFarland could gain passage of the bill in the Senate and enlist presidential support, but their combined power and influence did not carry over to the House of Representatives. In the House, California, with superior numbers and well-chosen committee assignments, successfully frustrated Arizona's CAP efforts. Moreover, California's representatives convinced enough congressmen that Arizona was attempting to use water that did not belong to it, that the project was a financial extravagance inconsistent with post-war spending policies, and that perhaps no water at all existed for Arizona given current uses.[47]

Hayden, in a variety of ways—especially in testimony before various committees in the House and Senate—sought to soften California's intractable opposition, while portraying CAP as benefiting the region, and therefore, the nation. On April 28, 1949, Hayden made one of his celebrated appearances in support of CAP before the Senate Interior and Insular Affairs Committee. As the *Arizona Republic* put it: "The appearance of a senior senator before a committee is rare enough but in the case of Senator Hayden it is extremely unusual, because the Arizonan is not only chairman of the power Rules Committee, which directs the order of legislation before the upper chamber, but is second in command, and virtually chairman of the ... Appropriations Committee." In short, his testimony in behalf of CAP carried significant political weight.[48]

He began by emphasizing that CAP was a small portion of a larger comprehensive plan for regional development of the Colorado River basin. He also reminded the committee that for the past thirty-five years he had supported numerous similar developments in California —the Los Angeles County Drainage Area, the Sacramento Flood Control Project, and water storage reservoirs at Whittier Narrows, Folsom, Pine Flat, and Table Mountain, to name a few. "Now not a soul in Arizona begrudges the appropriation by Congress of that $722,919,000 for use in the State of California," he told the senators. Yet, these were only projects built by the Army Corps of Engineers. Appropriations from the Bureau of Reclamation on the All-American Canal, the Central Valley Project and its irrigation systems, the California portion of the Klamath Project, the Orland Project, Parker Dam and power plant, the Santa Barbara Project, the Solano County Project, and the California portion of the Yuma Project amounted to another $694,981,137 of federal appropriations. Every one of these California water projects, Hayden allowed, was justified and created new wealth. He continued: "Out of deep sympathy for those people (Californians), I helped authorize the Central Valley Project, which is no less fantastic than the Arizona proposal now before the committee.... It is a perfect precedent for what we are asking." Arizona deserved similar consideration, especially because the benefits of CAP would far outweigh the costs. In effect, Hayden contended that the CAP and its $738,000,000 price tag, was neither a federal handout nor out of scale relative to similar California water projects.[49]

Hayden cast his arguments within a regional context, seeking to downplay differences with California. "As far as we are concerned in Arizona," he advised the committee, "our people like to have prosperous neighbors," and it mattered little whether a steer was fattened on one side of the river or the other, "he most likely went to the Los Angeles market." "Our mining products and agricultural products are all in greater demand," he continued, "because there are millions of people living in California who are prospering—they make a better market for what we produce." Recalling the early days of the fight for the compact in Arizona, Hayden concluded with a refrain from the Swing-Johnson debates: "We are all in one economic unit."[50]

The appeals for regional cooperation and emphasis on economic interdependence, however, gave way to an emotional discussion of one of the most divisive issues confronting lower basin leaders. The issue of III (b) water—the Gila River—took on renewed significance, for Congress once again faced the challenge of interpreting the specific meaning of that troublesome article of the Colorado River Compact. Senator Hayden told the committee, "Everybody knew that the Gila River water, the so-called III(b) water, was Arizona water. It is clear as a bell from the record that Arizona is entitled to 2.8 million acre-feet out of the 7.5 million acre-feet allocated to the lower basin." Hayden added a personal note: "I know how these figures came about. I was here in Congress at the time."

According to the Arizonan, Senator Key Pittman of Nevada, during the debates on the Boulder Canyon Project Act, was "the principal negotiator" in the settlement of the dispute over III (b) water. He recalled that Senator John Kendrick of Wyoming approached him in the cloakroom with the specific provisions of the Pittman Amendment. "Now this is what you have been talking about," Hayden recalled Kendrick saying. "You want a clear definition of Arizona's rights to water out of the Colorado River.... We have given it to you." Hayden insisted III (b) was Arizona water, and California's senators at the time, Hiram Johnson and Samuel Shortridge, "knew better than anybody else."[51]

Following the testimony a heated exchange between Hayden and Senator Downey of California punctuated the hearings. The Arizona senator had suggested that California was distorting the intent and meaning of previous legislation. "If there was so much as a whisper of what California is now contending here," Hayden had charged, "the Boulder Canyon Project Act would never have passed." He alleged that since the passage of the act, California had twisted historical events and abrogated solemn agreements, prompting a comparison between California and the "Politburo in Moscow." At that challenging remark, Downey protested: "What specific acts do you have in mind? I resent that insinuation." Hayden shot back, "The perfectly idiotic idea that California owns the whole of the Colorado River and the cockeyed idea that Arizona doesn't own the Gila.... It never was in the mind of Senator Johnson. It never was in the mind of Senator Shortridge. I know what I am talking about because I was there!" According to one newspaper account, the Arizona senator came close to losing his temper. Despite the rare public confrontation with the Californian, Hayden allowed that he had clearly stated Arizona's position as well as his intent in securing the desired legislation and on June 2, 1949, the Interior and Insular Affairs Committee reported out S 75 with a "Do Pass" recommendation. On July 1, 1949, it voted 9-3 to send the bill to the floor of the Senate for debate. The Senate took no action during that session, however, and further action on S 75 awaited the second session of the Eighty-first Congress.[52]

Much as he had done over twenty-five years earlier in support of the compact, Hayden campaigned within Arizona for CAP. He declared the project was "the future of Arizona" and counseled "we must banish the specter of drought with construction of CAP." Also, the normally circumspect senator singled out California as the chief obstacle to the enactment of desired legislation. In a 1950 radio address he discounted California's claims that CAP was economically and logistically infeasible, asserting, "by compact and by contract there is sufficient water in the Colorado River belonging to Arizona to provide an adequate supply for Arizona's agricultural and domestic needs." Also, he detected a distinct difference between the current struggles with California over CAP legislation and the earlier debates over the Swing-Johnson bill. During the earlier confrontation "the people of Arizona were divided and expended energy fighting each other," while the CAP effort saw the state united in its efforts.[53]

To an unprecedented degree local and state politicians, business leaders, and the general public actively supported the legislation. Governor Dan Garvey proclaimed a "CAP Week" while the CAPA and AISC churned out literature for popular consumption. State leaders also embarked upon a massive letter writing campaign reminiscent of earlier efforts to woo federal water projects. These cooperative public relations efforts were aimed not only at casting the CAP, "the most ambitious reclamation project yet proposed," in the most favorable light, but also discrediting California's much-publicized criticisms of the project.[54]

While a crowded calendar prohibited full Senate consideration of S 75 during the first session of the Eighty-first Congress, the groundwork had been laid. Senator Hayden, Chairman of the Rules Committee and de facto Chairman of the Appropriations Committee, assured its timely consideration in the second session. In addition, during the interim, he approached each senator asking for their support of his bill, subtly exercising the prerogatives of senate seniority. On February 6, 1950, as the full Senate began debate on S 75, Hayden delivered a ninety-minute presentation on the floor, summarizing and synthesizing earlier committee testimony. He also let it be known that President Harry Truman supported the measure despite rumors to the contrary. On the eve of the Senate vote, Arizona's senior senator felt secure that the bill would pass.[55]

On February 21, 1950, by a vote of 55-28, S 75 passed the U.S. Senate. Most observers agreed that the twenty-seven vote margin was a stunning victory for Arizona and its seventy-two-year-old senator. Hayden's influence on the vote was pronounced. Only five Democrats, including Senator Downey of California, voted against the measure. An overwhelming majority of western senators, grateful for Hayden's past political handiwork, supported the bill. Even Senator McCarran of Nevada, who spoke against S 75 and backed California's efforts to postpone consideration, voted for CAP. A political pragmatist, the Nevada Democrat saw the futility in casting a vote against the bill. Hayden praised his Arizona colleague, Senator McFarland, Senator Clinton P. Anderson of New Mexico, and Senator Robert Kerr of Oklahoma for their key votes. In this and future votes Hayden could count on this influential group for support.[56]

Predictably, jubilation spread throughout Arizona and news accounts singled out Hayden for his "brilliant" performance. *Newsweek* dryly informed its readers of "the lack of excitement" surrounding the vote, citing Hayden's traditionally effective cloakroom work and concluding that the venerable Arizonan "was one of the wiliest maneuverers" in the history of the Senate. Closer to home, the *Arizona Republic* optimistically declared, "The First Battle is Ours" and fashioned a front page headline, "Project Bill Is Special Victory for Carl Hayden." Included in most accounts was a legislative history of the bill, reviewing how Hayden, over a decade previously, "caused the U.S. Bureau of Reclamation to start engineering work on the CAP."[57]

At this point the legislation entered an especially politically charged period. In Arizona and California the election campaigns of 1950 centered on the much-publicized CAP bill. According to several accounts, Hayden and the CAP were as often mentioned in the the California campaigns as in those of Arizona's. California congressmen, seeking reelection, warned their constituents that because of Hayden, efforts to block enactment of CAP would be difficult. California representatives Norris Poulson and Claire Engle, for example, warned residents of San Diego against tying the completion of the much-awaited San Diego Aqueduct to the CAP fight because of "the formidable influence of Senator Hayden." Engle told several southern California audiences that "Hayden is the most powerful man in the U.S. Senate ... and as a top ranking member of the Senate Appropriations Committee—Hayden had done favors for everyone." As the political battle shifted to the House of Representatives, the Californians prepared strategy against the able Arizona congressman, John Murdock, a former history professor at Arizona State Teachers College who ranked second in seniority on the Public Lands Committee. California still clung to the hope that action on the bill could be delayed for several years when the House delegation from California would increase significantly. Preliminary reapportionment figures indicated that in the elections of 1952 California's representation in the House would grow from twenty-three to thirty members. The Golden State, therefore, would have exactly as many representatives as all the other reclamation states combined. Engle and Poulson suggested, somewhat cynically, that California then could exercise veto power in important water matters.[58]

Arizona's delegation, on the other hand, knew they faced an uphill battle in the House. The *Phoenix Gazette* lamented that "with no

Hayden in the House to steer the project, and a solid block of California representatives bitterly determined to stop it, the CAP had practically no chance of success." Indeed, Murdock, Chairman of the Subcommittee on Irrigation and Reclamation of the Public Lands Committee, faced serious challenges, especially from Californians Poulson, Engle, and Richard Welch, all outspoken opponents of the CAP who sat on the subcommittee.[59]

Hayden watched the House battle in frustration as California's delegation outmaneuvered Arizona's two congressmen, Murdock and Harold "Porky" Patten. During the Eighty-first Congress, California introduced an incredible twenty-three separate Colorado River bills, referring the entire question of water rights to the Judiciary Committee. Most observers close to the legislation knew the delay tactic was masterminded by Northcutt "Mike" Ely, the determined California lawyer who had orchestrated California's disciplined legislative strategy and had spent virtually his entire legal career on issues related to water law. Hayden believed he was carefully laying the groundwork for what he believed was the inevitable Supreme Court case. Despite Murdock's extraordinary efforts in both sessions of the Eighty-first Congress, the House counterpart of S 75 never emerged from the Public Lands Committee. Thus, as the second session adjourned in December 1950, CAP legislation had passed the Senate, languished in the House, and brought forth again the unresolved question of rights to Colorado River water.[60]

In January 1951, the Eighty-second Congress convened and Arizona's delegation reintroduced CAP bills in both houses of Congress. Naturally the focus of attention was on the House bill, where Arizonans hoped for quick action. Indeed close observers expressed cause for mild optimism because Murdock, due to the outcome of the 1950 elections, rose to chairman of the House Interior and Insular Affairs Committee. California and its supporters, nevertheless, still outnumbered Murdock and his allies on the committee. On February 21, 1951, Chairman Murdock called to order the first of twenty-three sessions on CAP legislation. For nearly two months the committee rehashed previous testimony, injected new reasons to sup-

Senator Hayden and Senator Ernest MacFarland welcome a delegation of Arizona Indians to the capitol, 1950 (ASU: CP CTH 1944).

port their respective positions, but made no real progress in addressing the central problem of water rights.[61]

Finally, California's representatives moved to break the stalemate. In mid-April, during the course of the hearings, California committee members Sam Yorty, Claire Engle, and Norris Poulson asked fellow member John Saylor of Pennsylvania to a breakfast meeting. The Californians convinced Saylor, a skeptic of the economic features of the legislation, to offer a preferential motion to postpone further consideration of the bill until the water rights issue had been adjudicated in the Supreme Court or an agreement among the lower basin states had been made. On the morning of April 18, 1951, Chairman Murdock, aware that he was losing control of his committee, reluctantly recognized Congressman Saylor. The Pennsylvanian announced: "I move you, Mr. Chairman, that H.R. 1500 and H.R. 1501 be postponed until such time as the use of the water in the lower Colorado River Basin is either adjudicated, or a binding mutual agreement as to the use of the water is reached by the states of the lower Colorado River Basin." The Californians quickly seconded the motion. Then, by a vote of 16-8, the committee shelved the bill. Arizona Governor Howard Pyle, who was waiting to testify in behalf of CAP, asked to address the committee after the stunning turn of events. Departing from his prepared statement, the governor said: "I think this is one of the most depressing moments of my life. A delaying action on the part of California has been the thing they have aspired to most of all."[62]

Arizona's senators were not so much surprised as disappointed at events in the House Interior and Insular Affairs Committee. They hoped that Murdock, despite being outnumbered, could override the opposition. Hayden, moreover, was especially perplexed at some of the paradoxes of recent events. Once again the issue of rights to the river might be referred to the Supreme Court, where previously the Court had concluded that Arizona could not obtain any means to divert water from the mainstream except by an act of Congress. Therefore, Hayden reasoned, the Saylor motion had trapped Arizona in a constitutional box. Representative Engle of California, whom

Hayden and capitol hill guard contemplate the Old Senate Chamber, 1950 (ASU: CP CTH 1931).

Arizonans placed most of the blame on for their setback in the House, declared, "This action is a signal victory for California." Yet senators Hayden and McFarland refused to abandon hopes for securing passage of CAP during the Eighty-second Congress.[63]

Hayden and McFarland quickly reintroduced S 75 in the Senate in a last ditch effort to salvage the legislation. This version carried an article providing for the adjudication of the water rights issue in the Supreme Court. Hayden agreed to the article knowing that, if necessary, he could have it struck out in conference committee before final approval of the legislation. Beginning on May 29, 1951, the Senate, for the second time within a year, conducted a floor debate on the Hayden-sponsored CAP bill.[64]

The "usually silent" Senator Hayden, on May 29, 1951, took the floor of the Senate to deliver one of the longer addresses of his career outside of the Swing-Johnson filibuster. He touched upon all aspects of the current legislation—legal, political, economic, technical. He also explained and interpreted for the Senate the recent events in the House of Representatives pertaining to the bill. Finally, he questioned California's "unjustified objection" to what was due water-poor Arizona and reminded California's two senators, Richard M. Nixon and William F. Knowland, how he had helped in securing funding for the Central Valley Project in their state. The majority of his remarks, however, were aimed at the unresolved question of water rights.[65]

The Arizonan told the Senate that the 1951 CAP bill contained, in Section 12, a provision for a Supreme Court determination of the water rights involved. That section of S 75 was drafted by two distinguished lawyers, Senators Joseph C. O'Mahoney of Wyoming and Eugene Milliken of Colorado, Upper Basin supporters of the bill. Echoing the lament of Arizona's governor, Hayden informed his colleagues that California wanted "delay and more delay; delay for many years to come in hope that in the meantime more people will go to southern California and that thereby a greater need for the water will be built up." Section 12 of the legislation thus addressed directly the intent of the Saylor motion in the House of Representatives, for it had the effect of withholding any appropriation for the construction of irrigation works intended to bring Colorado River water into central Arizona until the Supreme Court decided that enough water existed for CAP. It therefore provided a framework for compromise between Arizona and California.[66]

Despite a history of arguing that no justiciable issue existed concerning water rights, Hayden advised the Senate, "the Californians now say one exists." Indeed California had executed an about face, claiming it now wanted to follow a course long advocated by Arizona. "We in Arizona," Hayden claimed, "have a very good reason to believe that this is just another scheme to postpone action."[67]

If California succeeded in killing CAP, the Arizonan warned, it could conceivably apply the same tactics to hinder development in the upper states. The numbers were in California's favor; with at least thirty congressmen and two senators California could block further development anywhere in the basin. Hayden further predicted that if

CAP could be stalled for another ten years, "and the hoped for five million additional people moved to southern California, that state could gain its desired end; use of the entire Lower Basin streamflow." Instead of promoting that kind of selfishness, he said turning toward California's senators, the Arizonan suggested that southern California look elsewhere for its water supply. In that quest, Hayden promised "to assist California in its search for new sources of water."[68]

On June 5, 1951, the Senate, despite persuasive opposition arguments presented by senators Nixon and Knowland, voted 50-28 to authorize the $788,000,000 CAP. This action gave the bill new life in

Senator Hayden's campaign portrait, 1950 (ASU: CP CTH 1356).

the House, where, six weeks earlier, it had been left for dead. This version of S 75 not only authorized a Supreme Court test of water rights, but also provided that construction could not begin while any suit was pending before the Court. Unfortunately for Arizona and supporters of the project, and especially for Congressman Murdock whose political career hung in the balance, their hopes that the House would reconsider the legislation during the Eighty-second Congress did not materialize. The House adjourned without further deliberation on the bill. Again, Arizona appeared to have lost a major battle with California over Colorado River water.[69]

The results of this hard-fought phase for CAP were clear. Arizona had lost the overall congressional battle, despite winning major victories in the Senate. Still, Hayden plotted the next course of action. Arizona's strategy, he informed Governor Pyle, should include a new effort in the Supreme Court. Congressional hearings repeatedly brought forth the vexing question whether Arizona had title to the water necessary for CAP. The seventy-four-year-old senator, in the middle of the controversy since 1919, revised his long-held view that Arizona should avoid litigation. "If the Californians are sincere in their oft-repeated demands for court action," he announced in August 1952, "then they will welcome the opportunity to present their side of the case where its merits can be fully determined." In reality, preparations for the inevitable Supreme Court test had already begun, and Hayden's public pronouncement merely sounded this most recent challenge. Indeed, Arizona had found its justiciable issue, and the next phase of the struggle commenced.[70]

"My Patience Has Been Exhausted": Passage and Triumph

At 1:30 P.M. on August 13, 1952, Hayden welcomed a small group of somber-faced Arizonans to his office. After a brief exchange of pleasantries he stuck a battered white straw hat on his bald head, strode to the door and beckoned, "Come on boys, let's get this done." Together the group walked to the U.S. Supreme Court building. Among them was was J.H. "Hub" Moeur, chief counsel for the Arizona Interstate Stream Commission (AISC), who filed a bill of complaint against California, asking for a judicial apportionment of the waters of the lower Colorado River basin. After witnessing the filing the seventy-four-year-old senator issued a short statement to the press. "I believe this action," he told those gathered on the steps of the Supreme Court, "will make possible the settlement of a most serious controversy which is delaying the development of the Colorado River basin." "If the Californians are sincere in their oft-repeated demands for court action," he added, "then they will welcome the opportunity to present their side of the case." With that, Arizona launched the monumental *Arizona v. California* Supreme Court case.[1]

As several students of the case have noted, it was one of the most complex and fiercely contested in the history of the Court. Before its completion, 340 witnesses and fifty lawyers had produced 25,000 pages of testimony before a special master. The case took nearly eleven years and cost nearly $5 million. And when a sharply divided Court announced its opinion on June 3, 1963, followed by the decree on March 9, 1964, the river possessed a greatly modified legal framework governing its apportionment and use among the lower basin states.[2]

Arizona's contentions had changed little since the 1920s. She asserted that California had made contracts for delivery of over 5.3 million acre-feet of water annually in spite of laws limiting it to 4.4 million acre-feet. That limitation notwithstanding, Arizona's attorneys argued that California had constructed reclamation works capable of diverting 8 million acre-feet of water annually thereby posing a threat to Arizona and other basin states. According to Arizona's attorneys, for the state to sustain its existing economy it required 3.8 million acre-feet of Colorado River system water per year. Furthermore Arizona relied on and asserted its rights to water under a variety of federal and state actions including the Colorado River Compact, the Boulder Canyon Project Act, the California Limitation Act of 1929 and additionally, the state had entered into a water delivery contract with the federal government.[3]

California registered no objection to Arizona's motion. Her substantial team of attorneys, led by the brilliant and indefatigable Northcutt "Mike" Ely, agreed with the U.S. solicitor general, who advised the Supreme Court that the federal government had an interest in the case and would move to intervene if Arizona's motion were granted. On January 19, 1953, the Court granted Arizona's original motion and the bill of complaint was filed. Hayden hoped for prompt action because he knew that no further progress could be made on CAP, or any other lower-basin project, until the Court reached its decision.[4]

On May 20, 1953, California responded to Arizona's bill of complaint. In nearly 500 pages of narrative and supporting documentation, California's attorneys contended that it had a right to the beneficial and consumptive use of 5,362,000 acre-feet of Colorado River system water per year under the terms of the Boulder Canyon Project Act and her contracts with the secretary of interior. Moreover, she claimed prior appropriative rights to the use of that amount of water and that these rights were senior to Arizona's and therefore superior.

Finally, California argued that Arizona, by failing to ratify the Colorado River Compact within the specified six months when the other six states had done so in 1923, as well as her subsequent attempts to have the agreement declared invalid and the Boulder Canyon Project Act declared unconstitutional, precluded her right from interpreting these statutes.[5]

For the next four years California conducted a campaign of judicial delay. A blizzard of motions and filings delayed the start of proceedings, while the number and complexity of issues raised prompted the Court to appoint a special master to hear arguments. On January 1, 1954, George I. Haight assumed the position. After ruling on several preliminary motions, Haight died suddenly before formal hearings began. He was replaced by Judge Simon Rifkind, a sharp-witted federal jurist from the southern district of New York. Finally, on January 14, 1956, hearings on *Arizona v. California* began.[6]

In the meantime, Hayden, on September 14, 1955, and nearing the end of his fifth term in the Senate, announced at a Phoenix Press Club forum that he intended to seek reelection in 1956. The election, however, posed new challenges for the seventy-eight-year-old senior solon. Besides the election taking place against the backdrop of the Supreme Court case, Arizona during the 1950s was undergoing an unprecedented spurt of population growth, industrial development, and overall economic expansion. Indeed Arizona boomed during the post-war years, attracting people, industry, and capital. Much of this new money financed urban and agricultural expansion in the state's heartland embracing fast-growing Phoenix and Tucson. Moreover, the distinctive technological, commercial, and urban dimension of this growth brought forth growing expectations from an increasingly affluent electorate. Longtime politicians like Hayden took careful notice when the youthful conservative Republican upstart, Barry Goldwater, won a stunning upset victory over well-entrenched Democratic incumbent Ernest McFarland in the race for U.S. Senate in 1952. The conservative victory not only shattered the Democratic party's domination of state politics — which dated from the territorial period — but also signaled the onset of a new era of conservative hegemony in

Arizona. Furthermore, Arizonans old and new expected the economic boom to continue and the key to sustaining this growth was the continued expansion of water supplies and affordable power.[7]

By the mid-1950s, however, the rivers of Arizona were fully developed and irrigators had turned increasingly to groundwater supplies. In their efforts to keep pace with the boom, they pumped with such intensity that water tables dropped and aquifers were exhausted. Thus the stakes were high in 1956, with *Arizona v. California* and the apparent pressing need for expanded water and power supplies. Much like his election campaign for the U.S. Senate in 1926, Hayden's efforts at reelection in 1956 centered on water resource development generally, and the use and distribution of waters of the Colorado River system specifically.[8]

Hayden's 1956 election campaign was noteworthy for other reasons as well. His advancing age, questions about his health, and rumors of incipient senility emerged during the course of the primary campaign and carried over into the general election. His Democratic primary opponent, Robert "Doc" Miller, a forty-eight-year-old Phoenix-area druggist, suggested that "youth must be served and age must be retired," adding that Hayden, at age seventy-nine and with fifty-two years on the public payroll was desperately seeking another six years in office. Hayden and his staff responded to the anticipated criticism with resolve and innovation.[9]

After careful deliberation Hayden agreed to make his first television film for use in a political campaign. His appearance on "Personalities in Government" featured the veteran senator's views of various presidents and congressional leaders with whom he had served during his forty-four years in Congress. The show, and subsequent radio interviews and television appearances, not only helped Hayden dispel rumors about his poor health and failing mental abilities, but also raised public awareness of his considerable accomplishments. Moreover, during the course of the campaign Hayden convinced voters that McCarthy-era Vice-President Richard Nixon's charges that he was a dangerous left-leaning ideologue out of touch with modern American values were ridiculous and unfounded.

Additionally, the new technology reached the growing numbers of new Arizona voters who were made aware that Hayden, in December 1955, had advanced to head the powerful Senate Appropriations Committee thereby giving the Grand Canyon State unprecedented influence in federal affairs.[10]

Hayden's influence and stature in Congress were emphasized in the 1956 campaign as well as in his final campaign for the U.S. Senate in 1962. An especially flattering portrayal by former U.S. Senator and Assistant Secretary of State William Benton, published in the *New York Times Magazine* on July 24, 1955, was adapted and utilized by Hayden campaign strategists in a variety of ways. Benton sought to praise the unsung or unappreciated heroes on Capitol Hill who rarely received a "stick of news type for their pains." Chief among them were those senators and representatives who were committee specialists. They mastered the detailed and complex problems of legislation, worked long hours in solitary study, and attended faithfully often tedious committee sessions that lay behind the construction of appropriations bills, tax measures, and major substantive legislation in all fields. This was the non-glamorous drudgery which was the heart of effective work in Congress, and without injustice to anyone, Benton ventured, Senator Carl Hayden of Arizona was the person who symbolized those in Congress who had "performed magnificent services for years on end while remaining virtually unknown to the general public."[11]

Benton continued that although Hayden spoke seldom and never with a tinge of rhetoric or passion his influence within the Senate was enormous. He marveled also that his advice was sought and heeded by members of both parties and was trusted by everyone. Indeed Hayden's handlers used this and other laudatory pieces to full advantage, effectively countering political attacks from the right and questions about Hayden's age and mental acuity. On election night, November 6, 1956, Hayden, as usual, won each county in the state, defeating his Republican opponent, Ross F. Jones, 170,816 to 107,447.[12]

The central issue of Hayden's final election campaign—the election of 1962—remained CAP and the Colorado River. Despite the senator's age, state leaders convinced him to run for a seventh term. In that year, on the fiftieth anniversary of statehood, Hayden, in a special edition of "Arizona Days and Ways," the Sunday magazine for the *Arizona Republic*, assessed his contributions to his state: "The basic factor in making Arizona's spectacular agricultural and industrial development was the Reclamation Act of 1902, sponsored by that great and energetic president, Theodore Roosevelt." That law made possible the use of federal funds to develop water for irrigation and hydroelectric power. "Needless to say," he offered, "I helped that program move forward." A *Phoenix Gazette* editorial of September 21, 1962, put Hayden's reelection in another perspective: "The U.S. Supreme Court's impending decision on a master's report favorable to Arizona in the Colorado River controversy puts CAP just around the corner. Every ounce of California's political clout will be brought into play. It will take a unique combination of power to beat the project's enemies. Such a combination rests in the hands of Carl Hayden." Clearly Arizonans saw their hopes tied to Hayden and his seniority in the Senate.[13]

In spite of his distinguished record, his acknowledged leadership in Arizona's water struggle, and support from newspaper editors throughout the state—including conservative publishing mogul Eugene Pulliam—Hayden faced several serious challenges in his 1962 campaign for reelection. His bright and aggressive thirty-two-year-old administrative assistant, Roy Elson, who managed the campaign, acknowledged that the Arizona electorate had grown and changed significantly since 1956, adding that "there must have been a fifty percent increase in the voting population" during the six-year period. Elson, described by Capitol Hill colleagues and newspapermen as Hayden's "Rasputin or Machiavelli," knew that most of these newcomers had never heard of Hayden and still others questioned the wisdom of voting for an eighty-four-year-old man. Moreover, in the fall of 1961 Mrs. Hayden passed away, leaving many wondering whether the elderly senator would not have the strength, emotionally or physically, to conduct his public responsibilities effectively. Meanwhile the Republican party continued its unremitting growth in the state, building a powerful and well-financed organization. Indeed, Hayden's staff knew the senator was politically vulnerable in 1962.[14]

Elson took decisive action in early 1961, preparing a twenty-page confidential memorandum for Hayden that detailed the difficulty ahead if the senator chose to run for reelection. As the administrative aide put it, "I wrote to the senator on what we had to do if he was going to win, because of this whole change in the demographics of the population.... We couldn't rely anymore on his old organization, we had to do more press, get things into the can, do television spots." Throughout the year Elson, who for the first time in Hayden's electoral career hired a press secretary, executed a well-organized and effective campaign strategy.[15]

He convinced the new Democratic administration to visit Arizona to honor Carl Hayden. Indeed, one of the highlights of the campaign occurred in November 1961, when President John Kennedy and Vice-President Lyndon Johnson attended a fundraising dinner in Phoenix where they spoke glowingly of the veteran senator's accomplishments. In addition to the November gala, during the the fall of that year the Hayden campaign traveled throughout Arizona shooting newsreel footage of the senator at Glen Canyon Dam and at various military bases—film that proved crucial to the success of the campaign.[16]

Beginning in early 1962, however, Hayden experienced a series of nagging flus and infections which threatened to derail the reelection effort. First the senator contracted a stubborn flu, then a urinary tract infection struck. Elson recalled that Hayden convalesced in his apartment at the Methodist building across from the Capitol and "for a long time we had some people sitting in our office, some John Birchers, demanding to see the senator." As a result of these pesky ailments, during the fall of 1962 rumor spread that the senator had actually died, prompting a somewhat feeble Hayden to assert publicly that news of his death was simply not true.[17]

It was during this critical period that Elson's earlier campaign strategy came into play. The newsreel footage shot the previous year, along with help from local television station executives willing to air the footage, aided the faltering campaign. Also, on the Saturday before the 1962 general election, Elson orchestrated a media event that put to rest rumors surrounding Hayden's mortality. Vice-

President Lyndon Johnson and Senator Richard Russell of Georgia arrived at Bethesda Naval Hospital—where Hayden spent the final thirteen days of the campaign—to brief the ailing senator on the Cuban Missile Crisis. While photographers shot pictures, Hayden got out of his bed and the three veteran Democrats held a press conference. The newsmen quickly drafted stories that although Hayden was not well, he was nevertheless alive and alert.[18]

On the night of the election, Hayden, still at Bethesda, asked Elson what he thought was going to happen. The senator expressed concern that the Republicans nominated the mercurial and oddly charismatic Glendale car dealer and prominent conservative, Evan Mecham, to run against him. Elson told his mentor that although the future governor of Arizona had run a vigorous campaign, "I think you're going to win by twenty-six or twenty-seven thousand votes." Elson's prediction was on the mark as Hayden won the election by a count of 189,287 to 155,526—a small margin for him. Then that night, before the polls closed, Hayden phoned all his key campaign workers in Arizona and personally thanked them for their help. Many were in tears over the emotional victory as Hayden had been elected for an unprecedented seventh term to the U.S. Senate.[19]

Senator Hayden took little time to celebrate as he quickly refocused his energies on the Supreme Court decision in *Arizona v. California*. When the opinion was finally announced on June 3, 1963, Hayden considered it a tremendous victory for Arizona while local newspapers considered it "a personal triumph for Carl Hayden." The Court, Hayden was pleased to note, centered its opinion on the Boulder Canyon Project Act rather than the Colorado River Compact. Moreover Congress, the justices reasoned, in passing the legislation "intended to and did create its own comprehensive scheme for ... apportionment." In addition Congress had authorized the Secretary of Interior to utilize his contract power to implement a lower-basin agreement. Importantly for Arizona, each state retained exclusive rights to its tributaries, which meant exclusive rights to the Gila. Concerning mainstream apportionment, the Court gave Arizona what it and Hayden had argued for since the 1922 negotia-

Roy Elson, Hayden's able and controversial chief of staff during the fight for the Central Arizona Project (ASU: CP CTH 2136).

tions over the compact: "4,400,000 acre-feet to California, 2,800,000 acre-feet to Arizona, and 300,000 to Nevada." "That formula," wrote Ben Cole of the *Arizona Republic's* Washington Bureau, was "a personal triumph for Carl Hayden because the decision referred back twenty-five years to the December 12, 1928, debate in which Hayden pointed out that the Boulder Canyon bill and its allocation formula settled the dispute over lower basin waters."[20] After reading the ninety-five pages of opinion and dissent, Hayden informed newsman

Cole, "Naturally I am pleased that the Supreme Court has in general followed the Special Master's recommendations with reference to the division of the waters of the Colorado River. This is especially gratifying because it makes possible at last for us to put our rightful share of the waters to use in the Colorado River Basin."[21]

Understandably, Californians reacted with anger and apprehension to the decision. They charged the Court with misreading the intent of Congress, eroding the rights of the states, and argued that the ruling represented the first time that the Court had interpreted an act of Congress as apportioning water rights to interstate streams. Previously, rights had been determined only by interstate compact or by the Supreme Court itself. Thus this untoward judicial innovation threatened California, and Hayden and his senate staff quickly concluded that Golden State leaders would try to regain in the political arena what they had lost in the judicial decision. Elson described the situation on the heels of the ruling, "We knew that California and Northcutt Ely would try some way to stop this through the legislative process, even though they had lost.... What they couldn't accomplish in court they would try to do in the field of politics."[22]

Other aspects of the decision reflected a departure from previous judicial renderings. The Secretary of the Interior would allocate future surpluses and shortages among and within the states. The latter feature marked, as one expert on the Colorado has written, "an especially sharp break with tradition." Moreover, the Court ruled that Congress could invoke the navigation clause of the U.S. Constitution as well as the "general welfare" clause to divide the waters of non-navigable and navigable streams. This dimension of the ruling, as Justice William O. Douglas wrote in his scathing dissent, increased drastically federal control over the nation's rivers. For Hayden and Arizona, nevertheless, the ruling appeared to clear the way for legislative action on CAP.[23]

Besides the positive implications for CAP, *Arizona v. California* proved a victory for American Indians as well. As noted earlier, when Arizona filed suit in 1952, the federal government intervened not only to protect its interests on the river, but also to defend the rights of the Native Americans living on the twenty-five reservations within the lower basin. U.S. attorneys petitioned for adequate water for all irrigable lands on Indian reservations as well as national parks, forests, recreation areas, and other federal lands. In their decision the justices ruled in favor of the government although limiting their decision to five reservations abutting the mainstream of the river—Fort Mohave, Chemehuevi, Cocopah, Yuma, and Colorado River. Basing its reasoning on *Winters v. United States* (1908) the Court held that the five reservations were limited not just to their land but their rights also extended to water. The justices concluded that "It is impossible to believe that when Congress created the ... Colorado Indian Reservation and when the Executive Department of this Nation created the other reservations they were unaware that most of the lands were desert ... and that water from the river would be essential to the life of the Indian people."

Especially noteworthy was the fact that in determining the amount of water the Indians were to receive, the Court adopted the government's position. Thus the Indians were awarded water based upon irrigable acreage. And in a supplemental decree, the Court added that the Indians were not restricted in the uses to which they could put their water. As one scholar wryly observed, "Reason, rather than agriculture, seemed to emerge as the ultimate test."[24]

Although he agreed in principle with the Court's ruling pertaining to the affected tribes, Hayden expressed concern that Indian uses were to be charged against the state in which the reservation was located. Arizona, where most of the Indian land under the ruling was located, therefore, bore the majority of the burden of this "Indian" water. Moreover, the justices ruled that these rights dated from the establishment of a reservation and were superior to later non-Indian rights, including those rights based on uses initiated before the Indians had begun diverting water from the Colorado or its tributaries. Clearly, *Arizona v. California* left the tribes in a much stronger legal position than they previously maintained.[25]

Upon the announcement of the Supreme Court decision Hayden phoned Don Smith, a reporter for *U.S. News and World Report*, to issue a rare public statement. "The decision of the U.S. Supreme Court on the division of Colorado River water," he told Smith, "is the most significant federal action in history affecting the state of Arizona. This adjudication must now be followed by the construction of the long-awaited CAP." During his recent reelection effort, Hayden made authorization of CAP the centerpiece of his campaign, promising to work for the project's prompt authorization after the Supreme Court's decision. Toward this end the aging dean of the Senate sought and won a seat on the Senate Interior and Insular Affairs Committee as a very "junior" member. In addition to this parliamentary positioning, Hayden, in April 1963, prepared and sent a draft bill and strategy memo to the Arizona delegation in order to foster unity in the state's approach to Congress. And on June 4, 1963, one day after the Court's ruling, Arizona senators Hayden and Goldwater and the three House members of Arizona's delegation introduced legislation (S 1658; H.R. 6796, H.R. 6797, and H.R. 6798) to authorize CAP, one of the largest water project proposals ever to come before Congress.[26]

Hayden's bill authorized a diversion of 1.2 million acre-feet of water annually out of the Colorado River to provide supplemental irrigation and municipal water to central and southern Arizona. To do this, it provided for the construction of five dams and reservoirs, two power plants, and transmission and distribution facilities on the Colorado and its tributaries in Arizona and western New Mexico. A key feature of this first bill was a 740-foot-high dam at Bridge Canyon on the Colorado River at the headwaters of Lake Mead. If built, Bridge Canyon Dam promised to be the highest dam in the western hemisphere. The Bridge Canyon power plant would have an installed capacity of 1.5 million kilowatts, and one-third of its capacity would be transmitted south to pump water over a canal and aqueduct system from the existing Parker Dam on the Colorado 219 miles to the Phoenix area and 341 miles to Tucson.[27]

Shortly before introduction of S 1658, the Bureau of Reclamation completed a supplemental feasibility report on CAP in January 1962. It estimated that CAP would provide additional water to irrigate 880,000 acres of land in Arizona and would provide 303,000 acre-feet of municipal and industrial use water for 1.1 million people, primarily in the Phoenix-Tucson areas. In the fifteen-year period that elapsed between the two Bureau reports on CAP, Arizona's population had grown from 700,000 to approximately 1.4 million, and lands under irrigation in central Arizona from 566,000 to about 1 million acres. In addition, U.S. Geological Survey data indicated that Arizona had "mined" its groundwater basins in the state at an alarming rate. According to the survey, the groundwater level was dropping at the rate of ten feet per year in the Phoenix area and twenty feet per year in Pinal County, south of Phoenix. In some areas wells were going dry or saline water was seeping into them, making them unusable, and the ground was subsiding from over pumping. C.A. Pugh, area engineer for the Bureau of Reclamation at Phoenix, estimated that the overdraft of groundwater basins in the state totaled 2.2 million acre-feet annually. The net delivery of water from CAP would amount to only 1,070,000 per year, so it could not possibly replenish more than half

Arizona's powerful political leaders poised to carry the fight for the Central Arizona Project after the Arizona v. California *Supreme Court case, 1963. Left to right, Congressman John J. Rhodes, Senator Barry Goldwater, Governor Paul Fannin, Congressman Morris Udall, Senator Carl Hayden, and U.S. Secretary of the Interior, Stewart Udall (author's files).*

the water deficit in the state at that rate of use. If these statistics were accurate, Hayden reasoned that Arizona appeared to be heading into a water crisis that could be only partially addressed by CAP.[28]

Hayden knew well that in spite of Arizona's obvious need for additional water, Congress historically delayed final action on reclamation projects until leaders and all sections of the state and region were unified or had arrived at a general consensus. Thus looking for the broad support necessary for his bill, he made known past support for several big packages of upper-basin projects including the Colorado River Storage Project Act of 1956, which led to the construction of Glen Canyon Dam. He also played a prominent role in backing numerous individual state proposals such as New Mexico's San Juan Chama project which passed Congress in 1962. In light of these and other previous efforts in support of regional development, Senator Hayden believed he deserved the same kind of consideration for CAP within his state and throughout the region.[29]

Yet between 1960 and 1963 the anticipation of a Supreme Court decision favorable to Arizona prompted federal administrators and representatives in the basin states to begin formulating a regional plan acceptable to the entire basin—not just Arizona. In January 1962, for example, Secretary of the Interior Stewart Udall, an Arizonan and former congressman, encouraged Congressman Wayne Aspinall (D-Colorado), Chairman of the influential House Interior and Insular Affairs Committee, to request the Interior Department to conduct a comprehensive study of water development in the Colorado River in preparation for the expected pressure for authorization of individual state projects—including CAP—as soon as the decision in *Arizona v. California* was handed down.[30]

Indeed several studies were already under way and in November 1962 Aspinall asked Udall for an outline of the Interior Department's plans for a regional approach to water development in the basin. In an effort to practice "constructive water statesmanship," Secretary Udall, and his undersecretary James Carr of California, adopted this regional approach and by January 1963 he revealed a huge $8 billion plan which included projects in five western states. In announcing his regional program—the Pacific Southwest Water Plan (PSWP)—Udall hoped to "erase the outmoded concept limited by state lines, and concentrate on meeting the total water needs of a region." In addition to this lofty goal, he also sought to reconcile diverse interests and several multiple use water projects into one harmonious and comprehensive plan. In August 1963, after Hayden had introduced his CAP bill, the PSWP was sent to the seven basin states and to five federal departments for review and comment. No state with water entitlements below Lee's Ferry was left out of the scheme and seven of the proposed seventeen projects benefited Arizona, California, Nevada, New Mexico, and Utah. PSWP, moreover, sought to unify the interests of Arizona and southern California, with several programs aimed at easing California's concern over mainstream withdrawals by CAP. Water transfer from northern to southern California, water salvage projects, and several new reclamation programs were included in the plan to mitigate other California concerns. Beyond this, Udall tried to exploit common interests in PSWP by proposing two huge hydroelectric dams, Bridge Canyon and Marble Canyon, to be located near the Grand Canyon National Park. Revenues derived from these cash register dams would underwrite the cost of the entire plan, and guarantee the future growth and development of the Southwest.[31]

To Hayden PSWP and the comparatively simple CAP bill were competing legislative initiatives, and the senator and Arizona's political leadership were particularly incensed with the Kennedy administration and Secretary of the Interior Udall. During 1963 and 1964, in several exchanges of letters and memos between Hayden's office and Interior, an agitated Hayden let it be known in vivid and uncompromising language that he considered the overdrawn PSWP a method for delaying consideration of CAP that played into the hands of California and upper basin opponents of CAP, particularly Colorado. Then-governor of Arizona, Paul Fannin, added that he considered PSWP "a plot against Arizona born in California and formalized in the Interior Department by California's undersecretary." Fannin advocated the senator's approach: "We must and will go it alone with the CAP as proposed by Hayden in S 1658." In numerous correspondence through the next two years, Udall suggested to Hayden and other state leaders that CAP fit into his broader regional program. To one of these missives, dated December 19, 1963, in which Udall alerted the senator that he could not file a favorable report on a separate CAP bill, Hayden shot back, "I vigorously protest the failure to keep your commitment to me and to other officials of this state. I insist that language be included in the PSWP which will be a clear endorsement of the CAP as embodied in S 1658 and/or as a separate first segment in any regional program." According to Elson, " it irritated the hell out of Carl Hayden because there was nothing incompatible with a simple CAP to any regional plan."[32]

Several CAP supporters offered other more political explanations for the legislative standoff in 1963-64. Although not discussed openly, several Capitol Hill insiders suspected that an understanding had been struck between President John F. Kennedy and Secretary Udall. As Hayden aide Elson described the unwritten agreement: "Let's not rock the boat with anything that's going to cause a big problem with California, particularly southern California, at least until after the 1964 elections." The *Yuma Daily Sun* of June 16, 1963, seconded Elson's musings concerning the politics of PSWP: "The mounting opposition of the politically powerful state of California is another obstacle. There is also the task of getting the approval of the Kennedy administration which will be ardently courting California's 40 electoral votes in 1964, an election year." California was now the largest state in the nation; it counted thirty-seven more electoral votes than increasingly Republican Arizona and was doubtlessly a prize in the 1964 presidential sweepstakes. Many CAP proponents realized that Kennedy, as leader of the entire nation—and a practical and politically savvy leader as well—would not simply brush aside the arguments of Democratic Governor Edmund G. "Pat" Brown or the forty-member congressional delegation. Whether valid or not, the notion that Kennedy did not want Udall appearing to take sides with his state of Arizona and its small electoral vote as opposed to California and its substantial electoral vote was a topic of discussion during the early phase of CAP's legislative journey.[33]

Not surprisingly, Stewart Udall took a great deal of editorial abuse within Arizona over his "federalized regional project" that "placed all water and power of the Colorado under control of his department." One highly charged and exaggerated editorial in the *Arizona Republic* of August 18, 1963, asked "Udall, Where Are You?" suggesting that the grandiose plan (PSWP) meant that he had written off Arizona for his political future and that he had come under the influence of the California water lobby headed by Undersecretary of the Interior James Carr. Younger brother and Arizona congressman Morris Udall was the focus of similar harsh and unfair criticism. Observers questioned whether he supported CAP or the "empire-building plan unveiled" by his brother. As the influential *Arizona Republic* editorialized, "Voters know where Stewart Udall stands—he's against the Central Arizona Project.... Will Morris Udall align himself with the rest of the Arizona delegation, which unanimously supports the project. Or, will he, in deference to his brother, sit on the sidelines and refuse to help Arizona?" To an unsympathetic Hayden, Udall confided that "he had taken his weekly horsewhipping from the Phoenix newspapers," but he resented what he termed a personal attack by Senator Goldwater and the unwarranted attacks on his younger brother by powerful publisher Eugene Pulliam. Clearly, the administration's preference for a regional approach to Colorado River development in the form of PSWP posed unforeseen challenges to Hayden and his staff. In spite of the uncharacteristically harsh rhetoric between the two distinguished Arizonans and among state interests, Hayden agreed with Udall's notion that "It is largely up to the two of us to hold the whole thing together." As a result of the need to make progress on CAP both camps made a frosty pledge to confer at any time on strategy matters.[34]

Nevertheless, as Arizona's quest for CAP shifted to Congress, and as several proposals and counterproposals made their way through the maze of subcommittee and committee hearings, Hayden knew that his accumulated power and influence in the Senate bode well for the legislation. In 1966, moreover, an Arizona "Task Force" arrived in Washington to lend support to the the legislative effort, drawing staff and expertise from the state's water establishment: Arizona Interstate

Steam Commission, Arizona Public Service, the Central Arizona Project Association and the Salt River Project. Additionally, Hayden chaired the Senate Appropriations Committee, and he could, if he wanted, hold up every other water project in the country.

As usual he appeared before a variety of congressional committees adding to his already considerable record of testimony in behalf of the project. Typical of his statements between 1963 and 1968 was his testimony in support of his bill, S 1658, before the Senate Subcommittee on Irrigation and Reclamation of the Committee on Interior and Insular Affairs on August 27, 1963. "Arizona's efforts to obtain her full share of Colorado River water have been frustrated by the deliberate delaying tactics of California," he told the subcommittee, and "after fifteen years of separate consideration by Congress, the effort is being made to absorb the simple and readily understood Central Arizona Project into one of the most controversial, complex, and confusing water resource development plans ever presented to Congress." Hayden told this and other groups of legislators in subsequent testimony that he believed in a regional concept of water resource development, that he could support any features of a regional plan which were sound, but that he was opposed to anything that would complicate and delay authorization of CAP. The senator expressed serious concern for Secretary Udall's PSWP because if the plan was never constructed, the benefits to California would be greater than if the plan were constructed. Hayden posited that in the end it would be cheaper for California to use Arizona's water than it would be to participate in any comprehensive plan.[35]

The Arizona senator did not want the urgently needed and completely feasible CAP to be stalled because of controversy over a master plan. Nor did he want other worthy projects, like Utah's Dixie Project or California's Auburn-Folsom South Project, hindered because they have been included in the collection of separate projects which Secretary Udall called the PSWP. Hayden correctly predicted that senators and representatives would hear testimony that there would be insufficient water in the Colorado River to sustain CAP. In anticipating these arguments he pointed to previous statements made by Commissioner of the Bureau of Reclamation Floyd Dominy, who stated that despite rumors to the contrary "there is certainly enough water in the river for the CAP of 1.2 million acre-feet" under the *Arizona v. California* ruling.

Hayden also criticized the portion of the PSWP proposal to import 1.2 million acre-feet of water from northern California to southern California at a cost of billions of dollars while ignoring an equal amount of water that could be developed at a minimum cost through adequate conservation practices within the area. "This committee," he inveighed, "is being requested to provide funds for the import of water from northern California at a great cost to protect the right of southern California to waste water."[36]

What especially irked Hayden about PSWP or other "regional" initiatives that emerged over the four-and-a-half years of legislative wrangling in what came to be the Colorado River Basin Project Act of 1968, was the obvious efforts of certain interests within California to delay CAP or nullify *Arizona v. California.* Later he recalled that "it appeared a lifetime of labor was approaching fruition." The Court decision, combined with solemn assurances of California's former governor Earl Warren who in 1948 told Hayden, "whenever it is finally determined that water belongs to Arizona, it should be permitted to use that water in any manner or by any method considered best by Arizona," seemed to clear the way for authorization of CAP. Moreover, shortly after the opinion, Governor Pat Brown announced at a press conference that California, having lost the Supreme Court case, would not try to accomplish by obstructionism what she had failed to accomplish by litigation. As he stated on August 4, 1963, and reiterated on several occasions thereafter: "For forty years I have witnessed the thwarting of Arizona's effort to put to use its share of Colorado River water. At every turn Arizona has encountered the deliberate delaying tactics of California and there is every reason to believe that this plan of obstructionism will continue." To his dismay he found that "a small group of Californians, notwithstanding previous commitments, continued to nullify by delay, the Supreme Court's decision." Although California employed the politics of delay throughout the process of legislative consideration of the bill, Hayden firmly believed that the concept of equity would prevail in the end. Indeed, California had its water, Nevada had its water, the upper basin was developing its water, and Arizona had nothing. Thus as he told lawmakers at the outset of legislative consideration of CAP, "I think all of you know that I have always attempted to help in any way possible with every project of our western resources—even when I was being fought on my own project—but quite frankly my patience has been exhausted."[37]

In spite of California's continued opposition, Hayden had powerful allies in the Senate. His close and respected friend, Senator Henry Jackson (D-Washington), chaired the Senate Interior Committee. Jackson, whose state owed much of its post-war prosperity to Hayden-supported federal reclamation programs, monitored carefully natural resource development and federal reclamation. Moreover, Jackson's valued relationship with Senator Hayden and firm alliance with President Kennedy served Arizona well throughout CAP's various journeys through the Senate between 1963 and 1968. During the course of arriving at a measure suitable to all contending and conflicting interests, however, California and the upper basin looked to the Northwest and the Columbia River system to import and augment Colorado River water supplies in an effort to avoid water shortages made worse by CAP. At one point during the process, several senators and congressmen contemplated the importation of 8 million acre-feet of water per year from the Columbia River Basin and even as far north as Canada. Naturally, Jackson saw fit to protect the interests of his region and took actions to eliminate transbasin transfers of water during final consideration of the CAP bill. In its final form the legislation contained a provision that provided for a ten-year ban on inter-basin feasibility studies.[38]

Hayden also counted on support from Senator Clinton Anderson (D-New Mexico) who served as chairman of the Power and Reclamation Subcommittee of the Interior Committee. Anderson held considerable stature in the Senate as well as with groups concerned with water resource development and, besides, he had a stake in the bill as it pertained to protecting and extending water entitlements for his state. Moreover, his especially close relationship with Senator Jackson made Anderson an important ally in the CAP fight. Indeed, throughout his last term in the office, Hayden relied on these two powerful senators to counter the opposition arguments of California's two senators, Thomas Kuchel (R-California), the ranking Republican member of the Senate Interior Committee, and Claire Engle (R-California), who helped engineer the 1951 defeat of CAP in the House of Representatives.[39]

Thankful for the support he maintained in the Senate, Hayden and his staff nevertheless knew the real fight for passage remained in the House of Representatives. Between 1963 and 1968 Arizona, fortunately, had capable and bipartisan representation in the House. John Rhodes, a Republican, was a respected and influential leader among House Republicans who served on the House appropriations subcommittee which would ultimately provide money to build the project. George Senner, a northern Arizona Democrat from Arizona's newly created third district, was untested and soon lost his seat to the inimitable Sam Steiger of Prescott, a Republican. And Morris Udall, a member of the key Committee on Interior and Insular Affairs, maintained special responsibilities over the bill. Importantly for Arizona, her three-man team in the House worked well together during the final four and one-half year legislative history of the bill.[40]

Although Arizona's House delegation introduced CAP bills identical to Hayden's the day after the Supreme Court's decision, passage was another issue. Indeed nine out of ten bills introduced and referred to committee never saw a floor vote. The power of congressional committees in the House, moreover, could not be overstated and of special importance were the committee chairmen. Bills opposed by the chairman rarely emerged from committee for a floor vote. The chairman controlled the schedule of hearings on legislation, and undecided members often followed the chairman's lead. Since the principal obstacle to passage of CAP was in the House, the House Interior Committee—and its Irrigation and Reclamation Subcommittee where the CAP bill was referred—held vital importance for CAP proponents.[41]

For Hayden this meant CAP passing through the gauntlet of the House Interior Committee, chaired by Wayne N. Aspinall. According to most observers of Colorado River Basin affairs, Aspinall, the former schoolteacher with a testy disposition who had climbed from a small western Colorado town to chairman of this all-important committee, distrusted expansionist California and felt similarly about Arizona. In fact, the river ran under the window of his home on Aspinall Drive in Palisade, Colorado, and he sought to conserve every acre-foot of water before the lower basin states would take it and never give it back. Mo Udall considered the sixty-seven-year-old chairman who had served in Congress since 1948 "a superb legislative tactician." Of utmost concern to Aspinall was the obvious fact that although entitled to 2.8 million acre-feet of water, Arizona's use of this amount through CAP might cut sharply into water destined for upper-basin use but not yet developed. During one crucial phase of CAP's consideration in the House Interior Committee in 1967, Hayden, in an uncharacteristic display of power, threatened to eliminate funding for construction of the Frying Pan-Arkansas Project in Colorado and allowed that he would hold up other projects important to the House Interior chairman if Aspinall did not move the bill forward. Therefore, as Hayden knew from the outset of legislative consideration of his bill, if CAP was going to get past Aspinall and his committee, Colorado must be satisfied.[42]

In addition to Aspinall, John Saylor of Pennsylvania, ranking Republican on the House Interior Committee, continued to frustrate Arizona as he had in the 1950s. Described by one colleague as a "dynamic, hard-hitting protagonist," who had earned respect in the House, Saylor was an ardent conservationist who supported the growth and expansion of the National Park system and advocated programs for outdoor recreation. Saylor, moreover, advocated a strong wilderness bill, the "integrity of the national parks," and complained vigorously about the Bridge Canyon Dam provision of CAP because it threatened to back water into Grand Canyon National Park. While not opposed to sound reclamation projects he opposed increasing public power development and spotty financing and poor planning in "marginal reclamation projects." He voted against the Upper Colorado project in 1956 thereby gaining recognition and support among environmentalists for his efforts.[43]

Indeed in 1966 and 1967 environmentalist opposition to the construction of dams in and around the Grand Canyon brought nationwide attention to CAP and threatened to derail the entire project. Environmentalists waged a spirited campaign against the dams reminiscent of the great battle over Echo Park. By 1966 virtually everyone involved in the legislation—through hearings, meetings, and "confidential" parlays—knew that the river was over-allocated and most wanted to see augmentation from the Northwest, so they generally favored the Grand Canyon dams. As expressed in his first post-Supreme Court CAP bill, Hayden still advocated construction of Bridge Canyon Dam, as he had since 1947, and indicated that he also supported Marble Gorge Dam if indeed revenues were needed to finance augmentation and other development. Yet the previously fragmented environmentalist movement, representing diverse interests and a wide array of organizations, brought significant pressure to bear on Congress and the Johnson administration. They contended that the dams would flood scenic areas and inundate portions of Grand Canyon National Park and Grand Canyon National Monument. A few groups, including the Sierra Club, the National Parks Association, and the Arboretum, saw a great deal to lose with the inclusion of hydroelectric power dams in the bill.

The California-based Sierra Club, with a national membership of about 40,000 at the time of the battle, was the most prominent and well-organized of the anti-dam environmental groups. Led by its energetic and controversial director, David Brower, the Sierra Club spearheaded a broadly gauged effort to fight the construction of dams in the vicinity of the Grand Canyon. An impressive letter-writing campaign and an effective public-relations program, underscored by the strong emotional and symbolic appeal of "saving" the Grand Canyon from profit-mongering developers, accomplished much for their cause. Brower wrote President Johnson, Secretary Udall, and other members of the administration directly, protesting the dams. Soon

Johnson administration officials, members of congress, and Arizona's leaders began receiving thousands of letters daily from individuals and groups as diverse as the social science faculty at Dartmouth College in Hanover, New Hampshire, to first grade public school classes in Sandusky, Ohio.[44]

In the course of the advocacy campaign, a series of highly publicized well-attended public addresses brought further attention to the issue. In Denver, for example, Brower, speaking before an anti-Grand Canyon dams audience, quipped that he did not oppose dams in the Grand Canyon as long as the Bureau of Reclamation built a comparable canyon somewhere else. As one chronicler put it, "Never before had conservationists challenged the collective will of seven states."[45]

By early 1966 the public was suitably convinced that the most controversial aspect of the legislation involved the two proposed dams. And in the spring of that year, after *Reader's Digest*, *Life* and even *My Weekly Reader* ran stories attacking the Grand Canyon dams, Hayden realized that they posed insurmountable political obstacles. By early 1967 Hayden, as he met with senate leaders in efforts to further revise CAP, knew that an alternative source of energy would be required to pump CAP water to central Arizona. In a July 1967 memorandum to President Johnson advising him that the Senate Committee on Interior and Insular Affairs had overwhelmingly recommended passage of S 1004, the CAP bill—for the fourth time—he added that this legislation contained "no new Colorado River dams." As Elson interpreted the outcome of the the anti-dam fight: "Most people in the East and other places were for CAP, but they were against the dams because they had been informed by Brower and his operatives that within the region there existed adequate amounts of alternative energy sources, notably low-grade coal." As a result Hayden and Arizona were forced to accept an alternative to hydroelectric power. Yet, as historian Donald Worster explained in his analysis of this environmentalist victory, they lost something as well. In exchange for Grand Canyon dams, energy required for CAP was derived instead from coal strip-mined on Hopi lands at Black Mesa and burned in the Navajo generating station near Page "polluting crystalline desert air with ash and poison gas." As one reclamation official explained the paradox, "it didn't solve a damn thing except it gave us power to pump water to central Arizona."[46]

If acquiescing on the dam issue, incorporating aspects of Secretary Udall's regional plan, and jousting with Congressman Aspinall's upper basin demands in the House proved difficult but tolerable, Hayden had great difficulty with another necessary compromise. From the start of congressional negotiations California's senators made it clear that its central demand for dropping opposition to CAP would be a first priority of 4.4 million acre-feet awarded it in the Supreme Court decision. As Hayden's chief negotiator throughout the CAP legislative battle, Roy Elson, recalled: "For California ... it all became an argument about what to do about the shortages in the river ... we got into these early difficulties mainly over that issue." Hayden knew immediately the implications of the demand; California sought to regain some of what it had lost in the decision. In effect, California wanted Arizona to regulate their mainstream diversions so that California would never receive less than 4.4 million acre-feet out of the 7.5 million acre-feet lower-basin allocation. At first an intransigent Hayden refused to negotiate the issue with California senator Kuchel. By 1965, however, as time seemed to get shorter and the issues more complex, Hayden relented and subsequent versions of the bill in the Eighty-eighth and Eighty-ninth congresses carried provisions for twenty-five- and twenty-seven-year guarantees for California's 4.4 priority. In the final version of the bill, however, Arizona promised California that CAP diversions "shall be so limited as to assure the availability" of 4.4 million acre-feet annually in perpetuity.[47]

As Hayden neared the last year of his final term in office and CAP remained stalled in the House Interior Committee in spite of the numerous concessions already made, a frustrated and impatient state leadership triggered another minor complication for the senator. Rumors of an Arizona "Go-It-Alone" CAP, promoted by state conservatives and elements within the Arizona Power Authority (APA) first surfaced in 1963. A prominent feature of the state-financed and operated plan included the successful application of the Arizona Power Authority to the Federal Power Commission to finance, construct, and manage a hydroelectric power dam on the Colorado River. Hayden quickly thwarted this untimely effort by sheperding through Congress a bill (S 502) that preserved the jurisdiction of Congress over the construction of hydroelectric power works below Glen Canyon Dam on the Colorado River. With passage of S 502 on June 23, 1964, those Arizonans calling for a state-owned and operated CAP were effectively prohibited from taking action though they lobbied the senator and threatened continuously to take action as late as 1967. While the state "Go-It-Alone" plan reflected the lack of consensus within Arizona over CAP strategy, it was more accurately an illustration of the high degree of frustration over repeated legislative delays in the CAP bill.[48]

By the end of 1967 after seemingly endless negotiations among and within states, implementing selected provisions from over thirty Department of Interior studies and discarding others, crafting suitable and appropriate legal language, and including time-honored porkbarrel benefits for those politicians who needed to "bring home the bacon," CAP was finally ready to move. Key in breaking the political logjam in California was newly elected Republican governor Ronald Reagan, who began direct and productive negotiations with Arizona's Republican governor Jack Williams. Reagan informed his administrators that he had "become increasingly concerned over the serious impasse ... relative to the Colorado River legislation and with the adverse impact this stalemate is having on other programs in California and on reclamation throughout the West." Another crucial element in prompting final action was Hayden's pressure on House Interior Chairman Aspinall, who in the fall returned from a "vacation" in Colorado and was virtually forced to hold final hearings on the bill and report it out of committee. The legislation, depending on one's perspective, was either light enough or heavy enough to move. During the spring of 1968, as Hayden and his staff participated in fashioning the final compromises and details in conference committee, most of the key players who participated in creating the measure that emerged from Congress—even opponents of CAP like California's Thomas Kuchel—could not disguise their profound pleasure that Senator Hayden came away from the momentous struggle with one last political victory. On September 12, 1968, when the Senate agreed to the House version of the Colorado River Basin Project Act, the ninety-year-old Hayden received glowing tributes for his persistent efforts. The senator quietly acknowledged the accolades with nods of appreciation. On September 30, 1968, President Lyndon Johnson, at a ceremony attended by Senator Hayden and other Arizona dignitaries, signed CAP into law.[49]

Besides CAP, the legislation included authorization of several other controversial reclamation projects as well, including Hooker Dam in New Mexico, an aqueduct from Lake Mead to Las Vegas, the Dixie Project in Utah, and the Uintah Unit of the Central Utah Project. The Act also authorized the San Miguel, Dallas Creek, West Divide, Dolores, and Animas-La Plata projects in Aspinall's state of Colorado. Additionally, it authorized the establishment of a Lower Colorado River Development Fund to build a still-yet-to-be-defined augmentation project. Finally, the bill made delivery of Mexico's 1.5 million acre-feet of water a national, not regional, responsibility. This legislation, signed into law two days before Hayden's ninety-first birthday, was—at the time—the most expensive single congressional authorization in history, containing about $1.3 billion for implementation of the program.[50]

On May 6, 1968, shortly before the final touches were being completed on CAP, Hayden was led into the Appropriations Committee chamber jammed with senators, friends from Arizona, and a few representatives from the media. President Johnson arrived bearing a pair of walnut bookends and issued a short grandiloquent tribute. Senator Richard Russell of Georgia, Hayden's best friend in the Senate, then chaired a brief ceremony and introduced Hayden. The Arizona senator walked slowly to the dais and announced, "Among other things that fifty-six years in Congress have taught me is that contemporary events need contemporary men. Time actually makes specialists of us all. When a house is built there is a moment for the foundation,

President Lyndon Baines Johnson signs the Colorado River Basin Project Act into law as Hayden looks on, 1968 (ASU: CP CTH 1433).

another for the walls, the roof and so on. Arizona's foundation includes fast highways, adequate electric power, and abundant water, and these foundations have been laid. It is time for a new building crew to report, so I have decided to retire from office at the close of my term this year." Then as cameras clicked, Hayden burst into tears as did nearly everyone else in the crowded room. With the typically brief announcement, Hayden signaled the end of his service to Arizona and his country.[51]

And as he prepared for retirement, Hayden drafted his last "Arizona Report" for his constituents. He recounted his first impressions upon entering the House of Representatives in 1912, where he received the advice of senior Maryland Congressman, Fred Talbott, who explained that there were two ways to represent your people, "Being a show horse or being a work horse." Hayden informed Arizonans that throughout his career he had tried to be the latter and he had found it to be rewarding. He touched on some of the legislative highlights of his long service in the House and Senate, ending his

President Johnson celebrates with Hayden after the signing of the bill that provides Arizona with its Central Arizona Project, 1968 (ASU: CP CTH 2392).

last report with a statement that suggested a profound awareness of the significant historical role he played in the nation's history. "There is inscribed on the National Archives Building in Washington this motto," he wrote, "What is Past is Prologue." "Indeed it is!" "Although I grew to manhood during the 19th century," he continued, "I know full well our State and Country cannot return to the way of thinking of those years. The lesson is that while we can learn from the past, Arizona and the Nation needs a Senator who is in full step with the times and is willing to lead us into the future where the fulfillment of the good life awaits all our people. And so, this is my last report to the people of Arizona. I shall be home soon."[52]

"Arizona's Most Distinguished Citizen"

Amidst the mix of nostalgia surrounding Hayden's retirement and the general good feeling about the passage of CAP, those who knew and worked with Hayden waxed philosophic about the climax of his career. Mo Udall, who played such a crucial role in CAP's legislative fortunes in the House of Representatives, perhaps expressed it best when he offered that much of Hayden's public career and his tenacious pursuit of CAP related to his upbringing on the banks of the Salt River and his father's operation of the ferry. "Water being so crucial to his state and his connections with irrigation and water in this dry land in his very youngest years and all the work he had done for other states to get water brought there," Udall suggested in 1972, "I think that he felt that this one last monumental project was going to ensure the growth and prosperity of Arizona for the next one hundred years." For Carl Hayden, water, and its use and distribution in the American Southwest, provided a palpable thread of continuity from his childhood at Hayden's Ferry in the 1870s and 1880s through his career and into his retirement in east Tempe in the late 1960s and early 1970s. The Central Arizona Project, similarly, served as a fitting symbol of Hayden's southwestern society; the yearnings of its nineteenth-century dreamers, the realization of those hopes toward the end of the twentieth century, and the implications of his reclamation culture in the twenty-first.[1]

In the three years following his retirement in 1969, "Arizona's most distinguished citizen" lived in Tempe, remaining remarkably active. He established a three-room carpeted office on the top floor of the Charles Trumbull Hayden Library at Arizona State University, directing a three-person staff that organized his files, papers, and books that had accumulated from the early part of the twentieth century. Also, Hayden resumed work on an Arizona pioneers project begun in the 1920s while he served in the House of Representatives. James Chilton, the senator's chief aide in his transition to private citizen, noted that during his public career the senator compiled 2,500 dossiers on pioneer Arizona families. Answering mail and other correspondence, working on the Arizona pioneer project, and giving a modest number of interviews and speeches around the Phoenix area occupied much of Hayden's time in the months following his return from Washington.[2]

He spent his last years living on the edge of the Shalimar Golf Course with his longtime nurse and aide, Frances Doll, who came into

Senator Everett Dirksen shares a memory with Hayden during one of numerous 1968 farewell parties. President Johnson and Senator Mike Mansfield look on (ASU: CP CTH 2188).

Senator Barry Goldwater eulogizes Hayden at the memorial service at Grady Gammage Auditorium at Arizona State University as former president Lyndon Johnson prepares his final words, 1972 (ASU: CP CTH 1716).

Hayden's employment in the 1940s to care for the senator's wife, Nan. There he read the daily Senate summary in the *Congressional Record*, scanned the newspapers, devoted himself to private matters and spent his last energies writing a biography on his father, Charles Trumbull Hayden. Hayden completed the manuscript in late 1971 and received the galley proofs of the short biography toward the end of January 1972. As he reviewed the manuscript of *Charles Trumbull Hayden: Pioneer*, the ninety-four year-old Hayden took ill, lingered a few days, and died peacefully on January 25, 1972.[3]

* * *

In spite of a half-century struggle with her neighbors, Arizona's phenomenal rate of growth in the twentieth century testified to Hayden's efforts and marked the lower basin's success at utilizing Colorado River resources. When regional leaders first focused their attention on water resource development they were largely concerned with protecting their incipient agricultural economies from the vagaries of the desert and, if possible, expanding their enterprise. As it turned out an urban-suburban oasis civilization has sprung from the use of Colorado River system water. As Gerald D. Nash, one of the leading interpreters of the modern West has reminded us, one of the prime characteristics of the twentieth century West has been its urban aspect. Colorado River historian Norris Hundley agrees with this assertion and links the West's urbanness with water: "It is clear ... that the growth of the arid West's urban centers, with their universities, museums, art galleries, drive-ins, freeways, and other symbols of civilization has been intimately connected with success at obtaining water." For Hayden's Arizona, at least, the ability to transport water hundreds of miles from the mainstream of the Colorado to the state's two urban centers, Phoenix and Tucson, has meant more than the survival of these two rapidly expanding centers of population. It has signaled also the stabilization and, in some cases, further development of the agricultural and mining economies as well as the post-industrial economy based on high technology. Finally, federal reclamation in the form of CAP has eliminated, psychologically at least, one of the barriers of future economic and population growth in Arizona — the fear of water shortages.[4]

As important as putting water to use in the arid Southwest, hydroelectric power, publicly owned and operated, was an important related issue that drew Hayden's attention throughout his career. The commodity revolutionized the quality of human life during the first third of the twentieth century and played a critical role in Colorado River basin development. Hayden's involvement in the debates over power generated at proposed dams on the Colorado River revealed that the issue was far more complicated than merely pitting advocates of private power—the "power trust"—against proponents of inexpensive public power. Local, state, and federal agencies, reflected in groups like the City of Los Angeles, the State of Arizona, the Imperial Irrigation District, the Salt River Valley Water Users Association, and the U.S. Department of Interior, among others, battled over the production, administration, and distribution of this revolutionary source of power. Significantly, the debate was by no means limited to the

Southwest, for the multitude of issues raised affected reclamation projects and other energy resource developments throughout the country far into the future.[5]

In Hayden's involvement in the costly and time-consuming struggle over harnessing and distributing the Colorado River system's resources, distinct themes emerged that illuminated much about the nature of western politics in the twentieth century. The two most obvious themes—East-West continuity and the federal government's central role in addressing the theme of aridity—linked Hayden and his role in the history of the Colorado River controversy closer than ever to national historical processes. Eastern institutions—public and private—were ever-present throughout the history of the debates over the Colorado River. The Supreme Court, Congress, Wall Street investors, farmers, and East Coast journalists played prominent roles during various phases of the conflict. Hayden's role in the Colorado River controversy, furthermore, provided a prime example of the decisive role that government—local, state, and federal—played in this important dimension in the history of the West. Lastly, but perhaps most important among the overarching historical themes that embrace Hayden, Arizona, and the Colorado River, a strong argument can be made that the conflict altered the balance of power within the American political system. Federalism, the concept that embodies the unflagging attempt to reconcile local self-determination with national unity, underwent substantial modification during the long course of the Colorado River controversy. Specifically, the Colorado River basin states, in their attempt to work out an accord among themselves in concert with the government, precipitated a philosophical debate between the state governments and the federal government. Hayden, as a western lawmaker from an arid land state steeped in the history of the federal reclamation movement, saw the federal government as the ultimate arbiter in the political process. Clearly, Hayden's role in this half-century long debate provides unique insight into the process and helps further document a major evolution in national water policy. The consequences of this evolution facilitated the emergence of the federal government as the most powerful agency concerning the

Colorado River, and therefore, other interstate streams. This power shift bore major implications for Arizona and the other western states within the American federal system.[6]

More specifically, Hayden was in the forefront of those western congressmen and senators who tried to increase the region's share of federal expenditures by securing funds for irrigation, reclamation, and power projects. He helped harness the region's water resources to promote economic growth and development. Yet in the effort to foster environmental and economic change, conflict among competing groups of resource users emerged, prompting Hayden to play a variety of roles in lower-basin water politics. These internal conflicts, however, did not detract from Hayden's larger view of a common regional destiny that united the western states on issues of regional growth. Even while battling Phil Swing, Hiram Johnson, George Hunt, and Wayne Aspinall over vital issues of water distribution and use, Hayden accepted and encouraged the involvement of the federal government to play the primary role in underwriting the region's further development. It was not surprising therefore, that Arizona voters, like their fellow arid-states brethren, crossed party lines to repeatedly reelect Hayden and those like him who delivered on their commitment to secure federal support.

He began his public career riding a horse and buggy to his office and ended it voting for funds that ultimately enabled him to watch people walk on the moon. He observed his countrymen fight two great wars, participate in military actions all over the globe, noted Americans migrating from the farms to the city, and admired the resiliency of a nation that recovered from the Depression and other exacting social, political, and economic dislocations.[7]

Hayden's long life and career can be attributed in part to personal qualities that included, among other things, hard work and kindness to others. As several colleagues who described Hayden's work habits in college, local politics, the House of Representatives, and the Senate, he often labored long hours, familiarizing himself with the task at hand, and demonstrated tenacity and perseverance at achieving goals. In addition his diplomatic manner, kindness, humility, and warm sense

Hayden as drawn by an editorial cartoonist after the passage of the CAP leglislation (Arizona State University Libraries).

of humor added an important dimension that endeared him to his congressional colleagues. Senator and Vice-President Hubert Humphrey, in a rare tribute in the world of politics, avowed, "I have never heard Senator Hayden say an unkind word about his colleagues or about anyone." In 1940, President Harry Truman remembered that Hayden was one of the few people in Washington who treated the self-conscious senator-elect from Missouri, dubbed a "tool of the Pendergasts," as a genuine human being "with kindness and friendship." Arizona Congressman John Rhodes put it succinctly: "If there was one trait that predominates in the nature of Carl Hayden it would be humility." Mo Udall agreed that Hayden possessed the "quality of humility which was one of the essentials of greatness." Those who worked with him on committees claimed he was a wonderful chairman who was never autocratic. These personal attributes, combined with a broad intelligence and facile mind capable of grasping legal, engineering, and a wide variety of other concepts, contributed mightily to his overall effectiveness in representing Arizona and his region. This formula for political representation, moreover, was administered with an economy of oratory, or as Hayden so well described his political axiom to his father in 1896, "silence equals politics."[8]

Another explanation for Hayden's enduring political success, which added texture to his public career, was an uncanny ability to organize disparate groups behind an idea or program. In effect, he exercised unique skill at the engineering of consent. In issues of special importance to Arizona, with few exceptions, he refused to resort to political posturing or hyperbole. Instead he carefully defined objectives, researched the issues, modified objectives when necessary, decided upon a strategy, charted a plan, and implemented tactics. Numerous examples illustrate Hayden's ability at this: his early efforts at organizing Tempe townspeople for the construction of the municipally owned and operated water works in the 1890s; his success at organizing a letter-writing campaign in the struggle to secure the San Carlos Irrigation Project in the teens and twenties; his close and continuous ties to the state's newspaper editors—Republican and Democrat alike; his testimony and preparation for reclamation bills before hearings of subcommittees and committees; and his judiciously dispensed behind-the-scenes use of seniority so vividly illustrated in his papers at Arizona State University. In contrast to the image of Hayden as the "Silent Senator," he can be viewed from another perspective, that of the first-rate public relations man.[9]

Hayden called upon all of these abilities in his efforts to secure Arizona's rights to Colorado River resources and the CAP. Underlying the scramble for water from the Colorado was not only its necessity for economic survival in an arid region, but also a western obsession with economic growth and development. This myopic dedication to an ideology of growth and development in an environmentally sensitive desert ecology has come under increasing scrutiny in recent years. Scholars revisit the era of the western water wars and the orgy of dam building and question not only the validity of this environmental manipulation, but also lament the fate of the Colorado River; described by one interpreter as "A River No More."[10]

As scholars and political leaders continue to reassess and revise their environmental and economic interpretations of federal reclamation in the American West, Carl Hayden will stand out in their analyses as one public figure who championed, and in many ways symbolized, this movement in the history of the twentieth-century American West. His unwavering support for this massive federal program defines most accurately the significance of his long tenure in federal government. Without question water in the arid West is among the most crucial of the region's concerns in the nineteenth and twentieth centuries, and doubtlessly this environmental dictate will influence to a significant degree the direction of public policy in the twenty-first century. This vast, complex, and enigmatic issue, more than any other, gave Carl Hayden's life and career unity, continuity, and purpose. In the future, the use of water will underlie every public policy decision made in the American West. Hayden was a man who understood the need for water, and that, perhaps, is the greatest tribute to a western lawmaker.[11]

Notes

I—THE VISION

1. *Senate Document* 76, 87 Cong., 2 Sess., "Tribute to the Honorable Carl Hayden, Senator from Arizona, To Commemorate the Occasion of his Fiftieth Anniversary of Congressional Service, February 19, 1962" (Washington, D.C.: Government Printing Office, 1962), 29; Philip Fradkin, *A River No More: The Colorado River and the American West* (New York: Alfred A. Knopf, 1981); Howard Pyle interview with Jack L. August, Jr., November 9, 1982, Tempe, Arizona, Oral History Collection (OHC), Arizona Collection (AC), Arizona State University (ASU), Tempe, Arizona.

2. See Michael McGerr, "Is There a Twentieth Century West?" in William Cronon, George Miles, and Jay Gitlin, eds., *Under an Open Sky: Rethinking America's Western Past* (New York: W.W. Norton, 1992), 249, 251-56. McGerr, however, sees a post-World War II counter trend in which the West played a crucial role in the rise of the New Right, best illustrated in the public careers of Barry Goldwater and Ronald Reagan. See also, Barry Goldwater and J.J. Casserly, *Goldwater* (New York: Doubleday, 1988), and Lou Cannon, *Reagan* (New York: Putnam, 1982). For an uncritical, salutary overview of Hayden's political career see Ross R. Rice, *Carl Hayden: Builder of the American West* (Lanham, Maryland.: University Press of America, Inc., 1994).

3. Walter Prescott Webb, "The American West: Perpetual Mirage, *Harper's* 214 (May 1957); McGerr, "Is There a Twentieth Century West?" 246. Although Webb's description of the West as a gigantic fire provides compelling imagery, obviously not all of the West—not even all of Arizona—is a desert. See also, John Opie, "Environmental History of the West," in Gerald Nash and Richard Etulain,

eds., *The Twentieth Century West: Historical Interpretations* (Albuquerque: University of New Mexico Press, 1992) 213.

4. Donald Worster, *Rivers of Empire: Water, Aridity and the Growth of the American West* (New York: Pantheon Books, 1985); Gerald Nash, *The American West in the Twentieth Century: A Short History of an Urban Oasis* (Engelwood Cliffs, New Jersey: Prentice-Hall, 1973); Opie, "Environmental History of the West," 213. Opie suggests that the search for water has dominated the history and development of the American West for the last hundred years. He also notes that California water consumption, whether irrigation or urban, has received the majority of scholarly attention, citing the works of Norris Hundley, Jr., Donald Worster, William Kahrl, and Abraham Hoffman, among others. Notably, Opie's survey of the literature notes Arizona's recent success at securing long-awaited benefits from the Colorado River and the need for analysis of these developments.

5. McGerr, "Is There a Twentieth Century West?" 248; Kenneth Owens, "Pattern and Structure in Western Territorial Politics," *Western Historical Quarterly* 1 (October 1970), 373-92; Paul Kleppner, "Politics Without Parties in Western States, 1876-1900," *Western Historical Quarterly* 14 (January 1983), 459-83; Paul Kleppner, "Politics Without Parties: The Western States, 1900-1984," in Gerald Nash and Richard Etulain, eds., *The Twentieth Century West: Historical Interpretations* (Albuquerque: University of New Mexico Press, 1992), 259-338.

6. For Hayden's earliest bill calling for Colorado River flood control see H.R. 9421, *Cong Rec.*, 66 Cong., 1 Sess. (1919), 22, 24, 309. See also, Paul Bracken and Herman Kahn, *Arizona Tomorrow: A Precursor of Post-Industrial America* (Croton-on-Hudson, New York: The Hudson Institute, 1979), 14-61, 78-108.

7. For a biographical portrait of Charles Trumbull Hayden see Jack L. August, Jr., "A Vision in the Desert: Charles Trumbull Hayden, Salt River Pioneer," *Journal of Arizona History* 36 (Summer 1995), 109-34; Hayden Eulogy, February 7, 1900, Hayden Biographical File (HBF) Carl Hayden Papers Collection (CHPC), Hayden Library (HL), Arizona State University, Tempe, Arizona; Carl Hayden, *Charles Trumbull Hayden: Pioneer* (Tucson: Arizona Historical Society, 1972), 1; Bert Fireman, "Charles Trumbull Hayden," *Smoke Signal* (Tucson Corral of the Westerners, Spring 1969), 195; *Arizona Republic*, February 18. 1962.

8. August, "A Vision in the Desert," *Journal of Arizona History*, 111-14; Hayden, *Charles Trumbull Hayden*, 2; Charles T. Hayden to Mary Hanks Hayden Heath, July 8, 1844, Hayden Family Letters Collection (HFLC), CHPC, ASU; Fireman, "Charles Trumbull Hayden," *Smoke Signal*, 195; Norman Graebner, *Manifest Destiny* (New York: Bobbs-Merrill, 1968), passim.

9. August, "A Vision in the Desert," *Journal of Arizona History*, 114-17; Fireman, "Charles Trumbull Hayden," Arizona Crossroads, Bert Fireman Collection (BFC), Arizona Historical Foundation (AHF); Carl Hayden, "Address at Tempe," November 1, 1956, HBF; Charles T. Hayden to Brother, June 7, 1847, HFLC, ASU; Hayden, *Charles Trumbull Hayden*, 2.

10. August, "A Vision in the Desert," *Journal of Arizona History*, 117-24; Carl Hayden interview with Joe Frantz, October 28, 1968, Lyndon Baines Johnson Presidential Library, Austin, Texas; Hayden, *Charles Trumbull Hayden*, 5; Hayden, "Speech at Dedication of Hayden Library," HBF; *Arizona Miner* (Prescott), April 20, 1864, September 28, November 30, 1867, December 10, 21, 1870; Geoffrey Mawn, "Promoters, Speculators, and the Selection of the Phoenix Townsite," *Arizona and the West* 19 (Autumn 1977), 209-12; Carl Hayden, "Sallie Davis Hayden: Thoroughbred Pioneer," manuscript, n.d., HBF.

11. August, "A Vision in the Desert," *Journal of Arizona History*, 127-28; *Salt River Herald* (Phoenix), October 3, 1877; *Arizona Citizen* (Tucson), October 13, 1877; Charles Trumbull Hayden to Carl Hayden, March 14, 1897, HFLC.

12. August, "A Vision in the Desert," *Journal of Arizona History*, 128-29; Jack L. August, Jr., "Carl Hayden: Born a Politician, *Journal of Arizona History* 26 (Summer 1985), 130-32.

13. August, "Carl Hayden: Born a Politician," *Journal of Arizona History*, 127-28; Carl Hayden to Charles Trumbull Hayden, March 20, 1897; Josephine Alford to Sallie Davis Hayden, April 12, 1891, HFLC; *Arizona Citizen* (Tucson), February 18, 1897.

14. August, "Carl Hayden: Born a Politician," *Journal of Arizona History*, 128; Charles Trumbull Hayden to Carl Hayden, September 17, 1898, HFLC; *Arizona Republican* (Phoenix), April 20, 1900; *Tempe Daily News*, February 7, 1900; Stephen Shadegg, "The Miracle of Water in the Salt River Valley: Part II," *Arizona Highways*, 18 (August 1942), 29.

15. August, "Carl Hayden: Born a Politician," *Journal of Arizona History*, 128-29; Karen Smith, "The Campaign for Water in Central Arizona, 1890-1903," *Arizona and the West*, 23 (Summer 1981), 127-48; Ruby Haigler, "History of Tempe," unpublished manuscript (1930), Arizona Collection, Hayden Library, ASU.

16. August, "Carl Hayden: Born a Politician," *Journal of Arizona History*, 130-31; Carl Hayden to Charles Trumbull Hayden, March 29, 1897, HFLC; Hayden, "Sallie Davis Hayden: Thoroughbred Pioneer"; Hayden, "Remarks at Tenth Banquet of the National Reclamation Association," HBF, CHPC, ASU.

17. August, "Carl Hayden: Born a Politician," *Journal of Arizona History*, 130; Howard Pyle, "Carl Hayden: Friend and Neighbor," Speech Delivered at Annual

Meeting of Arizona State University Library Associates, May 2, 1975, Howard Pyle Family Papers.

18. August, "Carl Hayden: Born a Politician," *Journal of Arizona History*, 130-31; The Hayden Family Letters Collection (HFLC) are filled with correspondence describing the many trips taken by Hayden family members.

19. August, "Carl Hayden: Born a Politician," *Journal of Arizona History*, 132, Charles Trumbull Hayden to E.A. Ross, October 9, 1897; Charles Trumbull Hayden to Carl Hayden, September 21, 1897; Hayden, "Sallie Davis Hayden: Thoroughbred Pioneer"; Hayden, "Remarks at Tempe Chamber of Commerce Testimonial Dinner," n.d.; Hayden, "My Horse Bob"; Hayden, "The Initiative and Referendum, An Oration for Commencement Day," HBF, CHPC; Carl Hayden, Student No. 124, The Great Register, Arizona State University Archives, ASU. See also, Ernest Hopkins and Alfred Thomas, Jr., *The Arizona State University Story* (Phoenix: Southwest Publishing Company, 1960), 120.

20. August, "Carl Hayden: Born a Politician, *Journal of Arizona History*, 134-35; Kevin Starr, *Americans and the California Dream, 1850-1915* (New York: Oxford University Press, 1973), 307-44.

21. August, "Carl Hayden: Born a Politician," *Journal of Arizona History*, 135-37; Charles Trumbull Hayden to Carl Hayden, September 17, 21, 1898; Carl Hayden to Charles Trumbull Hayden, March 29, 1897, November 29, 1899, HFLC, ASU.

22. August, "Carl Hayden: Born a Politician," *Journal of Arizona History*, 137; Carl Hayden to Charles Trumbull Hayden, February 14, March 29, 1897, HFLC, ASU.

23. August, "Carl Hayden: Born a Politician," *Journal of Arizona History*, 137-38; Carl Hayden to Charles Trumbull Hayden, September 14, 1896; Carl Hayden to Sallie Davis Hayden, November 10, 1896, January 14, 1897; Roscoe W[illson] to Carl Hayden, April 15, 1899, HFLC, ASU.

24. August, "Carl Hayden: Born a Politician," *Journal of Arizona History*, 138; Carl Hayden to Sallie Davis Hayden, September 6, 13, November 10, 1897; M.E. Millay to Carl Hayden, November, HFLC; Hayden, "Address in Acceptance of the Herbert Hoover Medal," HBF, CHPC, ASU; *Tempe News*, September 25, 1897; *Phoenix Herald*, September 24, 1897.

25. August, "Carl Hayden: Born a Politician," *Journal of Arizona History*, 140-41; M.F. Hood to Carl Hayden, April 30, 1898, HFLC; Hayden, "Remarks by Senator Hayden Following Presentation of VFW Congressional Award"; Hayden, "Address in Acceptance of the Herbert Hoover Medal," HBF, CHPC, ASU.

26. *Tempe News*, June 15, 1900.

27. L.P. Moore to Carl Hayden, September 26, October 2, 1901; A.J. Peters to Hayden, October 23, 1901; W.H. Wilmer to Hayden, November 13, 1901, HFLC, ASU; *Tempe News*, August 16, 1901.

28. Hayden to J.T. Wilson, n.d., HFLC; Hayden to Dorothy Robinson, July 7, 1958, Folder 19, Box 701, CHPC, ASU. Many writers, including Hayden himself during his later years, perpetuated the historical inaccuracy that Hayden first ran for election to the Tempe Town Council in 1902. Charles Trumbull Hayden had also supported the concept of public ownership and operation of municipal water works.

29. Marsha Weiseiger, "History of Tempe," AC, ASU.

30. See William D. Rowley, *Reclaiming the Arid West: The Career of Francis G. Newlands* (Bloomington: Indiana University Press, 1996); For background on reclamation in the Salt River Valley see Karen Smith, *The Magnificent Experiment: Building the Salt River Reclamation Project, 1890-1917* (Tucson: University of Arizona Press, 1986). For the best recent account of the nineteenth century movement toward a federal reclamation program see Donald J. Pisani, *To Reclaim a Divided West: Water, Law, and Public Policy, 1848-1902* (Albuquerque: University of New Mexico Press, 1992).

31. Smith, *Magnificent Experiment*, 37-38. In 1898, south side residents had formed the Old Settlers Protective Association to defend the primacy of their water rights.

32. Hayden to Sallie Davis Hayden, February 2, 1903, HFLC, ASU.

33. Hayden to Sallie Davis Hayden, February 8, 1903; Hayden, "Speech Delivered Before Salt River Valley Water Storage Committee," Holograph Notes, n.d., HFLC, ASU.

34. Hayden to Sallie Davis Hayden, February 24, 1903.

35. Hayden to Sallie Davis Hayden, n.d., HFLC, ASU. Over the next eight years the federal government poured money and manpower into the Tonto Reservoir site, stimulating the local economy. Dedicated on March 18, 1911, the Theodore Roosevelt Dam, a huge masonry block structure, created the largest artificial lake in the world at that time. Ex-president Roosevelt presided over the ceremonies opening what became one of the nation's most successful reclamation projects. Smith, *Magnificent Experiment*, 70-91.

36. Hayden to Sallie Davis Hayden, March 17, 1903, HFLC, ASU.

37. *Tempe News*, April 29, 1904; Hayden to Sallie Davis Hayden, May 4, 1904, HFLC, ASU.

38. *Phoenix Daily Enterprise*, May 24, 1904.

39. Jeff Adams to Hayden, February 4, 1904; C.B. Wood to Hayden, April 29, 1904; Alexander O. Brodie to Hayden, June 29, 1904; Hayden to Sallie Davis Hayden, July 4, 1904, HFLC.

40. *Tempe News*, September 30, November 5, 1905; Hayden, "Speech at Dedication of Bliss Hospital," HBF, CHPC.

41. Hayden, "Speech in Acceptance of the Herbert Hoover Medal," HBF, CHPC; Hayden to Sallie Davis Hayden, HFLC, ASU.

42. Hayden, "Speech for Campaign for Sheriff" (1906), Holograph Notes, HFLC, ASU.

43. *Phoenix Daily Enterprise*, November 11, December 8 and 12, 1906.

44. "Memorial Address and Other Tributes in the Congress of the United States on the Life and Contributions of Carl T. Hayden," *Senate Document* 92-68, 92 Congress, 2 Session (Serial 12980-2), 133-34; "Tributes to Honorable Carl Hayden, Senator from Arizona," *Senate Document* 76, 87 Cong., 2 Sess. (Serial 12448), 8; *Arizona Republican*, April 17, 1907; Hayden, "Speech in Acceptance of the Herbert Hoover Medal," HBF, CHPC. For more on Hayden's tenure as sheriff, see Charles C. Colley, "Carl T. Hayden—Phoenician," *Journal of Arizona History* 18 (Autumn 1977), 247-58.

45. *Arizona Republican*, September 16, 1907; James H. McClintock to Hayden, September 16, 1907; A.M. Tuchill to Hayden, HFLC, ASU.

46. *Arizona Republican*, February 17, 20, 21, 1908.

47. Sallie Davis Hayden to Carl Hayden, November 10, 1903, HFLC, ASU; *Tempe News*, October 30, November 2, 1903; *Arizona Republican*, July 12, 27, 1909. One of Hayden's national guard duties was to lead the Arizona rifle team at annual competitions. In August 1911 Major Hayden led his men to a fifteenth place finish in the overall competition at Camp Perry, Ohio. When the team needed a flag to carry in the opening ceremonies, Nan—who was in attendence—fashioned one, using an emblem that later became the official Arizona state flag. See, *Arizona Gazette*, July 25, 1911; *Arizona Republican*, August 30, 1911; *Arizona Republic*, March 19, 1964.

48. Hayden to Nan Downing Hayden, September 1, 1911, HFLC; Hayden to Larry Hayden, December 4, 1967, Box 501, Folder 15, CHPC; Creasman, "Address to the Tempe Chamber of Commerce"; Hayden, "Address at Reception of the Herbert Hoover Medal"; Hayden, "Remarks Following Presentation of VFW Congressional Award"; Hayden, "Speech at Dedication of Bliss Hospital," all in HBF, ASU. In 1910, during the 61st Congress, 2nd Session, four bills were intro-

duced pertaining to statehood for New Mexico and Arizona, but only one received action. The bill, H.R. 18166, passed the House of Representatives on January 17, 1910; it was then referred to the Senate Committee on Territories and debated in the Senate on June 16, 1910 (45 C.R. 8237). The House then concurred with the Senate amendments, and the bill was signed into law on June 20, 1910 (Public Law 219, 61st Congress). This Act (36 Stat. 557) was the Enabling Act that admitted Arizona and New Mexico into the Union as separate states.

II—A MAN OF STERLING CHARACTER

1. Hayden to Larry Hayden, December 4, 1967, Box 501, Folder 15; Hayden, "Address in Acceptance of the Herbert Hoover Medal," HBF, both in CHPC; "Memorial Address," *Senate Document 92-68*, 14; *Arizona Republican*, May 1, 1911; *Jerome News*, October 21, 1911. Arizona's labor vote proved so formidable that in the 1912 presidential election, incumbent Taft finished fourth behind Democrat Woodrow Wilson, Progressive Theodore Roosevelt, and Socialist Eugene V. Debs.

2. Hayden to Nan Downing Hayden, August 31, 1911, HFLC; Hayden to Larry Hayden, December 4, 1967, Box 501, Folder 15, CHPC; *Arizona Republican*, October 11, 1911.

3. August, "A Sterling Young Democrat," *Journal of Arizona History*, 232.

4. Hayden, "To the Water Users of Yuma Valley," and "To the Members of the Salt River Valley Water Users Association," both in Box 502, Folder 3, CHPC; Hayden, "Address in Acceptance of the Herbert Hoover Medal," HBF, ASU.

5. Hayden, "To the Water Users of Yuma Valley," Box 502, Folder 3, CHPC; *Coconino Sun* (Flagstaff), November 10, 1911.

6. Hayden, "To the Water Users of Yuma Valley," Box 502, Folder 3, CHPC.

7. *Coconino Sun* (Flagstaff), November 10, 1911.

8. August, "A Sterling Young Democrat," *Journal of Arizona History*, 234; *Globe Silver Belt*, February 10, 1911.

9. Hayden, Holograph Notes, n.d., Box 501, Folder 15, CHPC; *Globe Silver Belt*, February 10, 1911.

10. Hayden to Nan Downing Hayden, September 1, 1911, HFLC; Hayden, Holograph Notes, n.d., Box 501, Folder 15, CHPC; "West Magazine," *Los Angeles Times*, January 5, 1969, 34-35. The best study of the impact of the labor movement on Arizona politics, 1900-1920, is James W. Byrkit, *Forging the Copper Collar: Arizona's Labor-Management War of 1901-1921* (Tucson: University of Arizona Press, 1982).

11. Willson to Hayden, February 21, 1961; Hayden to Willson, February 27, 1961, Box 701, Folder 19; Hayden to Larry Hayden, December 4, 1967, Box 501, Folder 15, CHPC; *Coconino Sun*, November 10, 1911; *Arizona Republican*, October 31, 1911; *Arizona Blade Tribune* (Florence), December 9, 1911. Hayden's caution may be attributed to his narrow defeat at Stanford.

12. Willson to Hayden, February 21, 1961; Hayden to Willson, February 27, 1961, Box 701, Folder 19, CHPC; *Globe Silver Belt*, November 11, 1911.

13. Hayden to Sam Jennings, May 7, 1964, Box 701, Folder 16; Sam Jennings, "The Story of the Clans," unpublished manuscript, HBF, both in CHPC; Hayden to David Brinegar, June 5, 1961, Folder 5, Carl Hayden Letters (CHL), Arizona Historical Society, Tucson; *Arizona Daily Star*, June 29, 1961.

14. Helen Harter and Ophelia Celaya interview with Carl Hayden, February 17, 1970, HBF, CHPC; *Tempe Daily News*, June 30, 1976.

15. *La Voz Del Pueblo* (Phoenix), November 8, 1911; *La Democracia* (Tucson), November 5, 1911; *Douglas Industrial Semenario Democrata*, October 8, 1911.

16. *Tempe News*, December 9, 1911.

17. E.W. Chapin, the Prohibitionist candidate, received 88 votes. *Denver Times* (Colorado), January 12, 1912; *Tombstone Daily Prospector*, January 5, 1912; *Arizona Democrat* (Phoenix), January 3, 1912; *Arizona Republican*, December 13, 14, 1912.

18. Hayden to David Brinegar, June 5, 1964, Folder 5, CHL; Hayden to Willson, January 27, 1961, Box 701, Folder 16, CHPC.

19. Hayden to Willson, January 27, 1961, Box 701, Folder 16, CHPC; *Arizona Republic*, November 1, 1961. In an article written by old acquaintance and *Republic* reporter Ben Avery, Hayden had met the writer's mother. She thanked Hayden for the periodic mailing of seeds from the U.S. Department of Agriculture that kept their dry farm producing Kentucky wonder beans and beefsteak tomatoes.

20. Joe Frantz interview with Carl Hayden, LBJ Library; *Phoenix Gazette*, October 28, 1957.

21. Because Article XVII, which amended the U.S. Constitution and established the procedure of direct election of senators, did not pass until 1913, and since the Arizona legislature could not convene until after statehood to elect two senators, Hayden was the lone representative from the new state for some time. "Tributes to the Honorable Carl Hayden," *Senate Document* 76, 36, 76.

III—THE INDIAN CARD

1. Udall, "Congressman's Report," 2; William E. Leuctenburg, *The Perils of Prosperity: 1914-1932* (Chicago: University of Chicago Press, 1958), 43.

2. Gene M. Gressley, "Arthur Powell Davis, Reclamation, and the West," *Agricultural History* 42 (July 1968), 246, 256; Paul W. Gates, *History of Public Land Law Development* (Washington D.C.: Zenger Publishing Company, 1968), 662; Carl Hayden to Otis T. Baughn, January 8, 1924, Box 624, Folder 4; E.C. LaRue to Carl Hayden, March 16, 1916, Box 513, Folder 15, CHPC, ASU.

3. *Arizona Blade Tribune* (Florence), November 30, 1912; Hayden, "Speech on my Eightieth Birthday," HBF, CHPC, ASU; Frantz interview with Hayden, LBJ library. Hayden received 11,830 votes, Thomas Campbell (R) won 3,152 votes, and "Bull" Fisher (Soc.) garnered 4,799.

4. Gressley, "Arthur Powell Davis, Reclamation, and the West," *Agricultural History*, 256; *Yuma Examiner*, November 10, 1914; *Arizona Republican*, November 29, 1914. See also Box 606, Folder 1, CHPC, ASU.

5. The interest charge amendment to the Reclamation Extension Act was defeated 140-81. Gates, *History of Public Land Law Development*, 669-70; Hayden, "Speech to the Salt River Valley Water Users Association," November 2, 1914, Phoenix, Arizona, Box 606, Folder 1, Hayden; "To the Water Users of Arizona Reclamation Projects," August 27, 1914, Box 642, Folder 20, CHPC, ASU.

6. The Underwood Amendment carried 178-49. Hayden explained that the amendment passed because it was proven that the Reclamation Service failed to complete projects promptly and that the service habitually underestimated the cost on all projects. See also Gates, *History of Public Land Law Development*, 670; Hayden, "Speech to the Salt River Valley Water Users Association," November 2, 1914, Box 606, Folder 1; John Orme to Hayden, July 30, 1914, Box 606, Folder 2, CHPC, ASU; *Congressional Record*, 63 Cong., 2 Sess. (1914), 12243.

7. *Congressional Record*, 63 Cong., 2 Sess. (1914), 13453-454; Gates, *History of Public Land Law Development*, 671-73.

8. L.B. Hitchcock to Hayden, September 18, 1914, Box 606, Folder 1, Hayden to John Orme, June 11, 1914, Box 606, Folder 2, CHPC, ASU.

9. In return for local control, the Salt River Valley Water Users Association agreed to repay the cost of construction in twenty installments. The debt was repaid in 1955. For brief general accounts of the shift from federal to local control see George L. Knapp, "Uncle Reuben Becomes a Power Magnet: Senator Carl Hayden Rates the Remarkable Achievements of the Farmers of the Salt River

Valley," *Railway Conductor* 45 (August 1928), 362; George Wharton James, "In the Egypt of America: The Salt River Project," *Twentieth Century Magazine* 4 (April 1911), 1-11; Hal R. Moore, "The Salt River Project—Beehive of Prosperity," unpublished manuscript, 1951, AC, ASU.

10. Franklin K. Lane to Hayden, December 9, 1916, Box 628, Folder 2; Hayden to John Orme, June 17, 1917, Box 628, Folder 2; Hayden to A.W. Ayers, October 12, 1917, Box 628, Folder 2, CHPC, ASU.

11. *Coolidge News*, souvenir edition, November 1, 1930; Carl Hayden, Holograph Notes, Box 597, Folder 1; Hayden to Frederick Newell, Box 597, Folder 2, CHPC, ASU.

12. Gressley, "Arthur Powell Davis, Reclamation and the West," *Agricultural History*, 246, 256; Paul W. Gates, *History of Public Land Law Development* (Washington, D.C.: Zenger Publishing Company, 1968), 62; Hayden to Otis Baughn, January 8, 1924, Box 624, Folder 4; E.C. LaRue to Hayden, March 16, 1916, No. 513, Folder 7, CHPC, ASU.

13. Juliet Day, "A Dam for Arizona's Indians," *Arizona Highways* 6 (July 1930), 7; Frank May, "Coolidge Dam Dedicated by former President to Irrigate Lands in Florence-Casa Grande Valley," ibid., 6 (July 1930), 11-12.

14. An account of the rivalry between the Salt River Valley and the Gila River Valley is in Karen Smith, "The Campaign for Water in Central Arizona," *Arizona and the West* 23 (Summer 1981), 127-48.

15. By the middle of the decade, construction of the Yuma Project on the lower Colorado was well underway. J.C. Dobbins to Hayden, November 24, 1919, CHPC, ASU.

16. Carl Hayden, "Speech on My Eightieth Birthday," in HBF, ASU; Carl Hayden, "Washington Conversation," CBS Television Transcript, February 18, 1962, reprinted in *Senate Document, 76*, 10.

17. Carl Hayden, Holograph Notes, Box 597, Folder 1, Hayden to Newell, August 16, 1912, Box 597, Folder 2, CHPC, ASU.

18. *House Document 521*, 61-65; Newell to Hayden, August 30, 1912, Box 613, Folder 6, CHPC, ASU; *Casa Grande Dispatch*, Twentieth Anniversary Issue, May 1, 1932.

19. *House Document 791*, 63 Congress, 2 Session (1913), 54-56; Hayden to Elmer Coker, March 17, 1914; T.R. Peart to Hayden, February 25, 1914; J.F. Brown to L.B. Wood, March 14, 1914, Box 613, Folder 8; A.P. Davis to Franklin K. Lane, n.d., Box 613, Folder 10, CHPC.

20. Hayden informed Graham County leaders, "I was of the opinion that I could serve the people of Graham County best by keeping them out of court." Newell to Hayden, March 14, 1914; Phil C. Merrill to Hayden, March 25, 1914, Box 613, Folder 10, CHPC; *Arizona Blade Tribune* (Florence), April 8, 1916; *Graham County Guardian* (Safford), February 27, 1914.

21. As late as 1919, A.P. Davis believed the technology necessary to complete the San Carlos Project was "too experimental." Hayden to E.P. Connell, March 30, 1914, Box 613, Folder 5, CHPC, ASU.

22. Hayden to Z.C. Prina, March 20, 1914, Box 613, Folder 1, J.F. Treat to Hayden, May 14, 1916; John F. Truesdell, "Memorandum on the Report of the Board of Army Engineers on the San Carlos Irrigation Project, Arizona, and Comments on Bill H.R. 17106 Introduced to Authorize the Project," August 7, 1916, Box 613, Folder 6, CHPC; *Casa Grande Dispatch*, October 19, 1915. Significantly, neither the Reclamation Service nor the rival Army Corps of Engineers was drawn directly into the legislative fray.

23. Hayden, "Speech at San Carlos Day," October 23, 1923, Box 597, Folder 1, CHPC. In the late stages of the legislative process, Hayden wrote and presented to Congress a ninety-one page report titled "The Pima Indians and the San Carlos Irrigation Project." The capstone of his argument, it proved to be one of the most celebrated aspects of the San Carlos Project legislation. The purpose of the report, Hayden informed historian and project consultant, Herbert Eugene Bolton, "was to prove that the Pimas had always been friends of the white people, and that they had an adequate water supply for irrigation of their lands until the Americans came to Arizona." The document also concluded that overgrazing on the Gila River watershed had denuded the terrain, further contributing to water problems. Originally issued to the House Indian Affairs Committee in April 1924, the House and Senate reprinted it in 1965 for its "historical value." Hayden, "The Pima Indians and the San Carlos Irrigation Project," Box 621, Folder 13; Hayden to Herbert Eugene Bolton, April 3, 1924, Box 621, Folder 19; Hayden, "Statement Upon Passage of the San Carlos Project Bill," Box 609, Folder 18, all in ibid.; *Arizona Republic*, May 16, 1965.

24. W.F. Haygood to Hayden, January 23, 1920, Box 613, Folder 2; Hayden to Haygood, February 20, 1920, Box 613, Folder 3; "An Appeal for the Pimas," n.d., Box 609, Folder 18, CHPC. Presbyterian and Catholic churches on the reservation lobbied especially hard for the bill.

25. Hayden, "Speech at San Carlos Day," October 23, 1923, Box 597, Folder 1, ibid.; *Arizona Daily Star*, May 2, 1924; *Arizona Gazette* (Phoenix), May 1, 1924.

26. Hayden to Frank Stewart, April 28, 1924; Charles Burke to Hayden, July 1, 1924, Box 609, Folder 22, CHPC; May, "Coolidge Dam Dedicated," *Arizona Highways*, 11-14.

27. *For Greater Arizona: A Clipping Sheet of University of Arizona News*, August 14, 1919; *Arizona Citizen* (Tucson), May 15, 1924; *Arizona Republican*, October 24, 1923. Hayden attended most annual San Carlos Day celebrations prior to passage of the bill.

28. P.G. Spilsbury to Hayden, December 6, 1924, Box 604, Folder 19, CHPC. An AIC report analyzing transportation and marketing conditions on the proposed project struck a favorable chord with Secretary of Commerce Herbert Hoover. Hoover informed Hayden that he thought the AIC was "the best source of information in the state" and "that the Indians and white farmers can dispose of their crops to advantage thereby insuring success of the project." The commerce secretary pointed out that the Salt River Project "demonstrates what can be done on the adjacent Gila River, and I therefore hope that Congress will authorize construction of San Carlos Dam." Hoover's recommendation helped gain bipartisan support for congressional action on the San Carlos Project. Herbert Hoover to Hayden, May 9, 1924, Box 609, Folder 18, ibid.

29. Hayden to Frank A. Thackery, January 20, 1916, Box 624, Folder 4; Vice-President of Western Wholesale to Charles H. Randall, n.d., Box 624, Folder 5; Thomas Marshall to Hayden, n.d., Box 613, Folder 10; Sam Rayburn to Hayden, January 21, 1921, Box 619, Folder 5, ibid.

30. *Casa Grande Dispatch*, October 25, 1915, May 1, 1932; Hayden to Ruth Bentley, September 13, 1918, Box 624, Folder 5, CHPC.

31. Hayden to Elmer Coker, February 4, 1916, Box 608, Folder 4; Hayden to R.A. Ward, May 17, 1916, Box 608, Folder 5; Hayden to F.B. Slagle, March 4, 1922, Box 608, Folder 7; "Pinal County Gives True History of the San Carlos Project, unpublished manuscript, n.d., Box 597, folder 2; CHPC; Clara T. Woody, "The San Carlos Irrigation Project-Pima Indian Irrigation," unpublished manuscript, AC, ASU; Day, "A Dam for Arizona's Indians," *Arizona Highways*, 7.

32. *Arizona Republican*, May 10, 1922; *Arizona Blade Tribune*, May 9, 1922; Hayden to Otis T. Baughn, n.d., Box 608, Folder 4, CHPC; Hayden to Elmer Coker, February 4, 1916, Box 624, Folder 4, CHPC. The Indian Weir Dam was a floating slab of concrete 396 feet long, 212 feet wide, and 265 feet thick.

33. "Pinal County Gives True History," Box 597, Folder 2; Hayden to O.W. Breustadt, September 28, 1923, Box 609, Folder 19; Hayden to Baughn, n.d., Box 608, Folder 4, CHPC, ASU; *Arizona Blade Tribune*, May 9, 10, 11, 1922; *Arizona*

Republican, October 24, 1923. Many Arizonans expected that President Harding would deliver an address "either written or reproduced by talking machine."

34. "Pinal County Gives True History," Box 597, Folder 2, CHPC; *Arizona Blade Tribune*, January 21, 1921.

35. Gates, *History of Public Land Law Development*, 675; Blaine Lamb, "A Many Checkered Toga: Arizona Senator Ralph Cameron, 1921-1927," *Arizona and the West* 19 (Spring 1977), 47-64.

36. Hayden, Holograph Notes, n.d., Box 597, Folder 1; "Pinal County Gives True History," Box 597, Folder 2; Louis Cramton to Hayden, April 15, 1922, Box 624, Folder 5, CHPC, ASU.

37. Hayden to J.B. Cook, January 3, 1917, Box 624, Folder 5; "Pinal County Gives True History," Box 597, Folder 2; Phil Swing to Hayden, January 21, 1921, Box 619, Folder 8, CHPC, ASU.

38. *Arizona Daily Star*, May 2, 1924; *Arizona Guardian* (Safford), June 13, 1924; *Arizona Republican*, May 2,3, 1924; Hayden, Holograph Notes, n.d., Box 609, Folder 18, CHPC.

39. *Arizona Republican*, December 12, 1923; *Phoenix Gazette*, May 1, 1924; *Tucson Citizen*, May 15, 1924.

40. *Arizona Blade Tribune*, July 27, 1912; *Nogales Daily Herald*, February 14, 1912; *Tombstone Prospector*, November 17, 1916; *Arizona Gazette*, November 1, 1918. See also Box 501, Folder 15 and Box 639, Folders 10, 14, 16, CHPC.

41. County election figures are in Box 639, Folder 4, CHPC.

42. Hayden to Sydney Sligh, May 26, 1924, Box 609, Folder 18, CHPC; *Arizona Republican*, May 2, 1924.

43. *Arizona Republican*, May 2, 1924; Hayden, Holograph Notes, n.d., Box 609, folder 18, CHPC.

44. *Arizona Republican*, June 5, 1924; "Pinal County Gives True History," Box 597, Folder 2, CHPC. Significantly, the Senate accepted the House version without change. The bill, as finally approved, was in the form that Hayden wrote it.

45. See James R. Kluger, *Turning on Water with a Shovel: The Career of Elwood Mead* (Albuquerque: University of New Mexico Press, 1992), passim; Paul Conkin, "The Vision of Elwood Mead," *Agricultural History* 34 (April 1960), 88-97; Hayden to A.T. Kilcrease, March 5, April 4, 1924, Box 609, Folder 21, CHPC. Another important amendment to the bill stipulated that construction charges for land under private ownership would be amortized at a reasonable five percent per annum.

46. Hayden, Holograph Notes, n.d., Box 609, folder 18, CHPC; "Pinal County Gives True History," Box 597, Folder 2, CHPC; "A Message from Carl Hayden," *Arizona Republican*, May 2, 1924.

47. *Arizona Republican*, June 5, 1924; Carlos Ronstadt to Hayden, June 10, 1924, Box 618, Folder 15, CHPC.

48. Oren Arnold, "America's Silent Senator," unpublished manuscript, 1958, AC; Hayden to P.G. Spilsbury, December 6, 1924 Box 604, Folder 19, CHPC; *Arizona Daily Star*, December 4, 1924.

49. See Smith, *Magnificent Experiment*; Jack L. August, Jr., *From Horseback to Helicopter: A History of Forest Management on the San Carlos Apache Reservation* (Mesa, Arizona: American Indian Resource Organization, 1985); Day, "A Dam for Arizona's Indians," *Arizona Highways*, 7; *Coolidge News*, November 1, 1930; C.R. Oldberg to Hayden, April 22, 1922, Box 608, Folder 4, CHPC. Nevada Consolidated Copper Company paid $155,000 in fiscal 1930 for electricity generated at the Coolidge Dam powerhouse.

50. *Arizona Republic*, March 5, 1930; *Phoenix Gazette*, April 17, 1979; *Arizona Daily Star*, March 5, 1930.

51. *Arizona Republic*, March 5, 1930; "Pinal County Gives True History," Box 597, Folder 2, CHPC; Beverly Moeller, *Phil Swing and Boulder Dam* (Berkeley: University of California Press, 1971), 90-91.

52. See Norris Hundley, Jr., *Water and the West: The Colorado River Compact and the Politics of Water in the American West* (Berkeley: University of California Press, 1975); Norris Hundley, Jr., "Clio Nods: *Arizona v California* and the Boulder Canyon Act—A Reassessment," *Western Historical Quarterly* 3 (January 1972), 17-51; *Arizona v. California et. al.*, 373 U.S. 546 (1963); Jack L. August, Jr., interview with Judge Simon Rifkind, October 9, 1986, author's files.

IV—ORIGINS OF THE COLORADO RIVER CONTROVERSY IN THE SOUTHWEST

1. For Hayden's earliest bill calling for Colorado River flood control see, H.R. 9421, *Congressional Record*, 66 Cong., 1 Sess. (1919), 22, 24, 309. Arizona, with Central Arizona Project water to augment existing supplies of surface and groundwater, anticipates a continued high rate of growth into the twenty-first century. See Paul Bracken and Herman Kahn's controversial treatise, *Arizona Tomorrow: A Precursor of Post-industrial America* (Croton-on-Hudson: The Hudson Institute, 1979), 14-61, 78-108; Carl Hayden, "Arizona Report," CHL, AHS, Tucson, Arizona.

2. *Arizona Daily Star*, December 24, 1927.

3. Committee on Water of the National Research Council, *Water and Choice in the Colorado River Basin* (Washington, D.C.: National Academy of Science Publications No. 1689, 1968), 1-47; Hundley, *Water and the West*, xiv-xvi; Norris Hundley, Jr., "The Colorado Waters Dispute," *Foreign Affairs* 42 (April 1964), 495; Moeller, *Phil Swing and Boulder Dam*, x-xi; Philip Fradkin, *A River No More: The Colorado River and the West* (New York: Alfred A. Knopf, 1981), 15.

4. An account of the Colorado's silt-carrying capacities appears in Hundley, "The Politics of Reclamation," *California Historical Quarterly*, 229; For a more extensive analysis of the Colorado and silt, see U.S. Department of Agriculture, "Silt in the Colorado and its Relation to Irrigation," *Technical Bulletin No. 67* (Washington, D.C.: 1928), copy available in CHPC, ASU.

5. John Wesley Powell, "Report on the Lands of the Arid Region of the United States," *House Executive Document 73*, 45 Congress, 2 Session (1878); John Wesley Powell, "Reservoirs in Arid Regions of the United States," *Senate Book of Arizona* (San Francisco: Payot, Upham and Company, 1878), 66; Hiram Chittenden, "Preliminary Examination of Reservoir Sites in Wyoming and Colorado," *House Document 141*, 55 Cong., 2 Sess. (1897), 58; Hundley, "Politics of Reclamation," *California Historical Quarterly*, 294.

6. Hundley, "Politics of Reclamation," *California Historical Quarterly*, 299-300; Hundley, *Water and the West*, 53; Barbara Ann Metcalf, "Oliver Wozencraft in California" (M.A. Thesis: University of Southern California, 1963), 81-96; *Weekly Arizona Miner* (Prescott), June 13, 1879; *Arizona Citizen* (Tucson), June 13, 1879.

7. See especially Hundley, *Water and the West*, chapters 1 and 2; Hundley, "The Politics of Reclamation," *California Historical Quarterly*, 301-06.

8. Hundley, *Water and the West*, 17-21.

9. Hundley, "Politics of Reclamation," *California Historical Quarterly*, 297-301; Arthur Powell Davis to J.B. Lippencott, October 10, 1902, Bureau of Reclamation Papers, File 187, Colorado River Project, 1902-1919, Record Group 115, National Archives and Records Service (NARS); U.S. Geological Survey, *First Annual Report of the Reclamation Service, 1902* (Washington, D.C., 1903), 106-07, 109; U.S. Department of the Interior, *Fourteenth Annual Report of the Reclamation Service, 1914-1915* (Washington, D.C., 1915), 323; House Committee on Irrigation of Arid Lands, "Hearings on All-American Canal in Imperial Valley, California, H.R. 6044," 66 Cong., 1 Sess. (1919), 98-99. For the best short essay on Arthur Powell Davis see Gene Gressley, "Arthur Powell Davis, Reclamation and the West," *Agricultural History* 42 (July 1968), 241-57.

10. Hundley, *Water and the West*, 53-82; *San Diego Union*, January 20, 1918; Rufus B. von Klein Smid, "The League of the Southwest: What It Is and Why," *Arizona: The State Magazine* 11 (May 1920). Additional support for reclamation on the Colorado came from a group meeting in Salt Lake City, Utah. The Soldiers, Sailors, and Marines Land Settlement Conference added an extra dimension when it endorsed an interior department proposal to reclaim several million acres in the West for veterans of World War I.

11. For the best account of Phil Swing's activities in the IID before his election to Congress from California's 11th District see Moeller, *Phil Swing and Boulder Dam*, 3-19. Also see Hundley, *Water and the West*, 38-39.

12. For the early bills submitted by Hayden, Kettner, and Randall, see *Congressional Record*, 65 Cong., 3 Sess. (1919), 2647, 2934, 3738; 66 Cong., 1 Sess. (1919), 22, 24, 1258. See also House Committee on Irrigation of Arid Lands, "Hearings on All-American Canal in Imperial Valley, California, H.R. 6044" (1919), 7-8, 48-51, 94, 142, 285-87.

13. Hayden to Epes Randolph, August 14, 1919; Randolph to Hayden, September 2, 1919, Box 600, Folder 6; B.F. Fly to Hayden, October 1, 18, 1919; Hayden to Fly, October 10, 1919, Box 600, Folder 5, CHPC, ASU.

14. Hayden to Fly, September 26, 1919, Box 600, Folder 5, CHPC, ASU.

15. *Mohave County Miner* (Kingman), December 1, 1894, January 12, 19, and February 12, 1895; Hundley, *Water and the West*, 14.

16. House Committee on Irrigation of Arid Lands, "Hearings on All-American Canal in Imperial Valley, California, H.R. 6044," 37, 40, 42, 48, 262, 264; James R. Kluger, "Elwood Mead: Irrigation Engineer and Social Planner" (Ph.D. dissertation, University of Arizona, 1970); Hayden to Fly, October 10, 1919, Box 600, Folder 5, CHPC, ASU.

17. *Congressional Record*, 66 Cong., 2 Sess. (1920), 7360; Hundley, *Water and the West*, 51. Kettner relied heavily on Hayden and Phil Swing to draft the added provisions to this 1920 bill. See Hayden to Fly, September 26, 1919, Box 600, Folder 6, CHPC, ASU.

18. *Tombstone Epitaph*, June 8, 1922. Certainly, by the early 1920s, basin-wide sentiment toward California could be summed up as the *Tombstone Epitaph's* editor put it: "California was in the game to hog it all."

19. Quotes included in Hundley, *Water and the West*, 96-98, 104.

20. *Wyoming v Colorado*, 259, U.S. 419 (1922); Hundley, *Water and the West*, 76, 78, 105, 106. Carpenter's role in subsequent Colorado River affairs was especially

noteworthy. Although he called for federal cooperation in river development, he shared the long-cherished, jealously guarded position many westerners held concerning the supremacy of state's rights. The Coloradan vigorously resisted the claim, argued in the *Wyoming v. Colorado* case, that the U.S. government owned all the unappropriated waters in unnavigable streams in the West. "There should be no super-government imposition established," he wrote Hayden during this period. Carpenter, like many of his contemporaries, saw the federal government as an arbiter, not a dictator, of Colorado River affairs.

21. Moeller, *Phil Swing and Boulder Dam*, 29; Hundley, *Water and the West*, 105, 110, 111. According to Moeller, Hoover's appointment came after Phil Swing protested the rumored appointment of "a Denver man," doubtlessly Delph Carpenter. Secretary Albert Fall, according to Moeller, persuaded President Harding to appoint Hoover.

22. *Senate Document 142*, appendix, "Problems of Imperial Valley and Vicinity," 67 Cong., 2 Sess. (1922), 238, 239; Hundley, *Water and the West*, 119-34; Moeller, *Phil Swing and Boulder Dam*, 21, 24, 25.

23. Moeller, *Phil Swing and Boulder Dam*, 21, 24, 25; Hundley, *Water and the West*, 110-13, 128.

24. Hayden to Thomas Campbell, May 14, 1921, Box 597, Folder 13, CHPC, ASU; Hundley, *Water and the West*, 121, 124, 134, House Committee on Irrigation of Arid Lands, "Hearings on Protection and Development of Lower Colorado River Basin, H.R. 11449," 67 Cong., 2 Sess. (1922), 26, 34. In June 1922, Hayden reported on preliminary discussions of the highline canal plan to the House Irrigation Committee. Also, on the eve of Colorado River Compact negotiations, Richard Sloan, former territorial governor and supreme court judge, summed up Arizona's stance on hydroelectric power. As one of Governor Campbell's representatives to the public hearings in San Diego, Sloan announced that Arizona was committed to any policy or program that met with the approval of the secretary of interior. Arizona wanted safeguards, however, that protected its "preferential right" to use power when needed, as well as authority to tax those using energy from a power-generating dam located wholly or partly within the state of Arizona. Like the upper states, Arizona favored development, yet at the same time sought protection from California. See Eleanor Sloan interview with Jack L. August, Jr., June 27, 1984, OHC, AC, ASU.

25. Hayden to W.S. Norviel, August 28, 1922, Box 598, Folder 7; Hayden to Ottamar Hamele, January 29, 1923, Box 598, Folder 9; Hayden to G.E.P. Smith, February 17, 1923, Box 598, Folder 19, CHPC, ASU.

26. *Tombstone Prospector,* March 15, April 9, 1922; *Arizona Republican*, September 10, 1922; Hayden to Norviel, August 28, 1922, Box 598, Folder 7, CHPC, ASU. See also Hundley, *Water and the West*, chapters 6 and 7; Moeller, *Phil Swing and Boulder Dam*, 33-34.

27. William S. Norviel to Hayden, May 1, October 5, 1922, Box 612, Folder 7, CHPC, ASU; Jack L. August, Jr., "Carl Hayden, Arizona, and the Politics of Water Development in the Southwest, 1923-1928," *Pacific Historical Review* 58 (May 1989), 195, 196; *House Doc*. 605, 67 Cong., 4 Sess. (1923), 8-12. A major influence that not only paved the way for a seven-state agreement, but also the two basin concept was the *Wyoming v. Colorado* Supreme Court decision rendered January 5, 1922. The Court reaffirmed the rule of priority over streams shared by states that adhered to the doctrine of prior appropriation. Thus water users in California, who had a head start on their upstream neighbors, gained first right to the water. In deciding the *Wyoming v. Colorado* case, the Supreme Court allowed the application of the priority rule on interstate streams, even if the water was transferred out of the basin for use. The decision favored fast-growing California and placed that state in a strong legal position to gain prior rights to Colorado River water. Therefore, upper-basin representatives felt "badly exposed" and believed they had to get a compact at the Santa Fe meetings.

28. August, "Carl Hayden and the Politics of Water," *Pacific Historical Review*, 197; Hundley, *Water and the West*, 142, 149, 200-03, 339; Norviel to Hayden, February 26, 1926, Box 598, Folder 7, CHPC, ASU.

29. Hayden to G.E.P. Smith, February 17, 1923, Box 598, Folder 10, CHPC, ASU; *House Doc*. 605, 8-12; Hundley, *Water and the West*, 196, 340.

30. Hayden to F.T. Pomeroy, December 22, 1924, Box 600, Folder 9, CHPC, ASU; House Committee on Irrigation of Arid Lands, "Hearings on Protection and Development of Lower Colorado River Basin, H.R. 11449," 67 Cong., 2 Sess. (1922), 18-19; *Arizona Republican*, November 25, 1922; Hundley, "Colorado Waters Dispute," *Foreign Affairs*, 195-200; Hundley, *Water and the West*, 177, 203.

31. Ottamar Hamale to Hayden, January 29, 1923, Box 598, Folder 9, CHPC, ASU; *Reno Journal* (Reno, Nevada), June 9, 1923; *Arizona Republican*, November 25, 1922. See also Hundley, "Clio Nods," *Western Historical Quarterly*, passim; Hundley, *Water and the West*, 212, 214.

32. Governor Campbell fulminated against California, "The Swing-Johnson bill has been drawn up to furnish Los Angeles with the power she needs as the seventh largest manufacturing center in the United States." Campbell advocated the Smith-McNary bill, which would authorize reclamation work in sixteen states. "In

the old days," Campbell noted, "a man needed to be quick on the draw in Arizona.... Today we must be quick on the draw against California." Norviel to Hayden, May 11, 1922, Box 598, Folder 7; Hayden to Phil Swing, Box 598, Folder 10; Bisbee Chamber of Commerce to Albert Fall, January 22, 1922, Box 611, Folder 2, CHPC, ASU; Moeller, *Phil Swing and Boulder Dam*, 30-35; House Committee on Irrigation of Arid Lands, "Hearings on ... H.R. 11449," passim; Hundley, *Water and the West*, chapter 7; *Tombstone Prospector*, June 23, 24, July 29, 1922; *Arizona Republican*, June 7, 10, 1922.

33. Typical of Hayden's statements concerning the Girand Project was a statement he made to the Phoenix Chamber of Commerce in May 1923: "In view of the protests now on file with the Federal Power Commission from the states of the Upper Basin against the issuance of any license for power development on the Colorado River until their rights are safeguarded.... I can see no other solution of the problem than there must be an agreement among the seven states of the Colorado River Basin." *Tombstone Epitaph*, May 20, 1923; *Tombstone Prospector*, August 9, 1922; P.G. Spilsbury to Hayden, July 6, 1922, Box 598, Folder 10; O.C. Merrill, "Power Development on the Colorado River and Its Relation to Irrigation and Flood Control," April 11, 1922, Box 598, Folder 11, CHPC, ASU; House Committee on Irrigation of Arid Lands, "Hearings on Protection and Development of Lower Colorado River Basin, H.R. 11449," 67 Cong., 2 Sess., passim.

34. House Committee on Irrigation of Arid Lands, "Hearings on ... H.R. 11449," 26-28.

35. House Committee on Irrigation of Arid Lands, "Hearings on ... H.R. 11449," 26; E.C. LaRue to Hayden, May 15, 1923, Box 598, Folder 10; LaRue to Hayden, "confidential," May 15, 1923, Box 598, Folder 2; Hayden to Mulford Winsor, February 12, 1923, Box 598, folder 12, in CHPC, ASU. LaRue, who felt ignored by Reclamation Director Davis, supported development of the Glen Canyon site. In May 1923 he urged Hayden to induce President Harding to visit Glen Canyon on his trip through the West. "If you will take him up on the plateau so he can look into the Glen Canyon and obtain a view of the plateau region, he can not help but recognize that there are possibilities for development at that point which should receive serious attention by government engineers." "Would it be possible," LaRue asked the Arizona congressman, "for you, Governor Hunt, ex-Governor Campbell, and Dwight Heard to get together and arrange a trip to Glen Canyon?"

36. In a short time the Salt River Valley Water Users Association would come out against Boulder Dam power because the association saw it as competing with its own development in central Arizona. House Committee on Arid Lands, "Hearings on ... H.R. 11449," 26-27.

37. Editorial, "Cheap Power Will Rebuild Cities: Tombstone Case In Point," *Arizona Daily Star*, August 19, 1922.

38. House Committee on Arid Lands, "Hearings on ... H.R. 11449," 34; *The Highline Book* (Phoenix: The Arizona Highline Reclamation Association, 1923), passim. Even before Hayden outlined the program to the committee, Arthur Powell Davis believed an Arizona Highline Canal was not within the realm of possibility. "Obviously," the reclamation director wrote Hayden, "this plan would be prohibitive in cost, both for construction and for maintenance after built." See Davis to Hayden, May 23, 1922, Box 598, Folder 9, CHPC.

39. August, "Hayden and the Politics of Water," *Pacific Historical Review*, 197; E.C. LaRue to Hayden, February 20, 1923, Box 598, Folder 4; Hayden to Kean St. Charles, January 11, February 7, 1923, Box 598, Folder 10; Ottamar Hamale to Hayden, January 27, 1923, Box 598, Folder 9; Hayden to LaRue, February 12, 1923, Box 598, Folder 3: Hayden to Albert Leyhe, February 20, 1923, Box 598, Folder 3; Hayden to W.C. Wyatt, May 21, 1923, Box 598, Folder 2, CHPC, ASU; *Congressional Record*, 67 Cong., 4 Sess. (1923), 2710-717. In February 1923 Hayden received an unsolicited opinion from reclamation service engineer E.C. LaRue. The seven-page missive delineated critical problems with the pact, yet LaRue, in the end, gave the agreement his lukewarm endorsement. "I have made this statement," LaRue wrote Hayden, "inasmuch as the seven states have agreed to something I suppose the Compact should be ratified. In making that statement, it was necessary for me to swallow a big lump. If you want to know my honest opinion of the Compact I can give it to you in one word—Rotten. The terms can never be enforced in actual practice."

40. Dwight Heard, a staunch supporter of ex-Governor Campbell, ran numerous articles and editorials urging the Arizona state legislature to ratify the pact as quickly as possible. "The federal government," he accurately predicted, "is going to establish flood control on the Colorado." That is going to be done, "Compact or no Compact." "And without a Compact," he continued, "we have reason to believe that it will be done with scant regard to the interests of Arizona in the waters of the Colorado, either for irrigation or power." See *Arizona Republican*, September 28, 1922, January 30, 1923; Malcolm Parsons, "Origins of the Colorado River Controversy in Arizona Politics, 1922-23," *Arizona and the West* 4 (Spring 1962), 28-31, 37.

41. Parsons, "Origins of the Colorado River Controversy," *Arizona and the West*, 30, 37; *Arizona Republican*, September 28, 1922; Hundley, *Water and the West*, 136, 37; N.D. Houghton, "Problems of the Colorado as Reflected in Arizona Politics," *Western Political Quarterly* 4 (December 1951), 638-39.

42. See Marjorie Haines Wilson, "The Gubernatorial Career of G.W.P. Hunt of Arizona" (Ph.D. dissertation: Arizona State University, 1973); John S. Goff, *George W.P. Hunt and His Arizona* (Pasadena, California: Socio Technical Publications, 1973); Malcolm Parsons, "Party and Pressure Politics in Arizona's Opposition to Colorado River Development," *Pacific Historical Review* 19 (February 1950), 50-51; G.W.P. Hunt, "Why I Oppose the Approval of the Colorado River Compact," Box 599, Folder 10, CHPC, ASU. One recent student of Hunt and the controversy concluded that the Arizona governor, like many other state and local politicians in Arizona in the 1920s, "ran on water for a long time." See Walter Rusinek, "In Response to the Compact: The Critical Opposition of George Hunt," unpublished manuscript, Small Collections File, AC, ASU.

43. *Arizona Republican*, January 7, 8, 9, 1923; *Arizona Daily Star*, January 8, 9. 1923.

V—THE BATTLE WITHIN

1. Carl Hayden, Holograph Notes, n.d., Box 22, Folder 4; Clarence Stetson to Hayden, October 15, 1923; Levi Udall to Hayden, June 4, 1923, Box 598, Folder 10, CHPC, ASU.

2. In fact, George Maxwell eventually traveled to Santa Fe and attended the final stages of the negotiations. For Hunt's wire to Hoover, dated November 21, 1922, see *Arizona Republican*, November 22, 1922. Hunt concluded his message to Hoover, "No compact or treaty can be agreed upon until ... engineering work is fully completed." Diaries of George Hunt, entries for November 28, 29, December 6, 8, 1922, AC, ASU; Goff, *George Hunt and His Arizona*, 242; Hundley, *Water and the West*, 232-33; Wilson, "The Gubernatorial Career of G.W.P. Hunt," 250-53; Parsons, "Origins of the Colorado River Controversy in Arizona Politics, 1922-23," *Arizona and the West*, 32.

3. Hoover had arrived earlier in the day from the Imperial Valley where he had delivered a similar speech tailored to the water users of southern California. Also, before the Friday night gathering, he met in informal conference at the Adams Hotel with members-elect of the Arizona State Legislature and with Hunt in order to explain the pact. Hunt emerged from the hotel and quipped to reporters that he had a pleasant meeting with the commerce secretary, but that his position regarding the pact remained unchanged. Herbert Hoover, "The Colorado River Pact: The Full Text of Secretary Hoover's Speech at the Columbia Theater in Phoenix, Arizona, Friday, December 8, 1922," Small Collections File, AC, ASU; *Arizona Republican*, December 9, 1922; Hunt Diaries, entry December 8, 1922, AC, ASU. Hunt wrote, "Today I met with Herbert Hoover Sec. of Commerce.

Came to town with my Sec. McCluskey went to call upon him by his appointment. He seems quite nice but I did not notice any dynamic force."

4. Dirk Lay to Hayden, December 14, 1922, Box 598, Folder 4, CHPC, ASU; "Hoover Speech," AC, ASU; *Arizona Republican*, December 9, 1922; Ellis Hawley, ed., *Herbert Hoover As Secretary of Commerce: Studies in New Era Thought and Practice* (Iowa City: University of Iowa Press, 1974), passim.

5. Before this portion of his speech, Hoover denied any Mexican claim to water from the Colorado, which obviously pleased his audience. Hoover, "Hoover Speech," AC, ASU; *Arizona Republican*, December 9, 1922.

6. Hoover, "Hoover Speech," AC, ASU; *Arizona Republican*, December 9, 1922; Hundley, *Water and the West*, 235-36. During this portion of his speech, Hoover, according to his handlers, departed significantly from his prepared text.

7. At this time Colter, like Hunt, held Maxwell in high regard. In a forward to an issue of his publication *Arizona Highline*, Colter wrote, "In behalf of present and future generations of people throughout the Southwest, we wish to extend our profound gratitude to George H. Maxwell, father of the National Reclamation Association, who has and is doing so much for Arizona and the United States." Fred Colter, "Introduction," *Arizona Highline* 1 (November 1923), 2; Hunt Diaries, November 29, 1922, AC, ASU; *Arizona Daily Star*, December 9, 10, 1922; *Tucson Citizen*, December 11, 1922; *Arizona Republican*, December 9, 1922; August, "Carl Hayden and the Politics of Water," *Pacific Historical Review*, 197.

8. W.S. Norviel to C.S. Curry, December 10, 1922, Box 600, Folder 6; Norviel to Hayden, January 26, 1923, Box 598, Folder 5, CHPC, ASU; *Tombstone Prospector*, April 19, 1922; George Maxwell, "George Maxwell's Brief," *Arizona Highline* 1 (November 1923), 15-17.

9. Hayden to Jack Gavin, "confidential," n.d., Box 600, Folder 6; Norviel to Hayden, December 14, 1922, January 26, 1923, Box 600, Folder 5; M.H. McCalla to Hayden, January 18, 1923, Box 598, Folder 6, CHPC, ASU; W.S. Norviel to G.W.P. Hunt, March 26, 1923; Box 3, Folder 16, G.W.P. Hunt Papers, ASU. Soon after Hunt was elected, Maxwell and Hunt forced Norviel to resign as state water commissioner. Norviel wrote a detailed account of his forced resignation.

10. August, "Carl Hayden and the Politics of Water," *Pacific Historical Review*, 199; George Maxwell to Hayden, February 8, 1923, Box 598, Folder 5; Hayden to Jack Gavin, "confidential," n.d., Box 600, Folder 6; M.H. McCalla to Hayden, January 18, 1923, Box 598, Folder 6; B.F. Fly to Hayden, February 6, 1923, Box 597, Folder 2, all in the Hayden Papers, CHPC, ASU; W.S. Norviel to G.W.P. Hunt, March 26, 1923, G.W.P. Hunt Papers, AC, ASU; *Tombstone Prospector*, April 19, 1922.

11. Hayden to Gavin, "confidential," n.d., Box 600, Folder 6; A.P. Davis to Hayden, March 4, May 3, 1922, Box 598, Folder 9; G. Otis Smith to Hayden, April 26, 1922, Box 599, Folder 10, CHPC, ASU; G. Otis Smith to W.S. Norviel, April 26, 1922; Norviel to Hunt, March 26, 1923, Box 3, Folder 16, Hunt Papers, ASU.

12. Maxwell to Hayden, February 8, 1923, Box 598, Folder 5; Hayden to Maxwell, February 10, 1923, Box 598, Folder 6, CHPC, ASU; Hayden to Maxwell, December 16, 1922, Box 1, Folder 48, George Maxwell Papers, Arizona Department of Library and Archives (ADLA), Phoenix, Arizona.

13. Hayden to F. Ward Bannister, November 24, 1922, Box 597, Folder 13; Bannister to Hayden, November 30, 1922, Box 597, Folder 14, in CHPC; Hunt Diary, entry for January 8, 1923, AC, ASU; Parsons, "Origins of the Colorado River Controversy," *Arizona and the West*, 38; *Journal of the Senate: Arizona* (1923), 22-23; *Arizona Republican*, January 9, 1923.

14. Norviel to Hunt, March 16, 1923, Box 3, Folder 16, Hunt Papers, AC, ASU; Hunt Diaries, January 8, 1923, AC, ASU; *Journal of the Senate: Arizona* (1923), 22; *Arizona Republican*, January 9, 1923; Walter Rusinek, "Against the Compact: The Critical Opposition of George W.P. Hunt," *Journal of Arizona History* 25 (Winter 1984), 155-70.

15. *Journal of the Senate: Arizona* (1923), 22-23; *Arizona Republican*, January 9, 1923; Norviel to Hunt, March 16, 1923, Hunt Papers; Kean St. Charles to Hayden, December 11, 1922, July 3, 1923, Box 598, Folder 10, Mulford Winsor to Hayden, December 25, 1922, Box 598, Folder 12, Hayden to G.E.P. Smith, February 17, 1923, Box 598, Folder 10, CHPC, ASU.

16. Dwight Mayo, "Arizona and the Colorado River Compact" (M.A. Thesis: Arizona State University, 1964), 27; Parsons, "Origins of the Colorado River Controversy," *Arizona and the West*, 36; *Journal of the House of Representatives* (1923), 25; Hundley, *Water and the West*, 238-39; Kean St. Charles to Hayden, December 11, 5922, July 3, 1923, Box 598, Folder 10, CHPC, ASU; "Official General Election Returns, State of Arizona, November 4, 1924," ADLA, Phoenix.

17. Winsor to Hayden, December 25, 1922, January 14, 1923, Box 598, Folder 12; B.F. Fly to Hayden, n.d., Box 600, Folder 5, CHPC, ASU; Parsons, "Origins of the Colorado River Controversy," *Arizona and the West*, 51; Thomas G. Smith, "Lewis Douglas, Arizona Politics, and the Colorado River Controversy," *Arizona and the West* 22 (Summer 1980), 131-36. Early in his public career Winsor served as Hunt's secretary.

18. As noted earlier, Hayden defeated Republican W.J. Galbreath in the general election of 1924, 1,608 to 32 in Yuma County. Like in Mohave County, Hunt lost to

Heard in Yuma, 1,706 to 1,496. "Official General Election Returns, State of Arizona, November 4, 1924," ADLA; B.F. Fly to Hayden, n.d., Box 600, Folder 5, CHPC, ASU.

19. Lewis Douglas succeeded Hayden in the U.S. House of Representatives. *Journal of the House of Representatives: Arizona* (1923), 299-300; *Journal of the Senate: Arizona* (1923), 613; Hundley, *Water and the West*, 242-43; Smith, "Lewis Douglas, Arizona, and the Colorado River Controversy," *Arizona and the West*, 139; August, "Carl Hayden and the Politics of Water," *Pacific Historical Review*, 199-200; Parsons, "Origins of the Colorado River Controversy," *Arizona and the West*, 40; *Arizona Republican*, February 16, March 12, 1923; *Tombstone Prospector*, March 7, 1923.

20. Rusinek, "Against the Compact: The Critical Opposition of George W. P. Hunt," *Journal of Arizona History*, 155-70; Hayden to Jack Gavin, "confidential," n.d., Box 600, Folder 5, CHPC, ASU.

21. *Journal of the House of Representatives: Arizona* (1923), 70, 75, 170-77, 210-11, 221-22; Parsons, "Party and Pressure Politics," *Pacific Historical Review,* 56; Smith, "Lewis Douglas," *Arizona and the West*, 133-34; *Jerome News* February 9, 13, 1923; *Arizona Daily Star*, January 17, 1923.

22. *Arizona Daily Star*, December 23, 1922; *Tucson Citizen*, November 2, 1924; Parsons, "Party and Pressure Politics," *Pacific Historical Review,* 53; Smith, "Lewis Douglas," *Arizona and the West*, 134; Mayo, "Arizona and the Colorado River Compact," 30-34; Hundley, *Water and the West*, 84-85.

23. *Journal of the House of Representatives: Arizona* (1923), 176; Cleon T. Knapp, "Diamond Creek Development Proposed for Immediate Action," *Arizona Mining Journal* 9 (1923), 62-63; Parsons, "Party and Pressure Politics," *Pacific Historical Review,* 54; Parsons, "Origins of the Colorado River Controversy," *Arizona and the West*, 41, Smith, "Lewis Douglas," *Arizona and the West*, 134-36; Hundley, *Water and the West*, 239-49; *Jerome News*, February 2, 1923.

24. Smith, "Lewis Douglas," *Arizona and the West*, 125, 134-36; Parsons, "Party and Pressure Politics," *Pacific Historical Review*, 54-56; F.A. Woodward, "Arizona Resources," *Arizona Magazine* 13 (November 1928), 5.

25. The highliners emerged as a potent political interest group in Arizona during the 1920s. Colter developed a devoted following and most subsequent legislatures had a thorough sprinkling of Colter followers. Colter's campaign had three goals: the highline canal, a dam at Glen Canyon for flood control, and a dam at Bridge Canyon for power to pump water into the highline canal. Fred Colter, "Facts Concerning the Pact and Growth in Arizona," *The Highline* 1 (November

1923), 25-30; *Arizona Daily Star*, September 19, 1923; *Arizona Republican*, September 19, 1923.

26. Colter, "Facts Concerning the Pact," 25-30; Smith, "Lewis Douglas," *Arizona and the West*, 133; Hundley, *Water and the West*, 243; August, "Hayden and the Politics of Water," *Pacific Historical Review*, 202.

27. *Arizona Republican*, February 24, May 5, 8, 9, and 10, 1923; Moeller, *Phil Swing and Boulder Dam*, 77.

28. *Arizona Republican*, May 9, 1923; *Tombstone Prospector*, March 23, 1923.

29. *Arizona Republican*, May 9, 1923; *Tombstone Prospector*, May 9, 1923.

30. *Arizona Republican*, May 10, 1923; *Tombstone Prospector*, May 10, 1923.

31. Hayden to L. Ward Bannister, November 24, 1922, Box 597, Folder 13; Hayden to George Maxwell, February 10, 1923, Box 598, Folder 12, CHPC, ASU; Hayden to Maxwell, December 16, 1922, Box 1, Folder 48, George Maxwell Papers, ADLA, Phoenix.

32. *Arizona Republican*, May 17, 1923; *Tombstone Prospector*, May 20, 1923; August, "Hayden and the Politics of Water," *Pacific Historical Review*, 205.

33. *Prescott Courier*, August 3, 1923.

34. *Prescott Courier*, August 3, 1923; Dwight Heard to Hayden, May 1, November 15, 1923, Box 598, Folder 2; Hayden to W.F. McClure, November 8, 1923, Box 598, Folder 6, CHPC, ASU.

35. Hugh Campbell to Hayden, February 28, 1923, Box 598, Folder 6, CHPC, ASU; *Prescott Courier*, August 3, 1923.

36. Levi S. Udall to Hayden, June 4, 1923, Box 598, Folder 11, L. Ward Bannister to Hayden, July 9, 1923, Box 597, Folder 13; Delph Carpenter to Hayden, August 8, 1923, Box 598, Folder 10; Hugh Campbell to Hayden, August 17, 1923, Box 600, Folder 10, CHPC, ASU; *Arizona Republican*, April 16, 1923.

37. Arizona Engineering Commission, *Reports Based on Reconnaissance Investigation of Arizona Land Irrigable from the Colorado River* (July 5, 1923), ADLA, Phoenix; *Tombstone Prospector*, August 6, 1922. Then state engineer, W.S. Norviel, under authority of an act passed by the Fifth Legislature in special session appointed the commission that consisted of LaRue, Porter J. Preston, project manager for the Yuma Irrigation Project for the U.S. Reclamation Service, and H.E. Turner, hydraulic engineer for the Arizona State Water Department. The legislature allotted $20,000 for the task.

38. Arizona Engineering Commission, *Investigation of Arizona Land*, passim; Harry E. Blake, "Reconnaissance Report on the Colorado River," in H.E. Blake to W.S. Norviel, December 1, 1921, Colorado River Papers, ADLA, Phoenix; *Arizona Republican*, July 6, 1923; Hundley, *Water and the West*, 159-60, 191, 249.

39. Arizona Engineering Commission, *Investigation of Arizona Land*, passim; Hundley, *Water and the West*, 159-60, 247, 249; Hayden to Winsor, February 12, 1923, Box 598, Folder 12, CHPC, ASU; *Coconino Sun* (Flagstaff), July 27, 1923.

40. *Coconino Sun*, July 27, 1923.

41. Ibid. The editor of the Flagstaff daily commented that "Mr. Hayden's talk was received with close attention and interest and the applause following it was long, continued, and sincere."

42. Hunt and six representatives of the Committee of Nine formed the Arizona delegation. They were Senator H.A. Elliott, John C. Greenway, A.G. McGregor, George W. Wilson, C.W. Hinchcliff, and Thomas Maddock. Also, George Maxwell accompanied the retinue. Hunt Diaries, entry for September 20, 1923, AC, ASU; Hundley, *Water and the West*, 249, 252; Moeller, *Phil Swing and Boulder Dam*, 45.

43. Hayden, Holograph Notes, n.d., Box 598, Folder 12, CHPC; Arizona Colorado River Conference Committee, "Statement Before the Federal Power Commission By the Arizona-Colorado River Conference Committee Concerning the Development and Utilization of the Resources of the Colorado River, September 24, 1923, AC, ASU; *Arizona Republican*, September 24, 25, 1923; Hundley, *Water and the West*, 249, 252; Moeller, *Phil Swing and Boulder Dam*, 45.

44. Mayo, "Arizona and the Colorado River Compact," 53; Friend Richardson to G.W.P. Hunt, November 22, 1923, Box 598, Folder 2, CHPC, ASU; *Arizona Republican*, October 17, November 1, 23, 1923.

45. Hayden to Heard, November 21, 1923; Box 599, Folder 10, CHPC, ASU; *Congressional Record* 70 Cong., 2 Sess. (1928), 459, 466-72; Hundley, *Water and the West*, 268-70; Moeller, *Phil Swing and Boulder Dam*, 118-19.

VI—LEADER OF THE OPPOSITION

1. *New York Times*, February 13, 1927.

2. Moeller, *Phil Swing and Boulder Dam*, 118.

3. Hayden to Dwight Heard, February 7, 1925, Box 598, Folder 12; Hayden to Heard, February 8, 1925, Box 600, Folder 5, CHPC, ASU.

4. Mayo, "Arizona and the Colorado River Compact," 39-40; *Journal of the House of Representatives: Arizona* (1925), 526; *Journal of the Senate: Arizona* (1925), 527; *Tucson Citizen*, March 12, 1925; *Graham County Guardian* (Safford), March 27, 1925.

5. *Tucson Citizen*, March 28, 1925; *Coconino Sun*, March 27, 1925; *Graham County Guardian*, March 27, 1925.

6. *Journal of the House of Representatives: Arizona* (1927), 22-23; Mayo, "Arizona and the Colorado River Compact," 45-46.

7. Moeller, *Phil Swing and Boulder Dam*, 80-81; Mayo, "Arizona and the Colorado River Compact," 55.

8. *Los Angeles Times*, August 25, 1925; *Arizona Republican*, August 18, 1925; *Official Report of the Proceedings of the Colorado River Conference*, August 17, 1925 (Phoenix: State of Arizona, 1925), 3-4; Moeller, *Phil Swing and Boulder Dam*, 80-81; Hundley, *Water and the West*, 258-59; Mayo, "Arizona and the Colorado River Compact," 55.

9. Hayden to Heard, August 19, 1925, and Hayden to Jack Gavin, August 19, 1925, Box 600, Folder 11, CHPC, ASU; *Arizona Republican*, August 18, 1925; Moeller, *Phil Swing and Boulder Dam*, 82; Hundley, *Water and the West*, 258-59.

10. Ultimately, Arizona rejected the California Plan of 1925 but doubtlessly noticed that her neighbor appeared genuinely interested in serious negotiations. At this time Arizona insisted on one-half of the mainstream after Nevada received 300,000 acre-feet. The state also rejected the Boulder Canyon damsite and believed it should receive a majority of the power revenues because the fall of the river was primarily in Arizona. Nevada opposed the latter Arizona contention. H.S. McCluskey to Hayden, January 22, 1926, Box 599, Folder 8, CHPC, ASU; Mayo, "Arizona and the Colorado River Compact," 55-56.

11. Hayden and other Arizona leaders were especially disturbed with the breakdown of the Los Angeles conference. One Maricopa County paper editorialized, "California is utterly selfish.... It was only on the point of royalty that the conference went on the rocks. Arizona holds that she is entitled to revenue from electric current generated within her borders." *Mesa Journal-Tribune*, January 6, 1927; Thomas Maddock and H.S. McCluskey to Hayden, January 27 and February 2, 1927; Hayden to Arizona Colorado River Commission, February 2, 1927, Box 599, Folder 8, CHPC, ASU.

12. Colorado River Commission of Arizona, *Second Report to the Eighth Legislature, December 31, 1928* (Phoenix: State of Arizona, 1928), 13-14; Mayo, "Arizona and the Colorado River Compact," 74.

13. Donald R. Van Petten, "Arizona's Stand on the Colorado River Compact," *New Mexico Historical Review* 17 (January 1942), 9-11; Moeller, *Phil Swing and Boulder Dam*, 101; Hundley, *Water and the West*, 260; Mayo, "Arizona and the Colorado River Compact," 74.

14. *Arizona Republican*, January 13, 1927; Mayo, "Arizona and the Colorado River Compact," 66-67; Hundley, *Water and the West*, 261-62. On January 11, 1927, Dern, in his annual message to the Utah state legislature, proclaimed: "The state owns its waters, which can never be alienated but to which rights can only be acquired through beneficial use. Second, the state owns the bed of the river because it is a navigable stream. If we own the water and the river bed, why should the federal government claim or assert any rights on the river? It is not a flagrant violation of state's rights for the federal government to come into a state and undertake to grab one of its primary natural resources?"

15. Pittman believed that his statement of principles should have been used as a guide for further negotiations. *The Daily Silver Belt* (Miami, Arizona), December 19, 1929; Mayo, "Arizona and the Colorado River Compact," 72; Hundley, *Water and the West*, 266; Hayden to H.S. McCluskey, October 11, 1927, Box 600, Folder 4, CHPC, ASU.

16. *Congressional Record*, 69 Cong., 2 Sess. (1926), 5822; Mayo, "Arizona and the Colorado River Compact," 99-100, 103; Hundley, *Water and the West*, 253-54; Moeller, *Phil Swing and Boulder Dam*, 75; *Arizona Daily Star*, March 3 and 6, 1925.

17. Hayden to Dwight Heard, May 10, 1926, Box 599, Folder 4; J.K. Ward to C.B. Hudspeth, May 18, 1926, Box 598, Folder 13.

18. Hayden to R.E. Ellinwood, May 11, 1926, Box 597, Folder 12; Hayden to *Prescott Courier*, May 22, 1926, Box 598, Folder 13; Hayden, "Statement by Mr. Hayden," May 22, 1926, Box 598, Folder 13; Hayden to J.J. Cox, n.d., Box 599, Folder 1, CHPC, ASU; Moeller, *Phil Swing and Boulder Dam*, 90-91.

19. Sinott from Oregon and Hill from Washington were absent the day of the committee vote. Moeller, *Phil Swing and Boulder Dam*, 90-91; *Arizona Republican*, May 23, 1926; C.B. Hudspeth to C.C. Cragin, May 26, 1926, Box 599, Folder 11, CHPC, ASU.

20. *Arizona Republican*, May 23, 1926; *San Francisco Daily News*, May 25, 1926.

21. Hayden to August F. Duclos, May 24, 1926, Box 599, Folder 2, CHPC, ASU.

22. Blaine Lamb, "A Many Checkered Toga: Arizona Senator Ralph Cameron, 1921-1927," *Arizona and the West* 19 (Spring 1977), 47-64; *Los Angeles Times*, June 6, 1926; *Benson News*, November 23, 1926; *Arizona Daily Star*, July 15, 1926;

Hayden to Kean St. Charles, January 22, 1925; Hayden to Isadore Dockweiler, May 8, 1926, Box 599, Folder 15; Hayden to Phil Swing, January 27, 1925, Box 601, Folder 4; Will Irwin to Hayden, n.d., Box 642, Folder 8; Ralph Cameron to Hayden, November 3, 1926, Box 642, Folder 10; C.W. Ingram to Hayden, January 19, 1927, Box 599, Folder 12; Henry D. Ross to Hayden, February 19, 1927, Box 599, Folder 11, CHPC, ASU. Hayden defeated Cameron for election to the Senate by a vote of 44,591 to 31,845.

23. Ibid.

24. *Arizona Daily Star*, December 24, 1927. Hayden's committee service in the Senate: Chairman, Senate Appropriations Committee, 1957-1969; Chairman of Interior and Related Agencies Subcommittee on Appropriations; Agriculture, 1927-1969, Defense, 1927-1952, District of Columbia, 1927-1969, and Public Works Subcommittees, 1927-1969; Ex-officio Member of all other Appropriations Subcommittees, 1957-1969; Chairman Joint Committee on Printing, 1949-1952, and again 1955-1969; Chairman Rules Committee, 1949-1952; Member, Interior and Insular Affairs, 1927-1969.

25. *House Rep. 1657*. 69 Cong., 2 Sess. (1926), part 3, 30; Hayden, "Boulder Canyon Project Act: Minority Views," Box 598, Folder 14, CHPC, ASU.

26. *Arizona Republican*, January 22, 1927; *New York Times*, January 22, 1927; House Committee on Rules and Administration, *Hearings on H.R. 9826*, 69 Cong., 2 Sess. (1927), 61-62.

27. House Committee on Rules, *Hearings on H.R. 9826*, 69 Cong., 2 Sess. (1927), 64-70; *Arizona Republican*, January 22, 1927; *Imperial Valley Farmer* (El Centro), January 13, 1927.

28. Ibid.

29. Ibid.

30. Ibid.

31. Hayden to George Dern, May 26, 1927, Box 601, Folder 4, CHPC, ASU; Moeller, *Phil Swing and Boulder Dam*, 94-95.

32. Hundley, *Water and the West*, 272-73; Richard Lowitt, *George W. Norris: The Persistence of a Progressive, 1913-1933* (Urbana: University of Illinois Press, 1971), 352-53.

33. Hayden to Dern, April 26, 1926, Box 601, Folder 4, CHPC, ASU; *Los Angeles Examiner*, October 12, 1927, April 20, 25, 26, 27, 1928; Moeller, *Phil Swing and Boulder Dam*, 111, 116; Hundley, *Water and the West*, 273.

34. Sibert Board, "Department of Interior Memorandum for the Press," December 3, 1928, Box 600, Folder 4, CHPC, ASU; Moeller, *Phil Swing and Boulder Dam*, 118, Hundley, *Water and the West*, 274; *House Doc.* 446, "Report of the Colorado River Board on the Boulder Dam Project," 70 Cong., 2 Sess. (1928), 9-14; *Arizona Republican*, December 5, 1928. According to the Sibert Report, "in general geologic conditions at Black Canyon are superior to those at Boulder Canyon.... The Board is of the opinion that the Black Canyon site is suitable for the proposed dam and is preferable to Boulder Canyon."

35. Moeller, *Phil Swing and Boulder Dam*, 112-14.

36. *Los Angeles Times*, May 29, 1928; *Los Angeles Examiner*, May 30, 1928; *Arizona Republican*, May 29, 1928; Moeller, *Phil Swing and Boulder Dam*, 115.

37. *Congressional Record*, 70 Cong., 2 Sess. (1928), 823, 836; Moeller, *Phil Swing and Boulder Dam*, 120; Hundley, *Water and the West*, 275-76.

38. Norris Hundley, Jr., "The Politics of Reclamation: California, the Federal Government, and the Origins of the Boulder Canyon Act," *California Historical Quarterly* 52, No. 2 (1973), 292; Hundley, *Water and the West*, passim.

39. This portion of the bill, in subsequent years, became most controversial. Hundley has argued that "thirty-five years later the U.S. Supreme Court would misconstrue this action and decide that the Boulder Canyon Act provided a statutory apportionment of the waters of the lower Colorado." According to Hundley, Congress was "merely suggesting a way in which the lower states might settle their problems themselves." Hundley, *Water and the West*, 270; Hundley, "Clio Nods: *Arizona v. California* and the Boulder Canyon Act—A Reassessment," *Western Historical Quarterly* 3, No. 1 (1972), 17-51.

40. Interview with Judge Simon Rifkind, October 9, 1986, author's files; *Arizona v. California et. al.*, 373 U.S. 546 (1963); *Congressional Record*, 70 Cong. 2 Sess. (1928), 459, 466-72; Hundley, *Water and the West*, 170, 268-70; Moeller, *Phil Swing and Boulder Dam*, 118-20.

41. For Hayden's view of the future of the West see "Statement by Mr. Hayden," May 22, 1926, Box 598, Folder 13, CHPC, ASU.

42. Ralph Murphy, "Arizona's Side of the Question," *Sunset Magazine* 56, No. 1 (1926), 34-37; Richard Newhall, "Arizona and the Colorado: How Not to Win a River by Trying Very Hard," *Phoenix Point West Magazine* 6 (1965), 31.

VII—ADVERSITY AND OPPORTUNITY

1. Mayo, "Arizona and the Colorado River Compact," 100-06; Hundley, *Water and the West*, 286-90; *Tucson Citizen*, January 16, 1929.

2. According to Hayden, when the California commission at Santa Fe heard that Utah would again approve the compact, the Californians quickly brought the tri-state meeting to an end. Subsequent meetings took place at Los Angeles, April 1929; Washington, D.C., May, June 1929; Salt Lake City, August, 1929; Reno, January 1930; Phoenix, February 1930. *Congressional Record*, 70 Cong., 2 Sess. (1929), 1770-771; Hundley, *Water and the West*, 286-88.

3. Mayo, "Arizona and the Colorado River Compact," 100, 106, 112, 113; *Arizona v. California et. al.*, 283 U.S. 423; 75 L. Ed. 1155 (1931); *Arizona Daily Star*, May 31, 1929; *The Daily Silver Belt* (Miami, Arizona), December 19, 1929.

4. Hayden, Holograph notes, n.d., Box 600, Folder 5, CHPC, ASU.

5. Arizona voters reelected Hayden to the U.S. Senate in 1932, 1938, 1944, and 1950 during this phase of the Arizona's struggle for water from the Colorado. In 1932 he joined the Democratic landslide of that year, defeating former senator Ralph Cameron for the second time. The final tally, 61,966 for Hayden and 28,619 for Cameron, reflected closely the margins of victory in subsequent elections. Hayden averaged nearly 70 percent of the vote in the elections of 1938, 1944, and 1950. In the 1938 general election, for example, he defeated Republican B.H. Clingan 82,714 to 25,378. The 1944 election results gave Hayden 90,335 votes to Republican Fred Fickett's 39,891. The 1950 results showed 116,246 for Hayden and 68,846 for his Republican opponent, Bruce Brocket. Moreover, in the four aforementioned elections, the Arizona Senator never lost a county in either a primary or general election. Thus, while Arizona and the Pacific Southwest grew, changed, and developed, Hayden remained a prominent feature in the state's political landscape. See Box 640, Folders 4-12, CHPC, ASU; Donald Swain, "The Bureau of Reclamation and the New Deal, 1933-1940," *Pacific Northwest Quarterly* 61 (July 1970), 146; *Arizona Daily Star*, August 21, 1931; *Arizona Republic*, July 19, 1932; *El Machete* (Phoenix), October 20, 1944; *State Farm News* (Glendale, Arizona), April 7, 1944.

6. *Arizona Daily Star*, February 8, 1935; A.H. Favour to Hayden, February 21, 1933; Favour to Robert T. Jones, February 11, 1939, Box 610, Folder 2, CHPC, ASU. Favour further complained that there was no continuity of membership on the Colorado River Commission and no harmony between the commission and the Attorney General's office. Moreover, the commissioners were political appointees

who served at the pleasure of the governor. Thus sometimes they were chosen not for their knowledge or expertise but for the repayment of campaign favors.

7. Swain, "The Bureau of Reclamation and the New Deal," *Pacific Northwest Quarterly*, 146; James R. Kluger, *Turning on Water with a Shovel: The Career of Elwood Mead* (Albuquerque: University of New Mexico Press, 1992), passim; Gates, *History of Public Land Law*, 681-83; *Arizona Daily Star*, June 22, 1930; *Yuma Sun*, October 24, 1933.

8. *Tucson Daily Citizen*, October 31, 1953; Gates, *History of Public Land Law*, 690; Lowitt, *New Deal and the West*, 85, 89; Swain, "The Bureau of Reclamation and the New Deal," *Pacific Northwest Quarterly*, 144-46; Hayden to Ruth Babbitt, June 14, 1937, Box 640, Folder 7, CHPC, ASU. Hayden supported the use of relief and public works funds in 1933 and subsequent years. In fact, he was unwilling to await funds from the diminishing payments into the reclamation revolving fund, and in 1936 he supported efforts by Congress to appropriate moneys from general revenues.

9. For Hayden's direct involvement in the Columbia River Basin Project see Box 603, Folder 2; for his role in California's Central Valley Project see Box 433, Folder 4, Box 40, Folder 13, CHPC, ASU; Swain, "Bureau of Reclamation and the New Deal," *Pacific Northwest Quarterly*, 143-44; Gates, *History of Public Land Law*, 681-83, 690.

10. In the closing days of the third session of the Seventy-fifth Congress, Hayden slipped the amendment into the appropriations bill. An immediate result of this action was to make available $26 million for use on irrigation projects throughout the West. See Box 640, Folders 3-7, CHPC, ASU; *Arizona Producer* (Phoenix), September 1, 1938.

11. Norris Hundley, Jr., "The West Against Itself: The Colorado River—An Institutional History," in Gary D. Weatherford and F. Lee Brown, eds., *New Courses for the Colorado River: Major Issues for the Next Century* (Albuquerque: University of New Mexico Press, 1985), 22-23. Hundley points out in this recent overview that construction of the dam, under the terms of the new law, could not begin until the federal government had obtained contracts for the hydroelectric power needed to pay for the project. Nevada had no market at the time; Arizona had neither the desire nor the market. Thus California, in 1930, agreed to purchase all the electricity to underwrite the cost of the dam and the power plant. Also the contracts provided that the government could buy back 36 percent of the power for use in Arizona and Nevada any time during the fifty years required to pay for the project, thus protecting potential future power needs of the two states.

12. Hundley, *Water and the West*, 291, 293; Mann, *Politics of Water in Arizona*, 85; Hayden to Jack Gavin, n.d., Box 615, Folder 3, CHPC, ASU; *Arizona Daily Star*, May 22, 1934; *Arizona Republic*, May 22, 1934; *Arizona v. California* 299, U.S. 341;78 L. Ed. 1298 (1934).

13. It is important to note that during this period of litigation, negotiation between states and the federal government were still taking place in an attempt at gaining a settlement. Hundley, *Water and the West*, 294-95; Mann, *Politics of Water in Arizona*, 86; *Arizona v. California et. al.*, 298 U.S. 558; 80 L. Ed. 1331, 1332-333 (1936).

14. Hearings on H.R. 6958, *Hearings Before a Subcommittee on the Committee on Appropriations* U.S. Senate, 75 Cong., 1 Sess., "A Bill for the Department of Interior for Fiscal Year Ending June 30, 1938, and for Other Purposes" (Washington, D.C.: Government Printing Office, 1937), 420; *Tucson Daily Citizen*, October 31, 1950; *Arizona Daily Star*, June 22, 1930.

15. *Hearings* on H.R. 6958, 420.

16. Benjamin B. Moeur to Ray Lyman Wilbur, February 16, 1934; Ray Lyman Wilbur to Hayden, February 28, 1934, Box 601, Folder 19, CHPC, ASU; Lowitt, *New Deal and the West*, 85; Hundley, *Water and the West*, 285-88. For further accounts of Arizona's opposition to construction of Parker Dam and the Colorado River Aqueduct see *Tucson Daily Citizen*, July 1, 1931; *Arizona Daily* Star, May 29, 1931.

17. *U.S. v. Arizona*, 295 U.S. 174; 79 L. Ed. 1374 (1935); *Tucson Daily Citizen*, November 10, 11, 1934; *Arizona Daily Star*, March 7, November 10, 11, 12, 1934; *Arizona Republic*, November 10-14, 1934. MWD officials issued a statement the day after Arizona declared martial law: "We are taking no part in the controversy—our job is to build the Colorado River Aqueduct to receive the water when it is impounded by the Bureau of Reclamation at Parker Dam." Ida Tarbell, the Progressive Era muckraker, covered the colorful affair for her readers in an article, "Arizona's Threat to Secede," in the *New York Tribune* of November 25, 1935. Tarbell defended Arizona's actions claiming the state had suffered "outrageous injustice" at the hands of California and the federal government, and labeling the conflict a "miniature war."

18. Hayden, Holograph Notes, n.d., Box 610, Folder 19, CHPC, ASU; *Arizona Daily Star*, December 7, 1934; *Holbrook Tribune* (Holbrook, Arizona), December 6, 1935; Hundley, *Water and the West*, 286. Hayden saw benefits for Arizona in the construction of Parker Dam, including storage, flood control, and a share of the power produced by the dam.

19. A.H. Favour to Robert T. Jones, February 11, 1939, Box 610, Folder 2; C.B. Ward to Hayden, January 23, 1933; Hayden to C.B. Ward, February 2, 1923, Box 601,

Folder 21; Charles Carson to Hayden, May 14, 1934, Box 611, Folder 12; A.H. Favour to Jack Gavin, July 2, 1934, Box 611, Folder 13; Ray Lyman Wilbur to Benjamin B. Moeur, February 10, 1933, Box 601, Folder 19, CHPC, ASU; U.S. Department of Interior, "News Release," February 13, 1933, Thomas Maddock Papers, Box 6, Folder 25, Arizona Historical Society, Tucson, Arizona; Hundley, *Water and the West*, 291; *Arizona Daily Star*, August 31, 1934; *Los Angeles Times*, August 26, December 1, 1934.

20. An articulate and able politician, Osborn was, as one scholar observed, "a Democrat who felt no obligation to maintain the opposition established by former governor Hunt." The elections of 1940 also brought change to Arizona's delegation in the Senate. Ernest W. McFarland, a lawyer from Oklahoma who moved to the Gila River valley in 1919, upset longtime senator Henry F. Ashurst in the Democratic primary, and coasted to victory in the general election. During his two terms in the Senate (1940-1952), McFarland added an important legal dimension to Arizona's legislative policy concerning the Colorado River. These and other changes in the state's political apparatus, Hayden observed, provided the foundation for a more constructive approach toward regional development.

21. California planned to increase its annual use by 2 million acre-feet through a proposed project at Pilot Knob. Even more disturbing to Arizonans, the Pilot Knob Project included selling additional water to Mexico at $1 per acre-foot. Moreover, the environmental calamity prompted farmers to pump groundwater in unprecedented quantities. By 1940 most of the state's water storage reservoirs were nearly empty. In fact, hydroelectric power generation dwindled to the point that, in 1939, state leaders faced a severe power shortage. In response to the pleas of Governor Jones and other lawmakers, Hayden contacted the interior department and Bureau of Reclamation officials, who hastily constructed a transmission line on wood poles from Parker Dam. Thus Hoover Dam power, through a connecting link at Parker Dam, brought much-needed electricity to the Salt River Valley in 1940-41. The irony of the situation was not lost on Hayden, who realized that the decision to accept Hoover power represented a sharp reversal of Arizona policy. The drought and its immediate consequences—overdrafting of groundwater supplies and power shortages—forced state leaders to move away from state's rights policies.

22. Margaret Finnerty, "Sidney P. Osborn, 1884-1940: The Making of an Arizona Governor" (M.A. Thesis: Arizona State University, 1983); *Arizona Republic*, September 8, 1950; U.S. Bureau of the Census, *Sixteenth Census of the United States: 1940-Population*, Vol. 1, *Number of Inhabitants* (Washington, D.C.: Government Printing Office, 1942), 89-91; *Journal of the Senate, Sixteenth Legislature of the State of Arizona, 1943* (Phoenix, 1943), 89-90; *Journal of the*

Senate, Sixteenth Legislature of the State of Arizona, First Special Session, 1944 (Phoenix, 1944), 1-39; *Arizona Republic*, February 25, 1944.

23. Hundley, *Dividing the Waters*, passim; Hundley, *Water and the West*, 295-97; Hayden to Jack Gavin, n.d., Box 614, Folder 7, CHPC, ASU.

24. Senate Committee on Foreign Relations, *Hearings on Water Treaty with Mexico*, 79 Cong., 1 Sess. (1945), 1760; "Water Supply Below Boulder Dam," *Senate Document* 39, 79 Cong., 1 Sess. (1945), part I, 5-8; Hundley, *Water and the West*, 297; Hayden to Sidney P. Osborn, February 15, 1943, Box 616, Folder 2, CHPC, ASU.

25. The Arizonan's commitment to regional development of water resources continued through the war years and beyond. This commitment extended even to California, Arizona's erstwhile antagonist. In 1942, for example, during one particularly difficult funding fight for California's Central Valley Project, Hayden, against the wishes of many Arizona veterans of the Colorado River controversy, came to the aid of California. Interior Secretary Harold Ickes, in his renowned diary, commented on Hayden's special role in securing funds for the project: "We have now established the principle that we were striving for in connection with the Central Valley Project," and "we have money for transmission lines and we have money to pay for the steam standby plant that we want at Antioch." "I suppose that we owe more to Senator Hayden of Arizona than any other man. It was he who got those items by in the Senate." Harold Ickes, "The Diary of Harold L. Ickes," Library of Congress (LC), Washington, D.C., entry July 5, 1942, Vol. 43, 6762; *Arizona Republic*, October 18, 1941; *Arizona Daily Star*, October 18, 1941; *Tucson Daily Citizen*, October 18, 1941. For a brief overview of reclamation policy during World War II see Gates, *History of Public Land Law*, 691-94.

26. The short-term historical context of these developments are significant and shed light on Hayden's relationship with the Bureau of Reclamation. As a result of the water shortage emergency in Arizona during the late 1930s and early 1940s, Secretary of the Interior Harold Ickes supported Hayden's request to have Bureau of Reclamation engineers survey various routes to direct water from Parker Dam to central Arizona. In fact, on October 4, 1940, Hayden met with President Roosevelt to discuss the desperate need for new sources of water. Although the wet year of 1941 eliminated the need for emergency surveys, these steps anticipated later developments. In connection with these preparations, and the resumption of the drought a year later, the Arizona state legislature, in early 1943, approved $200,000 for use by the Bureau to conduct investigations on various routes for an aqueduct from Colorado to central Arizona. Hayden recognized this action, prompted by Governor Osborn, as a virtual revolution in state water policy. Also, according to Marc Reisner, a critic of Bureau of Reclamation

activities in the American West, Hayden exercised "near-despotic rule" over the Bureau's authorizing committees by World War II. During the war, moreover, Hayden was the ranking member of the Senate Committee on Post-War Economic Policy and Planning. Arizonans viewed their senator's position on this Committee as crucial in their quest for water from the Colorado River. See Marc Reisner, *Cadillac Desert: The American West and Its Disappearing Water*, rev. ed. (Vancouver: Douglas and McIntyre, 1993), 118. See also, Gerald Nash, *The American West Transformed: The Impact of the Second World War* (Bloomington: Indiana University Press, 1985), passim. U.S. Senate, Hearings Before a Subcommittee on Irrigation and Reclamation, "Authorizing with Respect to Present and Future Need for Development of Projects for Irrigation and Hydroelectric Power," passim.

27. House Committee on Irrigation of Arid Lands, "Hearings H.R. 11449," 34. Even before Hayden outlined the proposal before the committee, Reclamation Commissioner Arthur Powell Davis believed the canal was not within the realm of possibility. "Obviously," Davis wrote Hayden, "this plan would be prohibitive in cost, both for construction and maintenance after built." Arthur Powell Davis to Hayden, May 23, 1922, Box 598, Folder 9, CHPC, ASU.

28. "Authorizing with Respect to Present and Future Need for Development of Projects for Irrigation and Hydroelectric Power," passim.

29. Of great help to Arizona during these hearings was Harold Ickes. By this time, Ickes and Hayden had developed a close personal and professional relationship. Ickes recalled the pleasant talks on matters of interest to the West and marveled at Hayden's persuasive powers in committee. On July 11, 1943, for example, Ickes, ruminating over a recent budgetary battle in one of the subcommittees on appropriations, confided to his diary: "Senator Hayden has never shown himself as much a useful friend to my department as he has shown in recent fiscal legislation. As chairman of the Sub-committee on Appropriations for the Interior, he succeeded in restoring many items that had been cut out.... And he put in additional items, especially for reclamation projects." In turn, Hayden received from Ickes special consideration for programs he favored. "Ickes Diary," entries July 11, 1943, Vol. 49, pp. 7970-971; July 20, 1941, Vol. 39, 5592; May 9, 1943, Vol. 47, 7705, LC; Hearings, *Sen. Res.* 304, 1-2; Ernest McFarland, *Mac: The Autobiography of Ernest W. McFarland* (Phoenix: Ernest W. McFarland, 1979), 200-07. McFarland recalled the significance of these hearings in his autobiography: "Looking back, I consider this to have been a most important move because it created an interested Arizona which had never existed before. We held five days of hearings in Phoenix, Florence, Safford, Yuma, and Kingman. Eighty-three persons appeared before the subcommittee, some representing different industries,

and including almost all sections of the state of Arizona, particularly those representing irrigation, electrical power districts, land corporations, and farmers."

30. Hearings, *Sen. Res. 304*, 12-15; *Arizona Republic*, August 22, 1944.

31. This portion of the hearings were held in Florence, Arizona. Hearings, *Sen. Res. 304*, 50-54; *Arizona Daily Star*, August 4, 1944.

32. If by mid-century Hayden had achieved institutional status in his home state, he had also attained a significant amount of seniority in the U.S. Senate. Arizonans, inordinately dependent upon federal programs and moneys, knew well the importance of Hayden's accumulated years in the upper chamber. In the context of the Colorado River controversy and related water issues, his seniority was viewed as Arizona's chief weapon against numerically superior California. Moreover, Hayden's use of the prerogatives of seniority were best manifested in committee work. By 1950 he had risen to Chairman of the Committee on Rules and Administration and ranked second on the powerful Committee on Appropriations. As chairman of the Rules Committee, he was, in effect, general manager of the Senate with power over the conduct of business and physical property. His position on Appropriations kept him close to the fiscal workings of government. Because of Hayden, wrote one Arizona newspaperman in 1950, "Arizona has much more to say about the way the U.S. Senate is run than states with vastly larger populations." A member of California's congressional delegation agreed with that observation and added: "Carl Hayden is the most powerful man in the U.S. Senate. On the Appropriations Committee he has done favors for everyone." Carl Hayden interview with Ross Rice, October 15, 1971, OHC, AC, ASU; *Arizona Republic*, August 27, 1950; *San Diego Union*, October 19, 1950; U.S. Bureau of Reclamation, *Comparison of Diversion Routes, Central Arizona Project, Project Planning Report No. 3-8b. 4-2* (Washington, D.C., 1948), 1-4; Richard L. Berkman and W. Kip Viscusi, *Damming the West* (New York: Grossman Publishers, 1973), 105-11. In 1944 an agreement between the Bureau and Arizona provided for joint financing of CAP investigations.

33. See U.S. Bureau of Reclamation, *Comparison of Diversion Routes, Central Arizona Project, Project Planning Report No. 3-8b. 4-0* (Washington, D.C., 1945), 1-46; Michael Straus to Hayden, February 6, 12, 1948; Charles Carson to Hayden, October 20, 1945, February 25, 1946, Box 652, Folder 21, CHPC, ASU. Supporters of these early feasibility studies argued that they were needed to rescue Arizona's agricultural economy.

34. Michael Straus to Hayden, February 5, 1948; Bureau of Reclamation, "News Release," February 5, 1948, Box 645, Folder 24, CHPC, ASU; *Arizona Republic*, August 30, 1947.

35. Bureau of Reclamation, *Report on the Central Arizona Project* ... 4-2, 4-6; *Arizona Daily Star*, February 6, 1948.

36. Bureau of Reclamation, *Report on the Central Arizona Project* ... 4-2, 13; *Arizona Republic*, February 6, 1948; *Arizona Daily Star*, February 6, 1948; Jack L. August, Jr., "Carl Hayden's 'Indian Card': Environmental Politics and the San Carlos Reclamation Project," *Journal of Arizona History* 33 (Winter 1992), 397-422; August, "Carl Hayden, Arizona, and the Politics of Water Development in the Southwest, 1923-1928," *Pacific Historical Review*, 196, 214.

37. Bureau of Reclamation, *Report on the Central Arizona Project* ... 4-2, 43; Walter Rusinek, "Bristor v. Cheatham: Conflict Over Groundwater Law in Arizona," *Arizona and the West* 24 (Summer 1985), 143-62. Indeed much remained unresolved, including the groundwater issue which resulted in a long series of State Supreme Court decisions that had the effect of limiting the right of private ownership of groundwater while increasing the power of state government in controlling withdrawals.

38. McFarland, *Mac*, 207; Hayden to Forrest Donnell, June 20, 1947, Box 662, Folder 4, CHPC, ASU. In the House of Representatives, John Murdock (D-Arizona) submitted a companion bill to accompany S 433. H.R. 1598 was offered on February 3, 1947.

39. Carl Hayden to Leveritt Saltonstall, June 20, 1947; Kenneth McKellar to Hayden, June 21, 1947; Joseph McCarthy to Hayden, June 21, 1947, Box 19, Folder 5, CHPC, ASU. In the spring of 1947 Bureau of Reclamation investigators began pushing the Parker Pump Plan over the Bridge Canyon Dam Plan. According to Vaude Larson, Assistant Regional Planner for Region III—the Southwest Region—either Bridge Canyon or Parker could be constructed but the preponderance of advantages were with the Parker route. With lower total cost, shorter construction time, and greater overall economic feasibility, subsequent CAP bills advocated the Parker route although a dam at Bridge Canyon remained an integral part of the CAP concept until 1968. See also *Bridge Canyon Project*, Hearings Before a Subcommittee of the Committee of Public Lands, U.S. Senate, 80 Cong., 1 Sess., on S 1175, "A Bill Authorizing Construction, Operation, and Maintenance of a Dam and Incidental Works on the Mainstream of the Colorado River at Bridge Canyon, Together with Certain Appurtenant Dams and Canals for Other Purposes" (Washington, D.C.: Government Printing Office, 1948), 35-45.

40. *Hearings S 1175*, 80 Cong., 1 Sess., 3-4. The bill proposed one significant change in federal reclamation law. It did not require a fifty-year repayment period. Instead repayment would take "a reasonable period of years not to exceed the life of the project."

41. California congressmen Norris Poulson and Harry Sheppard, at the same time, introduced the counterpart of SJR 145 in the House of Representatives. *Arizona Republic*, July 8, 1947; *Phoenix Gazette*, July 10, 1947. Only one western senator sat on the Judiciary Committee and he supported California's contentions. Arizona wanted the resolution sent to the Public Lands Committee where the measure could be defeated.

42. U.S. Senate, *Hearings Before a Subcommittee of the Committee on the Interior and Insular Affairs*, 80 Cong., 2 Sess., on SJR 145, "A Resolution Authorizing the Commencement of Action by the United States to Determine Interstate Rights on the Colorado River" (Washington, D.C.: Government Printing Office, 1948), 333; *Arizona Republic*, July 9, 10, 1947; *Phoenix Gazette*, July 9, 1947; *Los Angeles Times*, July 9, 1947; Hayden, Holograph Notes, n.d., Box 19, Folder 2, CHPC, ASU.

43. *Arizona Republic*, July 9, 1947; *Phoenix Gazette*, July 10, 1947; U.S. Senate, *Congressional Record*, July 8, 1947, 80 Cong., 1 Sess., Vol. 93, 8423-430; Central Arizona Project Association (CAPA), "Water" (pamphlet), October 18, 1948.

44. As California rekindled the fires of old animosities in Arizona, one Arizona newspaper editor fulminated: "California has indicated her intentions to block the project by whatever means she considers effective. She reveals herself as selfish, predatory, and unprincipled." *Arizona Republic*, July 9, 1947, May 27, 1948; *Phoenix Gazette*, July 9, 10, 1947; House of Representatives, *Hearings Before Subcommittee No. 4 of the Committee of the Judiciary*, 80 Cong., 2 Sess., on H.J.R. 225, 226, 227, 236, H.R. 4097, "To Authorize Commencement of Action by the United States to Determine Interstate Water Rights on the Colorado River" (Washington, D.C.: Government Printing Office, 1948), passim; Hayden, Holograph Notes, n.d., Box 19, Folder 2, CHPC, ASU.

45. T. Richmond Johnson, *The Central Arizona Project* (Tucson: University of Arizona Press, 1977), 18-19; Hayden to Jack Gavin, n.d., Box 19, Folder 8, CHPC, ASU.

46. Wayne M. Akin interview with Jack L. August, Jr., September 14, 1982, Phoenix, Arizona, OHC, AC, ASU; CAPA, *Scrapbook*, vol. I; CAPA, "Basic Information on the Central Arizona Project," n.d., Central Arizona Project Association Collection (CAPAC), ASU; Johnson, *Central Arizona Project*, 30; *Arizona Farmer* (Phoenix), July 13, 1946. California, in contrast to Arizona, had developed its political infrastructure pertaining to water resource development much earlier than Arizona. In 1937 the California legislature created the Colorado River Board, charged with protecting California's interest in the river.

47. *Arizona Republic*, May 27, 1948; Hundley, *Water and the West*, 300-02. In 1948 the upper-basin states—Wyoming, Colorado, Utah, and New Mexico—ratified an

upper-basin pact, creating an Upper Colorado River Commission. Hayden and Arizona water leaders realized that the supplementary pact paved the way for use of the entire upper-basin allocation.

48. Barry Goldwater interview with Jack L. August, Jr., September 15, 1985, Phoenix, Arizona, OHC, AC, ASU; *Arizona Republic*, April 28, 1949; *New York Times*, April 30, 1949; *Los Angeles Times*, April 29, 1949. For Hayden's testimony see U.S. Senate, *Hearings Before the Committee on Interior and Insular Affairs, The Central Arizona Project and Colorado River Water Rights*, 81 Cong., 1 Sess. (Washington, D.C.: Government Printing Office, 1949), 733-34.

49. Hayden also told the committee in characteristic fashion, "I say that the money will all be returned to the Treasury of the United States, with good interest, because when valuable farm lands are protected, when manufacturing and business enterprises in cities and towns are protected, Congress is preserving taxable wealth." U.S. Senate, *Hearings ... Central Arizona Project ... Colorado River Water Rights*, 81 Cong., 1 Sess., 734. Also note the increase in cost of CAP between 1947 and 1949.

50. U.S. Senate, *Hearings, S 75*, 81 Cong., 1 Sess., 735; *Arizona Republic*, April 29, 1949.

51. Hayden also advised the committee that the Hayden-Ashurst filibuster was directed at a single point, that there be written into the bill a clear definition of Arizona's rights to the river. U.S. Senate, *Hearings, S 75*, 81 Cong., 1 Sess., 738-39; *Arizona Republic*, April 29, 1949.

52. Senators on the Interior and Insular Affairs Committee met for twenty days on S 75 and the printed testimony amounted to 954 pages. U.S. Senate, *Hearings S 77*, 81 Cong., 1 Sess., 743-44; U.S. Senator, *Senate Report 832, The Bridge Canyon Project*, 81 Cong., 1 Sess. (Washington, D.C. Government Printing Office, 1949), passim; Hayden, Holograph Notes, n.d., Box 19, Folder 4, CHPC, ASU; *Arizona Republic*, April 29, 1949; Johnson, *Central Arizona Project*, 64-65, 69.

53. President Harry Truman to Hayden, February 16, 1949, Box 19, Folder 8; Hayden, "Address By Senator Carl Hayden Over Radio Station KOY, Phoenix," September 11, 1950, Box 19, Folder 6, CHPC, ASU; *Arizona Republic*, November 12, 1950; *Arizona Daily Star*, November 12, 1950.

54. Harry S. Truman, "Memo for Senator Hayden," February 16, 1949; Walter Bimson, "Statement of Walter Bimson, President of Valley National Bank, Phoenix, Arizona," n.d., Box 19, Folder 8; J.H. Moeur to Hayden, August 30, 1949, Box 19, Folder 4; Royal Marks to Hayden, January 24, 1949, Box 19, Folder 3, CHPC, ASU; CAPA, "Colorado River: A Factual Summary—Water for

Arizona," Box 1, Folder 7, CAPAC, ASU; *Arizona Republic*, February 18, 22, 1950; *Tempe Daily News*, July 14, 1949; Johnson, *Central Arizona Project*, 57-67.

55. *Newsweek Magazine*, March 6, 1950, described this aspect of the political process in vivid terms for its readers: "Carl Hayden who almost never speaks to newsmen but is articulate enough in the cloakrooms, had a couple of helpful talking points. As chairman of the Rules Committee he is in charge of all Capitol patronage in the Senate wing. This strategic spot also enables him to block funds for any special committee investigations voted by the Senate. In addition, Hayden is the ranking member and de facto head of Chairman Kenneth McKellar's Senate Appropriations Committee which passes on specific projects, some legitimate and some strictly porkbarrel, upon which the political life of many senators depends." *Arizona Republic*, February 22, 1950; U.S. Senate, *Congressional Record*, February 21, 1950, 81 Cong., 2 Sess., 2101-102; Walter Bimson to Hayden, February 22, 1950, Box 19, Folder 10, CHPC, ASU.

56. *Sen. Report 832*, passim; U.S. Senate, *Congressional Record*, February 21, 1950, 81 Cong., 2 Sess, 2102; *Los Angeles Times*, February 22, 1950; *Arizona Republic*, February 22, 1950.

57. *Newsweek Magazine*, March 6, 1950; *Prescott Courier*, February 23, 1950; *Arizona Republic*, February 22, 1950.

58. John Murdock to Hayden, June 7, 1950, Box 19, Folder 3, CHPC, ASU; *Phoenix Gazette*, October 25, 1950; Johnson, *Central Arizona Project*, 61-71.

59. *Phoenix Gazette*, October 25, 1950; Johnson, *Central Arizona Project*, 60, 67.

60. Akin interview with August; Roger Ernst interview with Jack L. August, Jr., March 23, 1983, Phoenix, Arizona, OHC, AC, ASU; *Arizona Republic*, September 7, 1950; Johnson, *Central Arizona Project*, 59-71.

61. In the Eighty-second Congress, the CAP bills, introduced by representatives Murdock and Fatten, were numbered H.R. 1500 and 1501. CAPA, "Progress Report: News of Arizona's Water Fight," June 20, 1949," CAPAC; "Memorandum for Senator Hayden," n.d., Box 19, Folder 7, CHPC, ASU; Johnson, *Central Arizona Project*, 74-80.

62. Howard Pyle interview with Jack L. August, Jr., November 9, 1982, Tempe, Arizona, OHC, AC, ASU; House of Representatives, Interior and Insular Affairs Committee, *Hearings on HR 1500, 1501*, 81 Cong., 2 Sess., 741-63; *Arizona Republic*, April 19, 1951; *Arizona Daily Star*, April 19, 1951; *Los Angeles Times*, April 19, 1951.

63. *Arizona Republic*, April 19, 1951; Ernest McFarland to Hayden, March 12, 1951, Box 20, Folder 2, CHPC, ASU; Johnson, *Central Arizona Project*, 72-73. The defeat in committee effectively ended Murdock's career according to his successor, John Rhodes. See John J. Rhodes interview with Jack L. August, Jr., November 4, 1985, Tempe, Arizona, OHC, AC, ASU.

64. On January 30, 1951, the Senate Interior and Insular Affairs Committee, once again gave S 75 a "Do Pass" recommendation by a vote of 8-2. U.S. Senate, *Congressional Record*, 82 Cong., 1 Sess., Vol. 97, May 31, 1951, 5974-975; *Arizona Republic*, June 1, 1951.

65. *Arizona Republic*, May 30, 31, 1951; U.S. Senate, *Congressional Record*, 82 Cong., 1 Sess., 5979-980.

66. U.S. Senate, *Congressional Record*, 82 Cong., 1 Sess., 5974-975.

67. *Arizona Daily Star*, May 31, 1951; U.S. Senate, *Congressional Record*, 82 Cong., 1 Sess., 5974-6210.

68. U.S. Senate, *Congressional Record*, 82 Cong., 1 Sess., 5976.

69. Ibid., 5979-980.

70. *Arizona Republic*, June 1, 6, 1951; *Los Angeles Times*, June 6, 1951; *Arizona Daily Star*, August 14, 1952; Hayden to Howard Pyle, August 13, 1952, Box 21, Folder 8, CHPC, ASU; Hundley, "The West Against Itself," in Weatherford and Brown, eds., *New Courses for the Colorado River*, 30-32.

VIII—"MY PATIENCE HAS BEEN EXHAUSTED"

1. *Arizona Daily Star*, August 14, 1952; *Arizona Republic*, August 14, 1952; Aiken interview with August, September 18, 1982, OHC, AC, ASU; Hundley, "The West Against Itself," in Weatherford and Brown, eds., *New Courses for the Colorado River*, 30; Donald Worster, *Rivers of Empire: Water, Aridity, and the Growth of the American West* (New York: Pantheon, 1985).

2. The Supreme Court voted 5-3 in favor of Arizona. *Arizona v. California et, al.*, 373 U.S. 564, 565 (1963); Hundley, "The West Against Itself," *New Courses for the Colorado River*, 275; *Washington Post*, June 4, 1963; *Arizona Republic*, June 4, 1963.

3. Arizona's 3.8 million acre-feet included the 1 million acre-feet of Gila River water put to beneficial use under the San Carlos Irrigation Project. Johnson, *Central Arizona Project*, 84, 94-95. See also the Boulder Canyon Project Act [45 Stat. 1057] and the California Limitation Act [Laws of California, 1929, ch. 16, 38-

39]; John G. Will, "Law and Water," *Project Rescue: A Seminar on the Central Arizona Project* (Tempe, Arizona: Arizona State University, 1964), 19-23.

4. The solicitor general advised the Court on October 17, 1952, that the federal government would move to intervene in the case. T. Richmond Johnson interview with Jack L. August, Jr., March 20, 1985, Phoenix, Arizona, OHC, ASU; *New York Times*, June 4, 1963; Hundley, "The West Against Itself," *New Courses for the Colorado River*, 32.

5. *Arizona v. California et. al.*, 373 U.S. 564, 565 (1963); Johnson, *Central Arizona Project*, 88-97.

6. Simon Rifkind interview with Jack L. August, Jr., October 12, 1986, Ruidoso, New Mexico, author's files.

7. Norris Hundley, Jr. *The Great Thirst: California and Water, 1770-1990* (Berkeley: University of California Press, 1992), 300-01; *Arizona Republic*, August 15, 1955.

8. Hundley, *The Great Thirst*, 301.

9. Roy L. Elson, Administrative Assistant to Senator Carl Hayden and Candidate for the United States Senate, 1955-1969, "Oral History Interviews April 27 to August 21, 1990," Senate Historical Office, Washington, D.C., 103. As long time administrative assistant, Elson put it in 1990, "A lot of people, particularly as he got older and his hearing got bad, thought he was senile. There was nothing senile about Carl Hayden. You'd think he was up there asleep, and then he'd ask the most penetrating questions. He'd cut all the shit out and get right to heart of the matter. He was superb at doing that. I mean people would marvel." Paul M. Butler to Carl Hayden, May 30, 1955, Box 716, Folder 3, Paul Eaton to Renz Jennings, February 14, 1956, Paul Eaton to Stephen Shadegg, February 24, 1956, CHPC, ASU.

10. *Arizona Daily Star*, October 27, 1956; *Phoenix Gazette*, October 3, 1956, January 11, 1956; *Arizona Republic*, November 22, 1956; *Newsweek*, November 12, 1956, 68; Stephen Shadegg to Paul Eaton, April 19, 1956, Box 716, Folder 11; Lyndon Johnson to Hayden, January 15, 1955, Box 716, Folder 3; Democratic Policy Committee, "News Release," January 16, 1955, Box 716, Folder 2, CHPC, ASU.

11. William Benton, "For Distinguished Service in Congress"; *New York Times Magazine*, July 24, 1955.

12. Secretary of State, "Official Canvass: General Election—November 6, 1956," Department of Library and Archives, Phoenix, Arizona; Benton, "For Distinguished Service in Congress," *Phoenix Gazette*, November 12, 1956; Lewis Douglas, "Statement By Lewis Douglas, Sr.," October 1, 1956; Hayden, "Election Night Speech" n.d., Box 716, Folder 8, CHPC, ASU.

13. *Arizona Republic*, "Arizona Days and Ways Fiftieth Anniversary Issue," February 14, 1962, 536; *Senate Document 76*, 87 Cong., 2 Sess., "Tributes to Honorable Carl Hayden, Senator from Arizona, To Commemorate the Occasion of his Fiftieth Anniversary of Congressional Service, February 19, 1962" (Washington, D.C.: Government Printing Office, 1962), 29, 42-43; *Phoenix Gazette*, September 21, 1962. The *Arizona Republic* of September 21, 1963, offered that "Arizona's congressional delegation is vastly outnumbered by California which wants the Colorado River for itself. Only the parliamentary skill of Senator Hayden supported by the universal esteem in which he is held in Congress will secure passage of CAP.... Senator Hayden stands above party politics. He should be reelected by overwhelming non-partisan support.... Senator Hayden deserves the vote of every citizen who wants Arizona to prosper."

14. Elson asserted that during his service to Hayden (1952-1962) "there wasn't a thing I did ... that wasn't with the approval of the senator, or he didn't know about. I was the hatchet man, I was the negotiator, and caught alot of hell for it because they didn't think [my actions] were what the senator wanted." Elson, "Oral History Interviews, April 27 to August 21, 1990," 122-23, 198; *Cervi's Rocky Mountain Journal* (Denver), July 27, 1967. Elson also commented that in 1962, "forty percent of the people in Arizona didn't even know who Carl Hayden was, because he didn't put out press releases."

15. Elson, "Oral History Interviews, April 27 to August 21, 1990," 124. Hayden initialed the memorandum and Elson took it as permission to do "everything that was in there, whether he agreed to it or not." Meanwhile, Elson had commissioned a poll that showed the senator in serious trouble throughout the state.

16. Ibid., 125-26.

17. *Los Angeles Times*, January 5, 1969; Elson, "Oral History Interviews, April 27 to August 21, 1990," 125-27; James Minotto interview with Barbara Van Norman, Carl Hayden Oral History Project, Arizona State University, July 5, 1973. According to Minotto, a longtime Democratic operative who was affiliated with the 1962 Hayden campaign asserted, "some of the people in this state said that the Senator had died and that the doctors would not divulge his death so that he would be elected regardless of the fact that he had passed away."

18. Ross Rice interview with James Minotto, July 5, 1973; Ross Rice interview with Morris Udall, December 30, 1972; Jack L. August, Jr., interview with William S. Gookin, July 20, 1982; Jack L. August, Jr., interview with Barry Goldwater September 15, 1985, OHC, AC, ASU; *Los Angeles Times*, January 5, 1969; *Arizona Republic*, November 4, 1962. Three years after the 1962 election, a recently published political science textbook written by Marvin H. Bernstein and

Wallace Murphy of Princeton University, in a footnote on page 312, reported that Hayden had died. Hayden took time to write the Princeton professors a letter informing them that their textbook, *American Democracy in Theory and in Practice* was not in accord with the latest edition of the *Congressional Directory* which indicated that "I had been reelected in 1962 to be a Senator from Arizona for a term of six years." Hayden included a wry postscript to the letter: "I have not determined whether I will be a candidate for reelection to the United States Senate for a term beginning in 1969." *Washington Post*, May 6, 1965.

19. Elson, "Oral History Interviews, April 27 to August 21, 1990," 128; *Los Angeles Times*, January 5, 1969.

20. The five justices upholding the recommendations of Special Master Simon Rifkind were Hugo L. Black, author of the opinion, Byron R. White, Arthur J. Goldberg, Tom C. Clark, and William Brennan, Jr. Justice William O. Douglas wrote a tart dissent and Justice John H. Harlan drafted a separate dissent which had the concurrence of Justice Potter Stewart. Chief Justice Earl Warren, who was governor of California at the time the suit was filed, did not participate in the decision. Douglas, whose dissent was extremely sharp, wrote in part: "Much is written these days about judicial lawmaking, and every scholar knows that judges who construe statutes must of necessity legislate interstitially ... the present case is different. It will, I think, be marked as the baldest attempt by judges in modern times to spin their own philosophy into the fabric of law in derogation to the will of the legislature. The present decision, as Mr. Justice Harlan shows, grants the federal bureaucracy a power and command over water rights in the seventeen western states that it has never had, that it always wanted, that it could never persuade Congress to grant, and that this court up to now has consistently refused to recognize." *Arizona v. California et al.*, 373 U.S. 587 (1963); Jack L. August, Jr., interview with Wesley Steiner, February 18, 1983, Phoenix, Arizona; August interview with Wayne Akin, September 18, 1982, Phoenix, Arizona; August interview with John J. Rhodes, November 4, 1985, Tempe, Arizona, OHC, AC, ASU; *Arizona Republic*, June 4, 1963.

21. *Arizona Republic*, June 4, 1963.

22. Hundley, "The West Against Itself," *New Courses for the Colorado River*, 32; Hundley, "Clio Nods: *Arizona v. California* and the Boulder Canyon Act," *Western Historical Quarterly*, 17-51; Elson, "Oral History Interviews, April 27 to August 21, 1990," 186.

23. Arizona's attorneys, who fought the eleven-year court battle, were equally jubilant over the decision. Two who laid the groundwork and who subsequently died during the hearings were Charles A. Carson, Sr., and J.H. "Hub" Moeur, who actually filed the lawsuit and served as chief Arizona counsel in its early stages. Many, however,

credited attorneys Charley Reed of Coolidge and Mark Wilmer of Phoenix, along with their backup staff of attorneys and engineers, for orchestrating the judicial victory. According to Colorado River historian Hundley, moreover, states had always determined water laws applicable to their citizens they had naturally also determined the water rights of those citizens. But now the Court held that Congress had empowered the Secretary of the Interior to determine those rights when water had been secured by contract from a federal reclamation project. This aspect of the ruling also eroded state's rights at the expense of the federal government; Hundley, "The West Against Itself," *New Courses for the Colorado River*, 32; *Arizona v. California et al.*, 373 U.S. 587 (1963); *Arizona Republic*, June 4, 1963.

24. August interview with Simon Rifkind, October 12, 1986, Ruidoso, New Mexico, author's files. Indeed the majority decision upheld Special Master Rifkind's apportionment of waters to Indian reservations as "present perfected rights" established prior to 1929. Arizona had argued against this part of the master's proposed decree and was therefore opposed by the federal government. See also Hundley, "The West Against Itself," *New Courses for the Colorado River,* 32-33; Norris Hundley, Jr., "The Winters' Decision and Indian Water Rights: A Mystery Reexamined," *Western Historical Quarterly* 13 (1982), 17-42; *Arizona v. California et al.*, 373 U.S. 587, 596, 598-601 (1963); *Winters v. United States*, 207 U.S. 564 (1908); *Arizona v. California et al.*, 439 U.S. 422 (1979).

25. The Court thus reaffirmed *Winters*, asserting that the Native American rights existed whether or not they were actually using the water and continued unimpaired even if they should cease their uses. Some of the lands along the lower reaches of the Colorado had been set aside as early as 1865 and none later than 1917. Indeed, legally, at least, the five tribes now rested on solid legal ground concerning rights to Colorado River water. See Norris Hundley, Jr., "The Dark and Bloody Ground of Indian Water Rights: Confusion Elevated to Principle," *Western Historical Quarterly* 9 (1978), 478-79; Hundley, "The West Against Itself," *New Courses for the Colorado River,* 33.

26. In his memorandum of April 10, 1963, Hayden wrote: "I feel that our bill should be as simple as possible, and as similar as practicable to the bill considered by Congress in the late 1940s and early 1950s and twice passed the Senate." Hayden, "Memorandum," May 10, 1963, Box 2, Folder 4, CHPC, ASU; "Arizona Seeks Billion Dollar Water Project," *Congressional Quarterly Fact Sheet*, June 5, 1963.

27. *New York Times*, June 13, 1963; Edward C. Johnson to Hayden, June 14, 1963; Hubert Humphrey to Hayden, June 4, 1963; Clay Simer to Hayden, n.d., Box 2, Folder 1, CHPC, ASU; Morris Udall, "Arizona's Water Fight Shifts to Congress," *Congressman's Report*, June 21, 1963. See also S 1658.

28. Elson, "Oral History Interviews, April 27 to August 21, 1990," 185-87; C.A. Pugh to Hayden, January 15, 1963; Roy Elson to Paul Fannin, June 3, 1963; Memorandum to Files, "Statement Made by Secretary Udall to Senator Hayden," July 11, 1963, Box 2, Folder 15, CHPC, ASU; "Arizona Seeks Billion Dollar Water Project," *Congressional Quarterly Fact Sheet,* June 5, 1963. The technical reports convinced Arizona leaders of the need for CAP and, for the most part, they stood together. The Arizona delegation worked together on the bill, and the three House members, representing both political parties, often issued joint releases. Both Democratic and Republican governors endorsed the bill. Moreover, early in 1966, a task force of Arizonans who maintained various areas of expertise gathered in Washington to assist the efforts of the congressional delegation. The members and staff were from the Arizona Interstate Stream Commission, Arizona Public Service, Salt River Project, and the Central Arizona Project Association.

29. Elson, "Oral History Interviews, April 27 to August 21, 1990," 185-86; Helen Ingram, *Water Politics: Continuity and Change* (Albuquerque: University of New Mexico Press, 1990), 46-47. As Helen Ingram explains, "The extent of Arizona's effort was commensurate with the perceptions within the state of the benefits to be gained from CAP. This was based partly on the felt need for additional water in some parts of the state. In large part, however, the belief in CAP was emotional and symbolic."

30. John Rhodes to Hayden, January 25, 1963, Box 3, Folder 8; Wayne Aspinall to Stewart Udall, November 27, 1962, Box 3, Folder 10, CHPC, ASU; *Washington Post*, January 22, 1962; *Arizona Republic*, January 22, 1963; *New York Times*, January 22, 1963; United States Secretary of the Interior, "News Release: Secretary Udall Announces Study for Regional Solution of Water and Power for Problems of the Pacific Southwest," January 22, 1963; Ingram, *Water Politics*, 48.

31. Udall also noted that the long-range Lower Colorado River Basin Plan (PSWP) was patterned in part on the successful Colorado River Basin Storage Project in the upper basin. In addition he said, "A critical period is at hand, a more critical period lies ahead for millions of people who are flocking to the Pacific Southwest to establish permanent homes. This burgeoning population will require vast quantities of additional water for industrial and municipal use; greater quantities of electricity and other basic services; and more irrigated lands. Piecemeal development cannot do the job. Only regional planning, and action will enable us to meet the growth of this area." See, U.S. Department of the Interior, "News Release," January 22, 1963; Ingram, *Water Politics*, 48; Ernest A. Englebert, *Policy Issues of the Pacific Southwest Water Plan* (Boulder: University of Colorado Press, 1965), 130-35; Hayden, "Fact Sheet on Interior's Pacific Southwest Water Plan," n.d., Box 2, Folder 14, CHPC, ASU; Carl Hayden to Stewart Udall, February 20, 1964,

White House Central Files (WHCF), NR 7, UT 4 (1963-64), Lyndon Baines Johnson Presidential Library (LBJ), Austin, Texas.

32. Elson, "Oral History Interviews, April 27 to August 21, 1990," 186-87. Elson recalled that Hayden wanted a simple CAP bill, but he noted, "Stewart Udall became Secretary of Interior ... in '61, during the Kennedy administration. As the thing proceeded from '62 to '63 we heard these rumbles that everyone was complaining whether there was enough water in the river, and immediately we got into a numbers game, and hydrology, what was coming down ... through Glen Canyon, and the runoffs of the Upper Basin and the Lower Basin, and the Mexican Water Treaty obligations. You had everything involved in this, international, interstate, the West." See also Stewart Udall to Carl Hayden, December 19, 1963, Box 2, Folder 14; Hayden to Udall, n.d., Box 3, Folder 14; Paul Fannin, "News Release," December 27, 1963, all in CHPC, ASU. Fannin also wrote that "it is already apparent that the report was cleverly written by someone in the Department of Interior to give California a logical excuse for delaying any and all favorable action on either a practical regional water plan or the CAP which is now before Congress." He worried that "in spite of the favorable Court decision ... California can and will continue to use our share of the river until we obtain congressional authorization of the CAP."

33. Elson, "Oral History interviews, April 27 to August 21, 1990," 187; *Yuma Daily Sun*, June 16, 1963.

34. Stewart Udall to Hayden, "Personal," August 20, 1963, Box 2, Folder 14; Hayden to Udall, December 5, 1963, Box 2, Folder 1, CHPC, ASU; *New York Times*, June 13, 1963; *Arizona Republic*, August 14, 1963. In his August 20, 1963, letter to Hayden, Udall declared, "From this point on I intend to give Goldwater and Pulliam blow for blow if that is what they want. I may be 1000% wrong but on the basis of my knowledge of the art of the possible in the House and my conversations with Chairman Aspinall and others, it has been my best judgment that some kind of regional approach will be absolutely essential if a Central Arizona Project is to pass in the House.... In my opinion, Governor Fannin and the Arizona water people have made a grievous mistake in failing to have any consultation whatsoever with the members of the House concerning basic strategy. The Pulliam-Goldwater tactics of attempting to bludgeon my brother and Rep. Senner into line with their strategy is outrageous and indefensible."

35. Hayden, "Statement Upon Resumption of Hearings on S 1658," n.d., Box 3, Folder 9, CHPC, ASU; Morris K. Udall, "Arizona's Water Fight Shifts to Congress, *Congressman's Report*, June 21, 1963; Reisner, *Cadillac Desert*, 272-73. According to Reisner, in his powerful critique of the Bureau of Reclamation, "pol-

itics demanded that [CAP] be built, and in the 1960s, Arizona had power. Barry Goldwater was the presidential candidate of the Republican Party; Carl Hayden was the chairman of the Senate Appropriations Committee."

36. Hayden also reminded the committee that before any water could be conveyed through proposed PSWP facilities, the federal government had to construct the Auburn-Folsom South Unit ($400 million), the East Side Division of the Central Valley Project ($1 billion) and the state of California needed to complete the aqueduct system under the California State Water Plan. Hayden stated that he opposed "any proposals that would permit consideration to be given to these two California projects in preference to consideration of CAP, which has been waiting before Congress for fifteen years." Hayden, "Statement Upon Resumption of Hearings on S 1658," n.d., Box 3, Folder 9, CHPC, ASU.

37. Reisner, *Cadillac Desert*, 273; Hayden to Henry Jackson, February 18, 1964; Hayden, "California and the Central Arizona Project," August 5, 1963, Box 2, Folder 15, CHPC. Hayden detailed ten methods in which California obstructed Arizona from putting water to beneficial use from the Colorado between 1924 and 1963. He included California's refusal to accept the division of water recommended by the Colorado River basin Governors in 1924 and their insistence on endless negotiations among lower-basin States. Hayden also pointed to California's strenuous resistance to ratifying the 1944 Mexican Treaty which settled Mexican rights to Colorado River Water and the state's consumption of eleven months instead of the ninety days required by law in commenting on Interior's Central Arizona Project Report of 1947.

38. See M. Udall to John Rhodes and Sam Steiger, February 2, 1967, Box 5, Folder 12, CHPC, ASU. Udall wrote his fellow Arizona representatives that "there will be no House bill passed this year (1967) without Arizona, California and Colorado working together." Indeed, by early 1967, Arizona's House delegation believed that the "Colorado-California" partnership had been thoroughly sealed. The partnership was based upon seeing a CAP bill that provided for a Northwest study of some kind. Because of this alliance, Arizona's representatives correctly predicted that their bill at the time (H.R. 4671) would be opposed by the three Northwest Republicans and two Northwest Democrats sitting on the subcommittee and the full committee. See also Roderick Nash, *Wilderness and the American Mind*, 3d ed. (New Haven: Yale University Press, 1982), 209-35; *Congressional Quarterly Fact Sheet* (November 1, 1969), 3019-31, Ingram, *Water Politics*, 52; Reisner, *Cadillac Desert*, 281-91; Hundley, "The West Against Itself," *New Courses for the Colorado River*, 36; M. Udall, "Congressman's Report," June 21, 1963; Henry M. Jackson to Hayden, August 15, 1963; Hayden to Henry M. Jackson, February 18, 1964, Box 2, Folder 15, CHPC, ASU.

39. Ingram, *Water Politics*, 52-53; Udall, "Congressman's Report," June 21, 1963.

40. Reisner, *Cadillac Desert*, 280-82, 29-93; Ingram, *Water Politics*, 48-52; M. Udall, "Congressman's Report," June 21, 1963.

41. The House Interior Committee was burdened with the heaviest workload of any committee in Congress. In fact, nearly 30 percent of all bills in the House were referred to this committee. At the time of CAP consideration, the committee was generally favorable to reclamation as a majority of its members had seen its benefits in their own districts. In recent years, however, reclamation projects had met increasing resistance both in committee and in the House itself due to the marginal quality of projects and to the reluctance of eastern and urban congressmen to put water to additional lands because of farm product surplus. Moreover, CAP was not the only reclamation bill before the Subcommittee of Irrigation and Reclamation. Since January 1963, no less than fifteen other projects had been proposed and these bills awaited action. The backlog was a critical problem. Udall, "Congressman's Report," June 21, 1963; Ingram, *Water Politics*, 48-50.

42. Elson, "Oral History Interviews, April 21 to August 27, 1990," 184-90; Reisner, *Cadillac Desert*, 290-91; Ingram, *Water Politics*, 50. Ingram describes Aspinall's role, interests, and motivation in CAP consideration as "mixed and complex." Besides serving as champion of Colorado's interest and especially the spokesman for the western slope in water matters, Ingram argues that he maintained "a general paternity of the whole Colorado River basin and felt a responsibility for peaceful and harmonious development of water resources."

43. Rhodes interview with August, OHC, ASU; Elson, "Oral History Interviews," 193-94; Udall, "Congressman's Report," June 21, 1963.

44. See David Brower to President Lyndon Johnson, to Stewart Udall, to Henry Jackson, January 30, 1967, Box 19, Folder NR 7-1, WHCF; Members of the Dartmouth Faculty to Lyndon Johnson, July 25, 1966, Box 145, Folder LE/NR 7-15, WHCF, LBJ Presidential Library. Democratic governor Sam Goddard and former Arizona senator, governor, and colleague of President Johnson, Ernest McFarland, made attempts to counter the environmentalist arguments in personal letters to the president. See Sam Goddard to Lyndon Johnson, August 22, 1966, Box 145, Folder LE NR 7-1; Ernest McFarland to Lyndon Johnson, August 5, 1966, Box 19, Folder EX NR7-1/U, WHCF, LBJ Presidential Library.

45. Elson, "Oral History Interviews," 193-94; Reisner, *Cadillac Desert*, 285; Ingram, *Water Politics*, 55. According to Reisner, Brower and the Sierra Club led the highly publicized fight. He recruited Luna Leopold, one of the country's best-known

hydrologists and the son of Aldo Leopold, to criticize the Bureau's flow calculations, and deserves the most credit for eliminating Grand Canyon dams from CAP.

46. Hayden wrote a friend in support of the Grand Canyon dams: "I was aware of this future need [hydroelectric power] when Grand Canyon National Park was created by Act of Congress in 1919 when I was a young congressman from Arizona and for that reason made certain that the reservation for future reclamation development was clearly understood. The same question arose when Grand Canyon National Monument was created by Executive Order in 1932 and a letter exists in the Department of Interior files from then-director of the National Park Service Horace M. Albright to the Commissioner of Reclamation Elwood Mead, stating positively that creation of the monument would not interfere with construction of Boulder Canyon Dam or other dams. See Hayden to Oakes, n.d., Box 5, Folder 9, CHPC; Hayden to Lyndon Johnson, "Statement of Carl Hayden of Arizona, July 26, 1967, Accompanying the filing of the Majority Report of the Senate Committee on Interior and Insular Affairs on S 1004 authorizing the Central Arizona Project," Box 1967, NR 7-1/6 FG 145, WHCF, LBJ Presidential Library; Rhodes interview with August; Goldwater interview with August, OHC, ASU; Elson, "Oral History Interviews, 194-95; Worster, *Rivers of Empire*, 276; Reisner, *Cadillac Desert*, 287, 290; Hundley, "The West Against Itself," *New Courses for the Colorado River*, 36, 37; Ingram, *Water Politics*, 55-56.

47. Elson, "Oral History Interviews, April 27 to August 21, 1990," 185-86; Hundley, "The West Against Itself," *New Courses for the Colorado River*, 35-36; Ingram, *Water Politics*, 60-65;

48. Rhodes interview with August, November 4, 1985; Rod McMullin interview with Jack L. August, Jr., Scottsdale, Arizona, August 24, 1984; Roger Ernst interview with Jack L. August, Jr., Paradise Valley, Arizona, March 23, 1983, OHC, AC, ASU; Carl Hayden to Lawrence Mehren, August 14, 1964, Box 4, Folder 10, CHPC, ASU; Hayden to Lyndon Johnson, August 4, 1964, Box 145, LE/NR 7-1, WHCF, LBJ Presidential Library.

49. Ronald Reagan to Raymond R. Rummonds, November 28, 1967, Box 600, Folder 6, CHPC, ASU; Barefoot Sanders to Lyndon Johnson, August 1, 1968; James R. Jones to Carl Hayden, August 19, 1968, Box 1968, CWH File, LBJ Presidential Library. See also House Committee on Interior and Insular Affairs, *Hearings on Lower Colorado River Basin Project, H.R. 4671 and Similar Bills*, 89 Cong. (1965-1966); *Hearings on Colorado River Basin Project*, 90 Cong., 1 Sess. (1967); *Hearings on Colorado River Basin Project, Part II*, 90 Cong., 2 Sess. (1968). For a narrative/chronological history of Arizona's struggle for CAP see Johnson, *The Central Arizona Project, 1918-1968*, passim; *Arizona Republic*, September 13, October 1, 1968.

50. For the best analysis of the intraregional bargaining process involved in the Colorado River Basin Project Act see Ingram, *Water Politics*, chapter 4; Helen M. Ingram, *Patterns of Politics in Water Resource Development: A Case Study of New Mexico's Role in the Colorado River Basin Bill* (Albuquerque: University of New Mexico Press, 1969). See also Hundley, "The West Against Itself," *New Courses for the Colorado River*, 36-37; Reisner, *Cadillac Desert*, 294-95.

51. On several occasions Hayden told close friends, "Dick Russell was my best friend in the Senate. We served together for 36 years. Coming from the South kept him from being President of the United States." Carl Hayden to James Chilton, February 24, 1971, James Chilton Papers, Los Angeles, California; U.S. Senate Committee on Appropriations, "Press Release, Monday, May 6, 1968"; *Los Angeles Times*, January 5, 1969; *Arizona Republic*, May 7, 1969; *Arizona Daily Star*, May 7, 1969.

52. Carl Hayden, "Arizona Report," 1968, Carl Hayden Letters, Folder 7, Arizona Historical Society, Tucson, Arizona; "In Memorium: Senator Carl Hayden, 1877-1972," HBF, CHPC, ASU.

IX—"ARIZONA'S MOST DISTINGUISHED CITIZEN"

1. M. Udall interview with Ross Rice, December 30, 1972, OHC, ASU.

2. Also, Senator Hayden kept his schedule "loose" during his retirement, yet followed the "same routine" which included "going to the Library three days a week to get my letters typewritten," spending three hours at his desk (which was shipped from his office in Washington) from noon to 3:00 P.M., then he took home the mail. He lamented that "never before have I had so many birthday letters to acknowledge." Carl Hayden to James Chilton, November 18, 1970, James Chilton Papers, Los Angeles, California; *Phoenix Gazette*, May 8, 1969; James Chilton interview with Jack L. August, Jr., July 1, 1993, author's files. In addition, Arizona State University began a Carl Hayden Project which included the organization of his voluminous public papers and an oral history project.

3. At Hayden's memorial service, former President Lyndon Johnson and Senator Barry Goldwater, who faced off in the 1964 presidential election, addressed those in attendance. "In Memorium: Senator Carl Hayden, 1877-1972," HBF, CHPC, ASU; *Los Angeles Times*, January 5, 1969; Hundley, *Water and the West*, 332.

4. Nash, *The American West in the Twentieth Century*, 3-5; Earl Pomeroy, "The Urban Frontier in the Far West," in John G. Clark, ed., *The Frontier Challenge: Responses to the Trans-Mississippi West* (Manhattan: University of Kansas Press, 1971), 13-

16; Hundley, *Water and the West*, x; Bracken and Kahn, *Arizona Tomorrow*, 87. For a short concise analysis of urban growth in Phoenix and Tucson see Bradford Luckingham, "Urban Development in Arizona: The Rise of Phoenix," *Journal of Arizona History* 22 (Summer 1981), 197-235; Bradford Luckingham, *The Urban Southwest: A Profile History of Albuquerque, El Paso, Phoenix, and Tucson* (El Paso: Texas Western Press, 1982).

5. Hundley, *Water and the West*, xv-xvi; Peter Wiley and Robert Gottlieb, *Empires in the Sun: The Rise of the New American West* (New York: G.P. Putnam and Sons, 1982), 5; *Tombstone Prospector*, May 9, 1923.

6. Much has been written on this topic yet the first major exponent of this theory of western history, Earl Pomeroy, initially published his ideas on East-West continuity in "Toward a Reorientation of Western History: Continuity and Environment," *Mississippi Valley Historical Review* 41 (March 1955), 579-99. He developed these ideas more thoroughly in Pomeroy, *The Pacific Slope: A History of California, Oregon, Washington, Idaho, Utah, and Nevada* (New York: Alfred A. Knopf, 1965). See also John Caughey, "The Insignificance of the Frontier in American History," *Western Historical Quarterly* 5 (January 1974), 5-16; Howard Lamar, "Persistent Frontier: The West in the Twentieth Century," *Western Historical Quarterly* 4 (January 1973), 5-25; Gene Gressley, *The American West: A Potpourri* (Columbia: University of Missouri Press, 1977); Frank Trelease, "Arizona v California: Allocation of Water Resources to People, States, and Nation," in Philip B. Kurtland, ed., *The Supreme Court Review, 1963* (Chicago: University of Chicago Press, 1963).

7. Roy Elson to Jack L. August, Jr., March 3, 1983, author's files; *New York Times*, February 19, 1962; *Senate Document 76*, 71, 123, 134.

8. Carl Hayden to Charles Hayden, September 14, 1896, HFLC, CHPC, ASU; *Tucson Daily Citizen*, October 2, 1957; *Senate Document 76*, 19, 27, 38, 65, 67-70, 81-82, 123, 130. Hayden also played a major role in having Truman appointed to chair the War Investigating Committee during World War II, thereby placing the midwestern senator in the public spotlight, which, with dramatic help from fate, elevated the Missourian to the White House.

9. See Edward L. Bernays, ed., *The Engineering of Consent* (Norman: University of Oklahoma Press, 1955), 3-7.

10. Hundley, "The West Against itself," *New Courses for the Colorado River*, 42.

11. Fradkin, *A River No More*, 250.

Selected Bibliography

INTERVIEWS

Akin, Wayne. Interview with author. Phoenix, Arizona, 14 September 1982, Oral History Collection, Arizona Collection, Arizona State University, Tempe.

Chilton, James. Interview with author. Los Angeles, California, 18, 19 June 1992, author's files.

Elson, Roy. Interview with author. Washington, D.C., 27 September 1987, author's files.

Goldwater, Barry. Interview with author. Paradise Valley, Arizona, 15 September 1985, Oral History Collection, Arizona Collection, Arizona State University, Tempe.

Hayden, Carl. Interview with Joe Frantz. Old Senate Office Building 133, Washington D.C., 28 October 1968, Lyndon Baines Johnson Presidential Library, Austin, Texas.

Hayden, Hayden C. Interview with author. Tempe, Arizona, 21 September 1983, author's files.

Hayden, Larry. Interview with author. Tucson, Arizona, 11 October 1983, author's files.

Pyle, Howard. Interview with author. Phoenix, Arizona, 9 November 1982, Oral History Collection, Arizona Collection, Arizona State University, Tempe.

Rhodes, John J. Interview with author. Tempe, Arizona, 21 October 1985, Oral History Collection, Arizona Collection, Arizona State University, Tempe.

Rifkind, Simon. Interview with author. Santa Fe, New Mexico, 9 October 1986, author's files.

Sloan, Eleanor. Interview with author. Phoenix, Arizona, 27 June 1984, Oral History Collection, Arizona Collection, Arizona State University, Tempe.

Steiner, Wesley. Interview with author. Phoenix, Arizona, 18 February 1983, Oral History Collection, Arizona Collection, Arizona State University, Tempe.

PAMPHLETS

Centennial Commission. Program. *Ferry–Tale: Century in the Sun, 1871–1971.* Tempe, Arizona.

Udall, Morris. "Carl Hayden: Quiet History Maker." *Congressman's Report*, 11 (March 1971).

COURT CASES

Arizona v. California, 298 U.S. 558; 80 L. Ed. 1331, 1332–33 (1936).

Arizona v. California, 299 U.S. 341; 78 L. Ed. 1298 (1934).

Arizona v. California et. al., 283 U.S. 423; 75 L. Ed. 115 (1931).

Arizona v. California et. al., 373 U.S. 546 (1963).

United States v. Arizona, 295 U.S. 174; 79 L. Ed. 1374 (1935).

Wyoming v. California, 259 U.S. 419 (1922).

GOVERNMENT DOCUMENTS

Arizona Engineering Commission. *Reports Based on Reconnaissance Investigation of Arizona Land Irrigable from the Colorado River.* Arizona Department of Library and Archives, Phoenix, 1923.

Chittenden, Hiram. *Preliminary Examination of Reservoir Sites in Wyoming and Colorado.* 55th Cong., 2nd sess., 1897. H. Doc. 141.

Colorado River Commission of Arizona. *Official Report of the Proceedings of the Colorado River Conference.* Phoenix: State of Arizona, 1925.

______. *Second Report to the Eighth Legislature, December 31, 1928.* Phoenix, Arizona, 1928.

Committee on Water of the National Research Council. *Water and Choice in the Colorado River Basin.* National Academy of Science Publications no. 1689, 1968.

Congressional Record. 62nd Cong., 2nd sess., 1912.

______. 63rd Cong., 2nd sess., 1914.

______. 65th Cong., 3rd sess., 1919.

______. 66th Cong., 1st sess., 1919.

______. 66th Cong., 2nd sess., 1920.

______. 69th Cong., 2nd sess., 1926.

______. 70th Cong., 2nd sess., 1928.

______. 90th Cong., 2nd sess., 1968.

The Great Register. Arizona State University Archives, Tempe.

Official General Election Returns, State of Arizona, 4 November, 1924. Arizona Department of Library, Archives, and Public Records, Phoenix.

Powell, John Wesley. *Report on the Lands of the Arid Region of the United States*. 45th Cong., 2nd sess., 1878. H. Ex. Doc. 73.

______. *Reservoirs in Arid Regions of the United States*. 50th Cong., 1st sess., 1888. S. Ex. Doc. 163.

State of Arizona. House. *Journal*. 1923.

______. *Journal*. 1925.

______. *Journal*. 1927.

______. *Journal*. 1944.

State of Arizona. Senate. *Journal*. 1923.

Territorial Censuses of Arizona, 1860, 1864, 1870. Washington, D.C.

United States Bureau of the Census. *Twelfth Census of the United States, Rev. ed., 1900*. Washington, D.C., 1903.

______. *Thirteenth Census of the United States, 1910*. Washington, D.C., 1913.

United States Congress. House. *Boulder Canyon Reclamation Project*. 69th Cong., 2nd sess., 1926. H. Rept. 1657, Part 3.

______. *Colorado River Compact*. 67th Cong., 4th sess., 1923. H. Doc. 605.

______. Committee on Irrigation and Reclamation. *Hearings on Protection and Development of the Lower Colorado River Basin, H.R. 2903*. 68th Cong., 1st sess., 1924.

______. Committee on Irrigation of Arid Lands. *Hearings on All–American Canal for Imperial and Coachella Valleys, California, H.R. 6044*. 66th Cong., 1st sess., 1919.

______. Committee on Irrigation of Arid Lands. *Hearings on Protection and Development of Lower Colorado River Basin, H.R. 11449*. 67th Cong., 2nd sess., 1922.

______. Committee on Rules. *Hearings on H.R. 9826*. 69th Cong., 2nd sess., 1927.

______. *Report of the Colorado River Board on the Boulder Dam Project*. 70th Cong., 2nd sess., 1928. H. Doc. 446.

United States Congress. Senate. *Memorial Addresses and Other Tributes in the Congress of the United States on the Life and Contribution of Carl T. Hayden*. 92nd Cong., 2nd sess., 1972. S. Doc. 92–68.

______. *Problems of Imperial Valley and Vicinity*. 67th Cong., 2nd sess., 1922. S. Doc. 142, appendix.

______. *Tributes to Commemorate the Occasion of Carl Hayden's Fiftieth Anniversary of Congressional Service*. 87th Cong., 2nd sess., 1962. S. Doc. 76.

United States Department of Agriculture. *Silt in the Colorado River and its Relation to Irrigation*. Technical Bulletin no. 67. Washington D.C., 1928.

United States Department of the Interior. *Fourteenth Annual Report of the Reclamation Service, 1914–15*. Washington, D.C., 1915.

United States Department of Reclamation. *Report on the Central Arizona Project, United States Department of the Interior Planning Report no. 3–8B, 4–2*. Washington, D.C.: GPO, 1948.

United States Geological Survey. *First Annual Report of the Reclamation Service, 1902*. Washington, D.C., 1903.

MANUSCRIPT COLLECTIONS

Arizona Colorado River Commission Papers. Arizona Department of Library, Archives and Public Records, Phoenix.

Bureau of Reclamation Papers. National Archives and Records Service, Washington, D.C.

Fireman, Bert. Bert Fireman Collection. Arizona Historical Foundation, Arizona State University, Tempe.

Hayden, Carl. Carl Hayden Letters Collection. Arizona Heritage Center, Tucson.

______. Carl Hayden Papers Collection. Hayden Biographical File. Arizona Collection, Arizona State University, Tempe.

Hayden Family Letters Collection. Arizona Collection, Arizona State University, Tempe.

Hunt, George W. P. George W. P. Hunt Diaries. Arizona Collection, Arizona State University, Tempe.

______. G. W. P. Hunt Papers. Arizona Collection, Arizona State University, Tempe.

Maxwell, George. George Maxwell Papers. Arizona Department of Library, Archives and Public Records, Phoenix.

Pyle, Howard. Papers. Tempe (Arizona) Historical Society.

Small Collections File. Arizona Collection, Arizona State University, Tempe.

UNPUBLISHED MATERIALS

Alkire, Frank T. "Committee of Nine (or Eleven)." Arizona State University, Tempe, n.d. Arizona Collection, Hayden Library, Arizona State University.

Haigler, Ruby. "History of Tempe." Arizona State University, Tempe, 1914. Arizona Collection, Hayden Library, Arizona State University.

Jones, Daniel P. "Autobiography." Arizona State University, Tempe, 1924. Arizona Collection, Hayden Library, Arizona State University.

Kluger, James R. "Elwood Mead: Irrigation Engineer and Social Planner." Ph.D. dissertation, University of Arizona, Tucson, 1970.

Mawn, Geoffry P. "Phoenix, Arizona: Central City of the Southwest, 1870–1920." Ph.D. dissertation, Arizona State University, Tempe, 1979.

Mayo, Dwight. "Arizona and the Colorado River Compact." M.A. thesis, Arizona State University, Tempe, 1964. Arizona Collection, Hayden Library, Arizona State University.

Metcalf, Barbara Ann. "Oliver Wozencraft in California, 1849–1887." M.A. thesis, University of Southern California, Los Angeles, 1963.

Moody, Clara. "The San Carlos Irrigation Project—Pima Indian Irrigation." Arizona State University, Tempe, 1954. Arizona Collection, Hayden Library, Arizona State University.

Moore, Hal. "The Salt River Project—Beehive of Prosperity." Arizona State University, Tempe, 1951. Arizona Collection, Hayden Library, Arizona State University.

______. "The Salt River Valley." Arizona State University, Tempe, 1951. Arizona Collection, Hayden Library, Arizona State University.

Smith, Karen. "The Magnificent Experiment: Building the Salt River Reclamation Project, 1890–1917." Ph.D. dissertation, University of California, Santa Barbara, 1982.

Weiseiger, Marsha. "The History of Tempe, Arizona, 1871–1930: A Preliminary Report." Arizona State University, Tempe, 1977. Arizona Collection, Hayden Library, Arizona State University.

Wilson, Marjorie Haines. "The Gubernatorial Career of G.W.P. Hunt of Arizona." Ph.D. dissertation, Arizona State University, Tempe, 1973.

NEWSPAPERS AND PERIODICALS

Arizona Blade Tribune (Florence)

Arizona Citizen (Tucson)

Arizona Daily Star (Tucson)

Arizona Democrat (Phoenix)

Arizona Gazette (Phoenix)

Arizona Guardian (Phoenix)

Arizona Miner (Prescott)

Arizona Republic (Phoenix)

Arizona Republican (Phoenix)

Arizona Statesman (Phoenix)

Benson News

Calexico Chronicle

Casa Grande Dispatch

Casa Grande Valley Dispatch

Chloride Herald

Coconino Sun (Flagstaff)

Coolidge News

The Daily Silver Belt (Globe)

Denver Times

Douglas Daily Dispatch

Douglas Industrial Semenario Democrata

For Greater Arizona: A Clipping Sheet of University of Arizona News

Globe Silver Belt

Graham County Guardian (Safford)

The Imperial Valley Farmer

Jerome News

La Democracia: Semenario de Politica, Comercio, Industria, Anuncias, y Variedades

La Voz Del Pueblo

Los Angeles Examiner

Los Angeles Times

Mesa Journal–Tribune

Mohave County Miner

New York Times

Nogales Daily Herald

Phoenix Daily Enterprise

Phoenix Daily Herald

Phoenix Gazette

Phoenix Herald

Prescott Courier

Prescott Journal–Miner

Reno Journal

Riverside Press

Roll Call: The Newspaper of Capitol Hill

Salt River Herald

San Diego Union

San Francisco Daily News

Tempe Daily News

Tempe News

Time Magazine (New York)

Tombstone Daily Prospector

Tombstone Epitaph

Tombstone Prospector

Tucson Citizen

Washington Star

Weekly Arizona Miner

Weekly Arizonan

Weekly Phoenix Herald

Yuma Examiner

JOURNAL ARTICLES

August, Jack L., Jr. "Carl Hayden: Born a Politician." *Journal of Arizona History* 26 (Summer 1985).

______. "A Sterling Young Democrat: Carl Hayden's Road to Congress, 1900–1912." *Journal of Arizona History* 28 (Autumn 1987).

______. "Carl Hayden, Arizona, and the Politics of Water Development in the Southwest, 1923–1928." *Pacific Historical Review* 58 (May 1989).

______. "Carl Hayden's 'Indian Card': Environmental Politics and the San Carlos Reclamation Project." *Journal of Arizona History* 34 (Winter 1993).

______. "A Vision in the Desert: Charles Trumbull Hayden, Salt River Pioneer." *Journal of Arizona History* 36 (Summer 1995).

______. "Desert Bloom or Desert Doom? Carl Hayden and the Origins of the Central Arizona Project, 1922–1952." *Cactus and Pine* 8 (Summer 1996).

Caughey, John. "The Insignificance of the Frontier in American History." *Western Historical Quarterly* 5 (January 1974).

Colley, Charles. "Carl Hayden—Phoenician." *Journal of Arizona History* 18 (Autumn 1977).

Conkin, Paul. "The Vision of Elwood Mead." *Agricultural History* 34 (April 1960).

Day, Juliet. "A Dam for Arizona's Indians." *Arizona Highways* 6 (July 1930).

Fireman, Bert. "Charles Trumbull Hayden." *The Smoke Signal* (Tucson Corral of the Westerners) 19 (Spring 1969).

Ganoe, John T. "The Origin of a National Reclamation Policy." *Mississippi Valley Historical Review* 18 (June 1931).

Gressley, Gene. "Arthur Powell Davis, Reclamation and the West." *Agricultural History* 42 (July 1968).

Hayden, Sallie. "The Haydens Came First." *Arizona Cattlelog* 13 (March 1957).

Houghton, N.D. "Problems of the Colorado River as Reflected in Arizona Politics." *Western Political Quarterly* 4 (December 1951).

Hundley, Norris, Jr. "Clio Nods: Arizona v. California and the Boulder Canyon Act—A Reassessment." *Western Historical Quarterly* 3 (January 1972).

______. "The Colorado Waters Dispute." *Foreign Affairs* 42 (April 1964).

______. "The Politics of Reclamation: California, the Federal Government, and the Origins of the Boulder Canyon Act." *California Historical Quarterly* 52 (Winter 1973).

James, George Wharton. "In the Egypt of America: The Salt River Project." *Twentieth Century Magazine* 4 (April 1911).

Knapp, Cleon T. "Diamond Creek Development Proposed for Immediate Action." *Arizona Mining Journal* 19 (January 1923).

Knapp, George W. "Uncle Reuben Becomes a Power Magnet: Senator Carl Hayden Rates the Remarkable Achievements of the Farmers of the Salt River Valley." *The Railway Conductor* 45 (August 1928).

Lamar, Howard R. "Persistent Frontier: The West in the Twentieth Century." *Western Historical Quarterly* 7 (January 1973).

Lamb, Blaine. "A Many Checkered Toga: Arizona Senator Ralph Cameron, 1921–1927." *Arizona and the West* 19 (Spring 1977).

Luckingham, Bradford. "Urban Development in Arizona: The Rise of Phoenix." *Journal of Arizona History* 22 (Summer 1981).

Mawn, Geoffry P. "Promoters, Speculators, and the Selection of the Phoenix Townsite." *Arizona and the West* 19 (Autumn 1977).

May, Frank. "Coolidge Dam Dedicated by Former President to Irrigate Lands in Florence–Casa Grand Valley." *Arizona Highways* 16 (March 1930).

Meredith, H. L. "Reclamation in the Salt River Valley, 1902–1917." *Journal of the West* 7 (January 1968).

Moore, Hal. "The Salt River Project: An Illustrious Chapter in U.S. Reclamation." *Arizona Highways* 37 (April 1961).

Murphy, Ralph. "Arizona's Side of the Question." *Sunset Magazine* 56 (April 1926).

Newhall, Richard. "Arizona and the Colorado: How Not to Win a River by Trying Very Hard." *Phoenix Point West* 6 (March 1965).

Parker, Charles Franklin. "Senator Carl Hayden: The Distinguished Gentleman From Arizona." *Arizona Highways* 38 (February–March 1962).

Parsons, Malcolm. "Origins of the Colorado River Controversy in Arizona Politics, 1922–23." *Arizona and the West* 4 (Spring 1962).

______. "Party and Pressure Politics in Arizona's Opposition to Colorado River Development." *Pacific Historical Review* 19 (February 1950).

Pomeroy, Earl. "Toward a Reorientation of Western History: Continuity and Environment." *Mississippi Valley Historical Review* 41 (March 1955).

Shadegg, Stephen. "The Miracle of Water in the Salt River Valley, Part I." *Arizona Highways* 18 (July 1942).

______. "The Miracle of Water in the Salt River Valley, Part II." *Arizona Highways* 18 (August 1942).

Smith, Karen. "The Campaign for Water in Central Arizona, 1890–1903." *Arizona and the West* 23 (Summer 1981).

Smith, Thomas G. "Lewis Douglas, Arizona Politics, and the Colorado River Controversy." *Arizona and the West* 22 (Summer 1980).

Trelease, Frank. "Arizona v. California: Allocation of Water Resources to People, States, and Nation." *The Supreme Court Review* (1963).

Van Petten, Donald R. "Arizona's Stand on the Colorado River Compact." *New Mexico Historical Review* 17 (January 1942).

Von Klein Smid, Rufus B. "The League of the Southwest: What It Is and Why." *Arizona: The State Magazine* 11 (May 1920).

Woodward, F.A. "Arizona Resources." *Arizona Magazine* 13 (November 1928).

BOOKS

Arizona Highline Reclamation Association. *The Highline Book*. Phoenix: The Arizona Highline Reclamation Association, 1923.

Berkman, Richard L., and W. Kip Viscusi. *Damming the West*. New York: Grossman Publishers, 1973.

Bernays, Edward L., ed. *The Engineering of Consent*. Norman: University of Oklahoma Press, 1955.

Bracken, Paul, and Herman Kahn. *Arizona Tomorrow: A Precursor of Post–Industrial America*. New York: The Hudson Institute, 1979.

Byrkit, James W. *Forging the Copper Collar: Arizona's Labor Management War of 1901–1921*. Tucson: University of Arizona Press, 1982.

Chairman Publishing Company. *Portrait and Biographical Record of Arizona Commemorating the Achievements of Citizens who Have Contributed to the Progress of Arizona and the Development of Its Resources*. Chicago: Chairman Publishing Co., 1901.

Connors, Jo. *Who's Who in Arizona*. Tucson: Connors Publishing Co., 1913.

Davis, Arthur Powell. *Irrigation Near Phoenix, Arizona*. Washington: GPO, 1897.

Etulain, Richard, ed. *The American West in the Twentieth Century: A Bibliography*. Norman: University of Oklahoma Press, 1994.

Farish, Thomas Edwin. *Arizona History*. Phoenix: Phoenix Manufacturing Co., 1920.

Fradkin, Philip L. *A River No More: The Colorado River and the West*. New York: Alfred A. Knopf, 1981.

Gates, Paul W. *History of Public Land Law Development*. Washington, D.C.: Zenger Publishing Co., 1968.

Goff, John S. *George W. P. Hunt and His Arizona*. Pasadena: Socio Technical Publications, 1973.

Graebner, Norman. *Manifest Destiny*. New York: Bobbs–Merrill, 1968.

Gressley, Gene. *The Twentieth Century American West: A Potpourri*. Columbia: University of Missouri Press, 1977.

Haber, Samuel. *Efficiency and Uplift: Scientific Management in the Progressive Era, 1890–1900*. New York: Oxford University Press, 1981.

Hawley, Ellis, ed. *Herbert Hoover As Secretary of Commerce: Studies in New Era Thought and Practice*. Iowa City: University of Iowa Press, 1974.

Hayden, Carl. *Charles Trumbull Hayden: Pioneer*. Tucson: Arizona Historical Society, 1972.

Hays, Samuel P. *Conservation and the Gospel of Efficiency: The Progressive Conservation Movement, 1890–1920*. New York: Atheneum Press, 1975.

Hinton, Richard J. *The Handbook of Arizona*. San Francisco: Payot, Upham and Co., 1978.

Hopkins, Ernest J., and Alfred Thomas, Jr. *The Arizona State University Story*. Phoenix: Southwest Publishing Co., 1960.

Hundley, Norris, Jr. *Water and the West: The Colorado River Compact and the Politics of Water in the American West*. Berkeley: University of California Press, 1975.

______. *The Great Thirst: Californians and Water, 1770s–1990s*. Berkeley: University of California Press, 1992.

Johnson, Rich. *The Central Arizona Project, 1918–1968*. Tucson: University of Arizona Press, 1977.

Karnes, Thomas. *William Gilpin: Western Nationalist.* Austin: University of Texas Press, 1970.

Lamar, Howard R. *The Far Southwest, 1846–1912: A Territorial History*. New Haven: Yale University Press, 1966.

Layton, Edwin T., Jr. *The Revolt of the Engineers: Social Responsibility and the Engineering Profession*. Cleveland: Case Western University Press, 1971.

Leuchtenburg, William E. *The Perils of Prosperity*. Chicago: University of Chicago Press, 1958.

Lilley, William, and Lewis Gould. "The Western Irrigation Movement, 1878–1902." In *The American West: A Reorientation*, Gene Gressley, ed. Laramie: University of Wyoming, 1966.

Lowitt, Richard. *George W. Norris: The Persistence of a Progressive, 1913–1933*. Urbana: University of Illinois Press, 1971.

______. *The New Deal and the West*. Bloomington: Indiana University Press, 1984.

Luckingham, Bradford. *The Urban Southwest: A Profile History of Albuquerque, El Paso, Phoenix, Tucson*. El Paso: Texas Western Press, 1982.

McClintock, James H. *Mormon Settlement in Arizona*. Phoenix: Manufacturing Stationers, Inc., 1921.

Moeller, Beverly. *Phil Swing and Boulder Dam*. Berkeley: University of California Press, 1971.

Mowry, George E. *The Era of Theodore Roosevelt and the Birth of Modern America, 1900–1912*. New York: Harper and Sons, 1958.

Nash, Gerald. *The American West in the Twentieth Century: A Short History of an Urban Oasis*. Albuquerque: University of New Mexico Press, 1973.

Nash, Gerald D., and Richard Etulain, eds. *The Twentieth Century West: Historical Interpretations*. Albuquerque: University of New Mexico Press, 1989.

______. *Researching Western History: Topics in the Twentieth Century*. Albuquerque: University of New Mexico Press, 1997.

Pisani, Donald. *To Reclaim a Divided West: Water, Law, and Public Policy, 1848–1902*. Albuquerque: University of New Mexico Press, 1992.

Pomeroy, Earl. "The Urban Frontier in the Far West." In *The Frontier Challenge: Responses to the Trans-Mississippi West*, John G. Clark, ed. Manhattan: University of Kansas Press, 1971.

______. *The Pacific Slope: A History of California, Oregon, Washington, Idaho, Utah, and Nevada*. New York: Alfred A. Knopf, 1965.

Rice, Ross. *Carl Hayden: Builder of the American West*. Lanham, Maryland: University Press of America, 1994.

Sheridan, Thomas E. *Arizona: A History*. Tucson: University of Arizona Press, 1995.

Skinner, A. P. *Phoenix and Maricopa County Directory: 1905–1906*. Phoenix: The Phoenix Printing Co., 1905.

Starr, Kevin. *Americans and the California Dream, 1850–1915*. New York: Oxford University Press, 1973.

Steffan, Jerome O., ed. *The American West: New Perspectives, New Dimensions*. Norman: University of Oklahoma Press, 1979.

Wiebe, Robert. *The Search for Order, 1877–1920*. New York: Hill and Wang, 1967.

Wiley, Peter, and Robert Gottlieb. *Empires in the Sun: The Rise of the New American West*. New York: G.P. Putnam and Sons, 1982.

Worster, Donald. *Under Western Skies: Nature and History in the American West*. New York: Oxford University Press, 1992.

______. *An Unsettled Country: Changing Landscapes of the American West* Albuquerque: University of New Mexico Press, 1994.

Zarbin, Earl. *Roosevelt Dam: A History to 1911*. Phoenix: Salt River Project, 1984.

______. *Salt River Project: Four Steps Forward, 1902–1910*. Phoenix: Salt River Project, 1986.

Index

Printed in the United States
41178LVS00004B/118-177